PUNISHMENT, RESTORATIVE JUSTICE AND THE MORALITY OF LAW

PUNISHMENT, RESTORATIVE JUSTICE AND THE MORALITY OF LAW

Edited by

ERIK CLAES
RENÉ FOQUÉ
TONY PETERS

intersentia
Antwerp – Oxford

Distribution for the UK:
Hart Publishing
Salter's Boat Yard
Folly Bridge
Abingdon Road
Oxford OX1 4LB
UK
Tel: + 44 1865 24 55 33
Fax: + 44 1865 79 48 82

Distribution for North America:
Gaunt Inc.
Gaunt Building
3011 Gulf Drive
Holmes Beach
Florida 34217-2199
USA
Tel: + 1 941 778 5211
Fax: + 1 941 778 5252

Distribution for Switzerland and Germany:
Schulthess Verlag
Zwingliplatz 2
CH-8022 Zürich
Switzerland
Tel: + 41 1 251 93 36
Fax: + 41 1 261 63 94

Distribution for other countries:
Intersentia Publishers
Groenstraat 31
2640 Mortsel
Belgium
Tel: + 32 3 680 15 50
Fax: + 32 3 658 71 21

Punishment, Restorative Justice and the Morality of Law
Erik Claes, René Foqué, Tony Peters (eds.)

ISBN 90-5095-423-5
D/2005/7849/18
NUR 824

PREFACE

In 1984, the Aquinas Foundation of New York donated funds to the International Society of Criminology, allowing it to establish its administrative offices at the University of Montreal.

Since then, a first series of conferences have been held at prestigious universities around the world on the global theme of responsibility and citizenship in the domain of mental health and criminal justice. In a stimulating interdisciplinary climate, distinguished philosophers such as Christian Atias (Aix-en-Provence), Bernard Williams (Oxford), Ottfried Höffe (Tübingen), as well as eminent jurists like Lombardi-Vallauri (Rome), Ignacio Berdugo Gomez de la Torre (Salamanca), and Andras Szabo (Budapest) have been invited to give their views on the subject. One of the main challenges for this cluster of activities was to rethink the concepts of citizenship and civic responsibility, in order to address the challenges, difficulties and complexities of post-modern societies which are characterised both by strong individualism and privatisation by the state. Considered as a counter-weight against these disquieting developments, a richer and fuller notion of the "responsible citizen" bearing the relevant rights and obligations could play an important role here in the restoration of the public sphere. Introduced into the context of criminal justice such notions, which would be connected with security, well-being and human dignity, could also provide for better legal protection of both victims and offenders.

With its 10th Conference, entitled "Punishment, Restorative Justice and the Morality of Law" held at the Catholic University of Leuven on 2-3 May 2003, the Aquinas Foundation started a second series of activities focussing on the topic of "Ethical Limits on Social Practices and Political Actions". This broad subject covers an almost unlimited range of issues spanning the topics of paternalism, the moral status of children, distributive justice, the limits of tolerance, sex, and pornography, international law, criminal justice, and so on. The variety of such issues notwithstanding, the Aquinas Foundation invites young and senior researchers to engage in common reflection on the moral values and normative standards against which social and political practices could be assessed and by means of which these same practices ought to be guided.

The 10th Aquinas Conference on "Punishment, Restorative Justice and the Morality of Law", the proceedings of which are presented in this volume, has taken this common reflection as its basic reference point by focussing on the ethical fundamentals and limits of criminal punishment and restorative justice practices within the framework of a democratic constitutional state. Through the contributions it has produced, the proceedings of the 10th Aquinas Conference are faithful to the intellectual spirit of the Aquinas Foundation, a spirit of resisting any subtle invitation to cynicism and cultural pessimism, combined with a deep and genuine attachment to the moral sources of our Judaeo-Christian civilisation.

On behalf of the Aquinas Foundation I would like to thank the Law Faculty of the Catholic University of Leuven, and more in particular Professor Erik Claes, Professor René Foqué and Professor Tony Peters, for succesfully having organised the Conference and edited its Proceedings.

Denis Szabo
Professor emeritus of Criminology
University of Montreal

TABLE OF CONTENTS

PREFACE v

INTRODUCTION
ERIK CLAES and TONY PETERS 1

1. Central Issues 1
2. Criminal Justice, Legality and Human Dignity 2
3. Restorative Justice and the Morality of Law 6
4. Punishment and the Morality of Law 9

PART ONE.
CRIMINAL JUSTICE, LEGALITY, HUMAN DIGNITY 15

1. CRIMINAL JUSTICE, LEGALITY AND HUMAN DIGNITY
ERIK CLAES 17

Introduction 17
1. Worries About Legality and the Rule of Law 19
2. Some Preliminary Remarks 23
3. Is Legality Still Adequate Enough for a Successful Administration of Criminal Justice? 24
4. Does Legality Still Contain Enough Justifying Power to Guide and Constrain the Administration of Criminal Justice? 29
5. The Idea of a Rights-conception of Legality 33
6. Can Legality Fit Person-relative Facts? 36
7. Legality, Predictability and Human Dignity 39
8. Two Faces of (Respect for) Human Dignity 44
9. The Idea of a "Capability"-conception of Legality 50
Conclusion 52

2. PUNISHMENT, HUMAN DIGNITY, AND THE SOCIOLOGICAL IMAGINATION: A REPLY TO CLAES
TOM DAEMS 57

1. The Challenge for Normative Theory 58
2. Punishment, Human Dignity, and Modernity 60
2.1. The Other Crisis: Punishment as a Public Issue 60

2.2. Respect for Human Dignity: "Private Trouble" or "Public Issue"? 65
Conclusion 67

3. BACK TO BASICS: A REPLY TO CLAES
Sandra Marshall 69

PART TWO.
RESTORATIVE JUSTICE AND THE MORALITY OF LAW 77

4. RESTORATIVE JUSTICE AND THE MORALITY OF LAW
Serge Brochu 79

1. Morality 79
2. Recent Evolution of the Doctrine of Punitive Justice 80
3. Restorative Justice 81
4. Restorative Justice and the Morality of Justice Process 83
4.1. Taking Care of the Victim 83
4.2. Taking Care of the Offender 83
4.3. Taking Care of Society 84
Conclusion 85

5. RESTORATIVE JUSTICE AND THE MORALITY OF THE FAIR TRIAL: A REPLY TO BROCHU
Mireille Hildebrandt 89

Introduction 89
1. Historical Perspective on Mediation and Fair Trial in Penal Matters 90
2. The Public Context of Restorative Justice and the Concept of the Legal Norm 91
3. Primacy of the Victim? 93
4. The Morality and Effectiveness of Fair Trial and Restorative Punishment 94
5. Person- and Norm-relative Sensitivities 97
Concluding Remarks 99

6. RESTORATIVE JUSTICE AND THE MORALITY OF LAW: A REPLY TO BROCHU
IVO AERTSEN and KRISTEL BEYENS 101

Introduction 101
1. Restorative Justice in Contemporary Context 101
1.1. Contemporary Punishment 101
1.2. Restorative Justice in Contemporary Society 102
1.2.1. The Appeal of the "Gemeinschaft" in Late Modern Societies 102
1.2.2. Victims and Moral Clarifications 104
1.2.3. The Questionable Legitimacy of Courts 105
1.2.4. Is there a Place for Restorative Justice Mechanisms in Contemporary Advanced-Urban Societies? 105
2. Restorative Justice and Sentencing 106
2.1. The Need for some Integration 106
2.2. Sentencing: Retributive and/or Restorative? 108
2.3. Types of Morality 111
3. A Belgian Proposal for Sentencing Reform 113
3.1. General Framework 114
3.2. Principles for a Communicative and Participative Sentencing / Criminal Justice System 115
3.3. A Place for Narratives in Court? 115
3.4. Some Conditions for a Successful Restorative, thus Communicative and Participative Sentencing Process 117

PART THREE.
PUNISHMENT AND THE MORALITY OF LAW 119

7. PUNISHMENT AND THE MORALITY OF LAW
ANTONY DUFF 121

1. How Can Citizens Punish Each Other? 122
2. Punishment and Communication 131
3. Retribution and Restoration 140

8. RETRIBUTIVISM AND THE QUALITY OF SOCIAL LIFE: A REPLY TO DUFF
LODE WALGRAVE 145

1. Retributivism and Instrumentalism 145
2. What is a Wrong? 147

3. Why Needs a Wrong to Be Punished? ... 149
4. Punishment A Priorism as an Obstacle for Communication ... 151
5. Duff's Communitarian Liberalism and the Top-down Approach in Retributivism ... 154

9. RETRIBUTIVE PUNISHMENT AND SYMBOLIC RESTORATION: A REPLY TO DUFF
ARNOLD BURMS ... 157

10. DOES PUNISHMENT NEED HARD TREATMENT? A REPLY TO DUFF
BAS VAN STOKKOM ... 165

1. Why Do We Have to Rely on Retribution? ... 166
2. What is Hard Treatment? ... 167
3. Duff's Account: Some Implausible Psychological Arguments ... 169
4. Repentance and Trust: Facilitating Two-way Communication ... 174
Conclusion ... 177

11. A RESPONSE TO WALGRAVE, VAN STOKKOM, AND BURMS
ANTONY DUFF ... 179

PUNISHMENT, RESTORATIVE JUSTICE, AND THE MORALITY OF LAW: CONCLUDING OBSERVATIONS
RENÉ FOQUÉ ... 183

1. Introductory Remarks ... 183
2. The Need for a Normative Theory of Law ... 184
3. A Plea for a Reconstructive Theory of Law and the Role of General Principles ... 184
4. How the Language of the Law Institutionalises a Sense of Others ... 186
5. The Law as *Symbolic Order* ... 187
6. Participatory Citizenship, Moral Agency and the Principle of Human Dignity: Towards a Personalistic Conception of Law ... 189
7. The Risks of an Absolute Victimological Turn in Criminal Justice ... 193

8. The Meaning of *Restorative* in Restorative Justice: What Must Be Repaired? 195
9. The Domain-specificity of Criminal Law as Public Law: A Necessary Condition for the Complementarity of Punishment and Restorative Justice 197

LIST OF THE CONTRIBUTORS 199

INTRODUCTION

ERIK CLAES and TONY PETERS

1. CENTRAL ISSUES

The last decade has seen an upsurge of academic interest among lawyers, criminologists and philosophers in restorative justice programmes and practices. What these programmes are precisely aiming at is far from clear, and depends largely on the shape they take and on the role they actually play within, or in the margin of, the criminal justice system. What these programmes should aim at is even more unclear. The recent literature issuing from advocates of restorative justice evidences a multiplicity of goals which restorative justice should simultaneously achieve, moving from the repairing of the harm done to the victim, to the restoring of the dignity of both victim and offender and of their relationship. The problem here is that these goals are vaguely formulated without specifying how they can consistently be related to each other and whether some need to be prioritised above others.[1]

Critics take the unclear status of restorative justice practices, along with their vagueness in meaning and purpose, as a clear invitation to a fundamental questioning of the legitimacy of these practices. Their supporters consider the experiment of restorative justice as a platform for reforming penal institutions and for rethinking the legitimacy of orthodox legal reasoning. Within the framework of a "*rechtsstaat*", a democratic state governed by fundamental rights and by the rule of law, both issues of legitimacy lead not only to reflection on concepts such as restoration, punishment, or on such notions as harm and wrong. Questioning the legitimacy both of restorative justice practices and of the prevailing penal system also inevitably involves some reflection on, and articulation of, the underlying values and normative aspirations of such a democratic constitutional state. What are these values and how can they be given appropriate expression in the leading concepts and principles of criminal law? To what extent are fundamental rights and principles of the rule of law sufficiently reflected in the practices of restorative justice? How are these practices to be related to the criminal justice system according to the normative aspirations of a democratic constitutional state? To what degree can current penal practices be made continuous with these aspirations?

---

[1] For this objection, see recently A. VON HIRSCH, A.J. ASHWORTH and C. SHEARING, "Specifying Aims and Limits for Restorative Justice: A 'Making Amends' Model?" in A. VAN HIRSCH, J. ROBERTS, A. BOTTOMS (eds), *Restorative Justice and Criminal Justice. Competing or Reconcilable Paradigms?*, Oxford, Hart Publishing, 2003, 21-41.

These fundamental questions formed the intellectual framework for the 10th Aquinas Conference on "Punishment, Restorative Justice and the Morality of Law", at which conference the larger part of the papers published in this volume were presented. Consistent with the structure of the conference, this collection of essays is organised into three parts, each focussing on one central topic and containing a lead essay and corresponding replies. The first part offers critical scrutiny of one of the cornerstones of a criminal justice system governed by the rule of law, namely the principle of legality. Efforts are made to empower this principle through reflection on its underlying values and aspirations, and this in order to meet some of the legitimate ideals and concerns of restorative justice. These efforts are subsequently assessed from both sociological and philosophical perspectives. In the second part, attention is drawn to the legitimacy of restorative justice practices. Here, the normative intuitions of a democratic constitutional state serve either as a critical framework to assess these practices, or, more optimistically, as ideals to whose realisation restorative justice is supposed to make a valuable contribution. And, finally, in the third part, reflection on the value of restorative justice brings us to a fundamental questioning of the legitimacy of punishment and penal practices. Central to the discussion is whether it is possible to interpret and normatively reconstruct the idea and practice of punishment so as to make them compatible with, and even continuous with, the underlying values of a democratic constitutional state.

In what follows, the contents of each of these three parts are briefly introduced and outlined. The contributions have a dual objective: first, they reflect a common effort to define the role of restorative justice in relation to the penal system, and second, they seek to uncover the fundamentals of a democratic state governed by fundamental rights, democratic principles, and the rule of law, as an appropriate means to estimate the legitimate prospects of restorative justice. This last goal will be referred to using Lon Fuller's well-known expression "the morality of law".

2. CRIMINAL JUSTICE, LEGALITY AND HUMAN DIGNITY

What are the basic values that underpin a *rechtsstaat*, or a democratic constitutional state, and to what extent are those values properly reflected in the familiar principles and concepts of the criminal law? The practice of restorative justice easily triggers this kind of reflection, for it is deeply rooted in a scepticism of these principles. According to the proponents of restorative justice, contemporary criminal justice systems are blind to the specific context of the crimes they deal with, thereby reducing the complexity of the conflict, and making an abstraction of the concrete lifeworlds of both victim and offender. These shortcomings are not only due to deficiencies related to the specific organisation of penal institutions.

They also derive more dramatically from the underlying concepts and principles around which the entire system is built, and from which that system draws its rationale and reasonableness. One such precept is the principle of legality. This principle holds, at least according to its classical continental conception, that only the legislator may define which actions constitute a criminal wrong. This very principle, considered to be one of the core elements of the rule, prevents the criminal judge from being context-sensitive in his dealing with crime. It prevents him from being attentive to the concrete lifeworlds of victim and offender, since it prevents him from creatively filling out the scope of the criminal offence in light of the particular circumstances of the case.

In his "Criminal Justice, Legality and Human Dignity" Erik Claes takes up this topic in earnest by examining to what extent the principle of legality can be restyled so as to give appropriate expression to the underlying intuitions and aspirations of the rule of law, while at the same time giving sufficient weight to the concrete circumstances of the criminal offence and to the personal perceptions of both victim and offender. An inquiry into the structure of legal reasoning, as well as into the intrinsic relationship between legality and human rights standards, brings Claes to a rights-conception of legality that, at least in an important respect, claims to be context-sensitive and to articulate adequately its deeper normative point. To retrieve legality's normative potential is, according to Claes, to conceive it in terms of the capacity of each legal subject to trust in the rule- and rights-governed behaviour of his fellow-citizens. Public officials who fail to accord this capacity to their citizens fail to respect their individual human dignity.

Claes' attempts to revitalise legality in a way that gives appropriate expression to the aspirations of a democratic constitutional state and simultaneously satisfy the worries of criminologists and proponents of restorative justice, brings him simultaneously to the very limits of a legality-based criminal justice system. For Claes, one should not prevent a criminal judge from being sensitive to the particulars of the case if he proves faithful to a more refined principle of legality, and, accordingly, if he makes efforts to interpret the scope of a criminal offence in light of one or more fundamental rights that are at stake in the circumstances of the case. But according to the principle of legality, only these circumstances are to be taken as relevant insofar as they help to determine the general scope of the criminal offence. Other circumstances, such as those revealing or expressing the personal perspective of the particular victim or offender with regard to the criminal offence, are cut off from the process of legal interpretation. Or to use Claes' terminology, the context-sensitivity of the criminal judge confines itself to being norm-relative and thereby fails to be person-relative.

In order to obtain a more substantial account of why legality resists being continuous with the kind of context-sensitivity which is at stake in restorative justice practices, Claes distinguishes two types of respect for human dignity, each of which tends to suppress the other. According to Claes, concern with the personal perspective of victim and offender, with their respective desires to express and communicate to each other their stance in the conflict can be traced back to what he calls a "particularistic conception" of respect for human dignity, entailing full recognition of each other's radical uniqueness. Restorative justice programmes, and more in particular, victim-offender mediation schemes, aim at an instauration of a context in which victim and offender can rediscover each other's dignity by growing sensitive to the concrete details, facts, stories, and so on, through which the other appears as radically unique and tries to assume his uniqueness.

According to Claes, this particularistic conception of human dignity underlying restorative justice worries can hardly be integrated with a rights-conception of legality, since the latter conception is ultimately grounded in a different, generalist type of respect for human dignity. Attention is drawn not to the details revealing the unique perspectives of victim and offender, but to their equal capacity to trust in the rule- and rights-guided behaviour of the government and of each other.

The project of revitalising the principle of legality, however promising it might seem, appears to encounter many obstacles on its route. These obstacles need to be cleared away if the project is to have any hope of success. In the replies of Tom Daems and Sandra Marshall at least two hurdles were pointed out.

The first challenge to be addressed relates to the viability of such a project in light of current socio-political circumstances and developments. In his "Punishment, Human Dignity and the Sociological Imagination" Daems argues that Claes' attempt to articulate the normative point of the principle of legality, by linking it to such notions as trust, human dignity, and fundamental rights, is utterly fragile because it lacks in its actual form sociological imagination. As it stands, Claes' project falls short in paying sufficient attention to the specific socio-political context of a late modern society in which penal institutions and modern law are embedded. Without this kind of sociological context-sensitivity, any ambition of reconstructing the principle legality will end up a highly theoretical and normative enterprise. It will fail to serve as a viable instrument capable of critically guiding and governing actual criminal justice practice under present societal conditions. According to Daems, a blindness to the background of penal institutions is also not without risk in the present societal context marked by a culture of control and in which penal institutions cannot be seen in isolation from mechanisms of recycling and disposal of "wasted humans". Normative rethinking of the principle of legality could then easily serve as a mere legitimation of the status quo.

The second challenge relates to Claes' ambition to reconnect the principle of legality with some of the concerns of restorative justice, more particularly the full recognition of the private worries and concerns of victims and offenders. Claes sees this reconnection as an answer to what he takes to be one of the core aspects of the present penal crisis: the abstracting and alienating aspect of the legal framework of criminal law. For Daems, Claes overrates the legitimacy of these private worries, thereby obscuring some pressing public aspects of the penal crisis, such as the rise of punishment which is bound up with a broader context of power strategies of social exclusion and human engineering in the service of a particular social order. Daems here suggests refining the idea of legality based on human dignity in close connection with the principle of subsidiarity. Central to this refinement would be the answering of the following question: if one takes into consideration the potentially oppressive and interest-based character of legal norms, to what extent can the concept of human dignity inform decisions as to what type of behaviour deserves to fall within the scope of criminal law and criminal punishment?

In "Back to Basics", Sandra Marshall shares Daems' doubts in taking particularistic restorative justice worries as a legitimate standard for refining the principle of legality. Marshall engages in a constructive reading of Claes' objective to adjust the principle of legality to the complex process of legal reasoning and to ground it in the idea of human dignity. But this brings her to discover that the refinement of legality, however legitimate it may be, appears to broaden the gap with restorative justice instead of narrowing it. For Marshall, the grounding of legality in human dignity makes it all the more difficult to establish a legitimate place for private feelings and worries of both victims and offenders.

According to Marshall, to affirm the person-relativity of, for instance, the desire of the victim to enter into a dialogue with the offender, inevitably means recognising that this desire is not necessarily reasonable and that one cannot require the victim to have these communicative wants. But essential for a criminal justice system governed by legality, human dignity, privacy, and equality, is that such a system requires those communicative desires to be reasonable, and to be desired if reasonable. Marshall here draws special attention to what seems to be an incompatibility between the valorising of the person-relativity of the victim perspective on the one hand, and a commitment to the principle of equality and equal treatment, on the other.

3. RESTORATIVE JUSTICE AND THE MORALITY OF LAW

Daems' and Marshall's scepticism about the importance and legitimacy of the personal perspectives of victims and offenders with regard to restoring principles in the criminal law, can also be taken as a broader invitation to reflect critically on the underlying values of restorative justice. To what extent do restorative justice practices and their normative ideas contribute to the realisation of the ideals of a democratic constitutional state? On what normative grounds do we have to grant restorative justice ideas and practices a central role in the reform of our penal institutions and principles of the criminal law? These broader reflections are the subject of the second part of this volume.

In his "Restorative Justice and the Morality of Law", Serge Brochu parts from the idea that restorative justice and the traditional punitive system each provide different answers to the underlying fundamentals of a democratic constitutional state. Brochu summarises the morality of law in three basic principles: first, the principle of care for the well-being and the dignity of the victim; second, the principle of care for the well-being and the dignity of the offender; third, the principle of care for the safety and well-being of society. For Brochu, at least two arguments can be given why restorative justice, compared to the traditional punitive system, reflects these three principles in a more satisfying way. In the first, restorative justice, understood primarily as involved with the reparation of harm to the victim, gives full weight to the well-being and the dignity of the victim; whereas traditional criminal procedure is primarily characterised by the absence of the victim (first principle). In the second, when compared with the punitive system, restorative justice also acts more in accordance with the second principle (care for the dignity of the offender) for it seeks to empower the offender in his "responsibility-ability", in his capacity to assume his obligations toward the victim and toward society.

While reaffirming that restorative justice constitutes from the perspective of the morality of law an interesting alternative and better approach to the traditional system, Brochu ends his essay, with some critical points relating to the importance of restorative justice in present-day penal culture. In a contemporary society marked by the increase in punishment and by an obsession for security, safety, and control, restorative justice can only gain significance if it pays sufficient attention to the reality of recidivism. In addition, Brochu points out the undeniable, and perhaps unfortunate, reality of punitive desires on the victims' side, and the need to reconcile these desires with the values of restorative justice.

Mireille Hildebrandt is less confident about the potentials of restorative justice practice to meet the underlying aspirations of a democratic constitutional state and to offer a better view of criminal justice than that of the traditional penal system. Like Claes, Hildebrandt undertakes a considerable effort to retrieve the morality of a rule-of law-based criminal justice system by articulating the importance of state intervention in criminal affairs and by articulating the morality of a fair trial.

For Hildebrandt, an interesting entry point for understanding the deeper meaning of criminal justice governed by the rule of law is to understand the meaning of mediation in non-state societies. In these societies the success of these mediation practices is crucial to the further existence of the entire social fabric. The alternative is war, revenge, or feud, endangering thereby the coherence of the society. What constitutes the inner morality of a modern criminal justice system is that its rules and principles presuppose delegation of violence into the hands of the state. This mechanism of delegation makes the social fabric less vulnerable to war and revenge. In light of these insights, Hildebrandt remarks that there is no reason to be romantic with regard to mediation in a non-state society, and that in our contemporary society, there is no reason to overstate the role and importance of informal, consensual dealings with crime.

As a next step, Hildebrandt assesses the prospects of restorative justice by drawing attention to the values of a fair trial, recognised as one of the essentials of a "*rechtsstaat*", or a democratic constitutional state. Hildebrandt starts her analysis by reflecting on the concept of a legal norm.[2] According to her, legal norms cannot be reduced to their imperative status or to regular behaviour patterns; they are the expression of normative and mutual expectations holding together the ever-changing fabric of society. The meaning of legal norms therefore depends on the way citizens interpret these mutual expectations in their concrete actions; i.e. legal rules and actions are mutually constitutive. Each citizen has the power in undertaking an action to relate himself to the prevailing normative expectations of his society, and this by interpreting, affirming, or denying the legitimate status of these expectations and the legal norms in which they are embodied. One of the essentials of a democratic constitutional state is that it aspires to organising institutions, especially its penal apparatus, so as to confer on each legal subject charged with committing a legal wrong the capacity to reconstitute his actions as reasonable, and thus likewise his stance regarding the status of the legal norm. Such an aspiration calls for the implementation of a fair trial: a public, accusatorial procedure where the suspect is called to answer for his actions and is judged by an independent judicial body. The inner morality Hildebrandt has so far uncovered in the idea of a fair trial is that it obliges the state to recognise the norm-creating and norm-defying power of the citizen and,

---

2 For a profound analysis, see M. HILDEBRANDT, *Straf(begrip) en procesbeginsel,* Deventer, Kluwer, 2002.

accordingly, his capability to take a power-critical attitude to prevailing norms and expectations.

Hildebrandt's ideas around the deep aspirations of a fair trial and of a democratic constitutional state are of course not without consequences for her ideas about the role of restorative justice in the criminal justice system. First, Hildebrandt seems to reject Brochu's claim that restorative justice offers a fuller realisation to the aspirations of a democratic constitutional state. Indeed, she raises many doubts as to the idea of the primacy of the victim. If, from the perspective of the morality of law, criminal justice is about protecting, reaffirming, reinterpreting, and even recognising the possibility of defying the legal norm's authority, the criminal justice system puts both the citizen as *potential* victim and *potential* offender in the centre of the criminal justice system.

Second, as to the compatibility of restorative justice with the values of a fair trial, Hildebrandt notes that the confidential, informal nature of restorative justice annuls the offender's capacity to interpret or contest the authority of the legal norm. The confidentiality of these practices also opens the way for a secondary victimisation of the offender. Therefore Hildebrandt makes a plea for qualifying restorative justice practices as restorative punishment, thereby according the offender sufficient legal protection.

Despite her scepticism towards restorative justice, Hildebrandt concedes that from the perspective of the morality of law, reasons can still be found in favour of restorative justice as a complementary part of the criminal justice system. "Not because the victim should be in the centre, but because both victim and offender should be given the opportunity to restore their self-confidence, to demand respect for their person." (see p. 98 in this volume)

Ivo Aertsen and Kristel Beyens do not seem to share Hildebrandt's scepticism concerning the legitimate prospects for restorative justice. Taking as a starting point their experience as members of the Belgian commission for sentencing reform and from their experience with the Belgian practice of victim-offender mediation, they state that restorative justice can and should be integrated into the very heart of the actual criminal justice system. For them, restorative justice should not be promoted as an alternative system apart from the traditional penal apparatus. The practice of mediation, for example, shows that both offender and victim still want a connection with the traditional system. The victim expects the outcome of the mediation to be reaffirmed by a judicial body and translated into a public condemnation of the wrong committed. The offender still expects from the criminal justice system a framework of legal protection to which he can appeal when necessary. Against the background of these expectations Aertsen and Beyens plead for restorative justice seen both as a kind of intermediary level of penal intervention and as a platform for a rethinking and reshaping of the face of the criminal justice system. Depending on the conditions of the present penal culture, the notion of restoration could in many respects contribute to a fuller realisation of constitutional and democratic values in actual penal institutions. Restorative justice, and the underlying ideas of communication and consensus, would bring the criminal justice system closer to its ideals of democracy and public autonomy. In a world in which the court takes into consideration the outcome of the mediation process, there is a greater chance that both victim and offender will feel recognised in their capacity to have an actual stake in the shape and content of the state's response to criminal wrongdoing. In addition to this and in line with the Belgian proposals for sentencing reform, Aertsen and Beyens plead for the idea of restoration seen as an independent purpose of punishment. Such an introduction would temper, and perhaps in the long run abolish, the retributive vein of deliberate pain delivery which is still prominent in existing penal practice.

4. PUNISHMENT AND THE MORALITY OF LAW

Like many proponents of restorative justice, the view of Aertsen and Beyens reflects a deep scepticism about the justifiability of retributive punishment pictured as a practice of deliberate pain delivery. This scepticism seems to be particularly appropriate in states that purport to be liberal democracies. In such a state-form, citizens are supposed to rely on the state's non-interference with their basic liberties, but at the same time they have to acknowledge the existence of penal institutions. These institutions, through the criminal sanctions they impose, are granted the power to restrict and suspend basic liberties. How is all this consistent? Which grounds provide a liberal state with a right to punish without betraying its own liberal intuitions? What proper role can criminal punishment play in a liberal democracy? These questions bring us to the third and last part of this volume, which focuses mainly on the justification of criminal punishment.

In his "Punishment and the Morality of Law" Antony Duff tries to resolve this tension between criminal punishment and the values of liberal democracies, by radicalising the nature of this tension. The conception of punishment he offers, claims to be compatible with, and even expressive of, the intuitions of a liberal polity, while a the same time accommodating some legitimate concerns of advocates of restorative justice. Basically, his line of argument proceeds in four steps.

In a first step, Duff reflects on the basic values of a liberal democracy governed by the rule of law. Duff's starting point is the traditional liberal view on the meaning of the law, and more in particular of the criminal law. According to such a view the system of criminal law remains in essence the sovereign's law: it is a set of commands that issues from a (superior) sovereign and that is imposed on an inferior subject. The morality of law refers to the existence of legal principles, the purpose of which is to prevent the citizen from arbitrary state intervention. Duff dissociates himself from such a traditional liberal view. For him the law needs to be portrayed as a law fit for citizens, not for subjects; speaking in the voice of equal citizens, not in the voice of a superior sovereign. A liberal democracy governed by legal rules and principles is then more than the organisation of a limited exercise of state power. In a liberal democracy the law, and consequently the criminal law, ultimately strives to recognise each legal subject as a full and equal citizen. According to Duff, treating every member of the political community as a full and equal citizen means protecting the political values which define their citizenship and treating them as responsible agents capable of practical reasoning in the light of these values.

In the second step, Duff's argument consists of radicalising the liberal puzzle of punishment. The question of how to justify criminal punishment and its corresponding encroachment on basic liberties in a state that claims to prioritize these same liberties is reframed here into one of how, under the law of a liberal polity, to treat those punished as fellow citizens, citizens who are respected as responsible agents and who are protected and bound by the polity's defining values.

In the third, Duff prepares the way for his normative theory of punishment. He argues as follows. If a liberal democracy, with its legal norms, institutions and procedures, ultimately seeks to respect each citizen as a responsible citizen committed to the values of his political community, then it necessarily follows that each citizen can be criticised and made answerable for actions which, at first sight, seem to flout these values. According to Duff, taking seriously citizens and their allegiance to the polity's essential values presupposes law-making institutions that understand the criminal law's definitions of offences, not as brute orders, but as public wrongs; the kinds of conduct which violate the community's central values. Respecting citizens as full responsible agents also involves the existence of a criminal trial in which citizens can be called on to answer publicly for the alleged wrongs. Such a trial would allow the suspect to give reasons for acting as he did, excusing or justifying why he disregarded the defining values of his polity. If no such reasons exist, then any respectable liberal polity must establish institutions which are allowed to engage in a double strategy of persuasion: first, to try to convince the offender on reasonable grounds that he has committed a public wrong and, accordingly, has fallen short in his citizenship; second to persuade him on reasonable grounds to reform his future behaviour and to restore his allegiance to his political values in the future.

In the fourth and final step, Duff tries to conceive of a normative conception of criminal punishment which is continuous with this double strategy of persuasion. Duff sketches here a communicative theory of punishment which is more substantially worked out in other publications.[3] This conception takes its consistency from at least three notions – censure, repentance, hard treatment – all of which are bound up with each other through a communicative perspective.

In Duff's approach, criminal punishment is taken to be a distinctive mode of communication: it conveys a message of *censure* or condemnation for the wrong committed by the offender. According to Duff, such an account is continuous with, and even expressive of, the aspirations of a liberal democracy, to the extent that the censure appeals to those flouted values which the offender shares with the other members of his political community. If the state aspires to speak in the voice of its citizens and also takes seriously its commitment to the polity's essential values, then the offender deserves to be censured for having violated these values. The state owes this practice of censure to all the members of the polity, to the victim, but also to the offender in his capacity as a full and equal citizen.

But a state which purports to be a liberal democracy needs to do more than just reaffirm the polity's essential values. It requires the existence of a practice which engages in a strategy of persuasion to convince the offender to recognise his wrong-doing and to see the need for self-reform. In order to satisfy these requirements, Duff refines his account of criminal punishment by introducing the notion of *repentance*. To be continuous with the aspirations of a liberal democracy, criminal punishment ought to be a two-way communication, one which seeks an appropriate response from the offender, hoping to induce in the offender a willingness to make amends in a way that does justice to the public wrong he has committed. Duff calls this a process of penitential communication, in which the offender owns up to the wrong as his own, and at the same time disowns it as something he now repudiates.

By introducing a notion of repentance, Duff claims not only to satisfy the requirements of a liberal polity, but also to satisfy some of the legitimate concerns of advocates of restorative justice. Against those who criticise criminal punishment for a lack of concern for emotions like forgiveness, and reconciliation between the victim, the offender, and the other parties involved, Duff can easily reply that his normative account of criminal punishment pays sufficient attention to these concerns. If punishment adopts the inducing of repentance as its central aim, then it is necessarily connected to the notion of apology, which itself expresses a desire to seek forgiveness from, and reconciliation with, the person who has been wronged.

---

[3] For the most elaborate version of his communicative conception of punishment, see R.A. DUFF, *Punishment, Communication, and Community*, Oxford, Oxford University Press, 2001.

To complete his normative account of punishment, Duff still has to justify why the current system of criminal law imposes punishments which are onerous, independently of their censorious intent, and why such punishments intend to induce a kind of suffering which goes beyond mere verbal apology. According to Duff, at least three reasons can be given to explain why criminal punishment necessarily involves hard treatment. First, any strategy of inducing an apology for serious wrongs committed must take more than merely a verbal form. To be taken seriously by the victim and the community such a strategy must take a material form that keeps the offender's attention focussed on the wrongdoing and its implications. Second, in a liberal democracy that seeks through its rules and principles to promote the political values which define the citizenship of every member of the political community, any kind of apology must be proportionate to the seriousness of the public wrong committed. To be expressive of a liberal type of polity, an apology necessarily involves hard treatment, for the public apology must take the form of a required one, even if the offender does not mean it. Third, in a liberal democracy that promotes the value of privacy of autonomy, it is still up to the offender to decide whether to make a genuine apology or refuse to do so. Criminal punishment necessarily involves hard treatment, seen as the public ritual of apology which the political community owes to its citizens and the victim, thereby expressing the hope that the offender will come genuinely to repent without forcing him to do so.

Of course, like every normative and theoretical enterprise, Duff's communicative theory of punishment is not immune to critique. The variety of objections which are formulated in this volume (especially in the replies of Walgrave and van Stokkom) confront Duff with at least three challenges. The first relates to the distance separating Duff's normative account from the penal system under present conditions. The second focuses on the relation between communitarianism and state criminal punishment. The third concerns Duff's attempt to encapsulate restorative justice's concern with emotions like repentance and apology within the idea of penal hard treatment.

In "Criminal Punishment and the Morality of Law", like elsewhere, Duff tries to make his theory immune to the first challenge by admitting from the start that his communicative approach to punishment proposes an ideal theory which could be far removed from our current penal practices. Nonetheless it has the advantage of serving potentially as a critical reference point when it comes to the reform of these practices.[4]

[4] See in particular R.A. DUFF, *Punishment, Communication, and Community*, Oxford, Oxford University Press, 2001, especially chapter 5.

This immunisation strategy does not prevent Walgrave from pointing out the very fact that punishment, as it reveals itself in the real world, serves many societal functions and has an undeniable instrumental value. Any appropriate penal theory has to accommodate this multifunctional and instrumental meaning of punishment, and, correspondingly, has to address the question whether penal practices effectively help realise the purposes they are supposed to serve. For Walgrave, social science has delivered enough evidence to suggest that criminal punishment does not meet this efficiency test. The time has come, then, to unchain the criminal justice system from its penal fetters.

Here Burms' reply can be read both as a defence of Duff's non-instrumental theory of punishment and as a critique of Walgrave's response. Burms traces here a distinction between Duff's normative account of criminal punishment and a more descriptive account implied in Duff's anti-consequentialist view of punishment. The latter aspect engages Duff in what Burms calls an "understanding of the immanent meaning of criminal punishment". With "immanent meaning" Burms seems to refer to those aspects of retributive punishment which it is necessary to articulate if one wants to have any understanding at all of the practice of punishment. Thus immanent to the meaning of any practice of criminal punishment is, first, its continuity with emotions of indignation expressed in blame and censure and intended to induce remorse. Also immanent thereto is, secondly, its fit into the larger phenomenon of symbolic restoration through which the dignity of the victim is symbolically reaffirmed. Punishing the offender symbolically restores the dignity of the victim by preventing the offender from continuing with life as if the victim's standing as a full person is of no value whatsoever.

If Burms' understanding of the immanent meaning of punishment is correct, then there is plenty of room to argue that a communicative view of punishment is not all that far removed from actual penal practices. A communicative approach has a firm grounding in the existing practice of criminal punishment, which is undeniably expressive of such moral feelings as indignation and remorse. Burms could thus provide the basis to counter Walgrave's plea for abolitionism, namely that it is completely irrational to deny the appropriateness of punishment as such, just as it is completely irrational to deny the appropriateness of the emotions of indignation and remorse.

As a second challenge to Duff, Walgrave objects that Duff's communitarianism is not sufficiently sensitive to the very fact that it is not easy to identify in practice what the essential values of a liberal polity are, let alone to define which type of actions are in breach of these values. Duff would seem to ignore the consideration that criminal facts are in reality social constructions in which power and exclusion mechanisms often play a determining role. Therefore Walgrave prefers harm, not criminal wrong, to serve as the ultimate basis for an official response to crime. To this objection to a communitarian conception of punishment one could easily argue with Duff that the sheer fact that in criminalising behaviour a government can impose oppressive or unacceptable conceptions of criminal wrong, does not in itself rule out the state's general obligation to condemn certain kinds of wrong.

A third and final challenge is found in Walgrave's reply and is more extensively treated in the comment of Bas van Stokkom. This challenge relates to Duff's attempt to introduce the concern of restorative justice with emotions like remorse, apology, repentance, self-reform, and reconciliation, into the framework of hard treatment. According to van Stokkom (and Walgrave) an appropriate two-way communication between state and offender is undermined from the start when the invitation to self-reform and to making reparations is embedded in a context of hard treatment. The offender focuses on the hardship inflicted upon him, instead of on the moral message conveyed to him. The suffering involved in hard treatment cuts the offender off from a kind of opening up of the self which is necessary for moral self-reform. Taking the form of a regime of hard treatment, the moral communication expressed through punishment can easily degenerate into bullying. Repentance and moral repair ought therefore to be separated from the framework of hard treatment. For van Stokkom restorative sanctions have to be reserved for those offenders who do show genuine remorse and are sincerely repentant. The criminal justice system is only required to engage in punitive treatment in order to temper public rage when serious crime has been committed and where the offender proves to be untrustworthy in his willingness for moral self-reform. Against this alternative strategy of bifurcation, as proposed by van Stokkom, one can counter with Duff that such a strategy risks coming into conflict with one of the basic values of a liberal democracy: concern and respect for the privacy of each citizen. To judge the trustworthiness of the offender and the sincerity of his goodwill is to assess the character of the offender, to enter into the secrets of his moral self, and to engage in a moral book-keeping of his ultimate moral worth. These kinds of intrusive assessments would exceed the limits of what is tolerable in a state which intends to promote the values of a liberal democracy.

PART ONE.
CRIMINAL JUSTICE, LEGALITY, HUMAN DIGNITY

1. CRIMINAL JUSTICE, LEGALITY AND HUMAN DIGNITY

ERIK CLAES

INTRODUCTION

For several decades criminal lawyers have been confronted with an all-embracing problem that is often identified as "the penal crisis". This term refers to an almost inextricable knot of shortcomings and inadequacies weighing down many contemporary criminal justice systems. Since the birth of their science criminologists have made a considerable effort to map this penal deficit. By drawing attention to the often pernicious repercussions of that deficit on the lives of individuals, many criminologists have stepped into the role of scientific spokesmen for victims and offenders, as well as for their respective frustrations and dissatisfactions with the criminal justice system.

These dissatisfactions of victims and offenders concern both our current penal system and the very idea of criminal punishment. They also appear to be related to the legal framework of criminal law in which penal intervention takes place. In this context, the abstract concepts, principles and technocratic legal language by which public officials justify their actions are criticised here.

It is equally important to note that criminologists by virtue of their scientific knowledge have played, and are still playing, an important role in the development of alternative initiatives seeking to remedy the shortcomings of the criminal justice system. Particularly relevant are the rise of programmes and practices commonly known under the heading of "restorative justice", including, for instance, victim-offender mediation and conferencing techniques.

The core of restorative justice in all its different forms seems to be that it (a) seeks to take seriously the desires, wants and needs of victims and offenders, (b) interprets the phenomenon of criminality in terms of restoration, (c) aims to be an alternative for punishment or, at least, perceives itself as complementary to the penal apparatus, (d) aspires either to offer an alternative to the strongly legalistic framework in which penal practice takes place, or exert a considerable influence over the meaning and functioning of its legal concepts and principles.

Despite the critical diagnosis of the criminal justice system made by criminologists, and despite the evolving success of the restorative justice movement and the optimistic belief that its practices work, the bulk of criminal lawyers do not feel inclined to examine their system in the light of its concrete impact on the lives of victims and offenders. Legal practitioners within the criminal justice system, in their capacity of magistrates, barristers or doctrinal writers, adhere at least unconsciously to a sort of confidence in the meaningfulness, and even in the necessity of punishment. They also demonstrate a kind of fidelity to the necessity of a complex legal structure that constrains and regulates the behaviour of public officials.

This fidelity to the legal aspects of criminal justice, which is so common to legal practitioners, is far more than a somewhat blind reflex due to their profession. For it is to be traced back to a set of deep intuitions associated either with the term "rechtsstaat" and "droit d'état" in continental legal traditions, or with the concept of "the rule of law" in the common law tradition. Especially in continental legal reasoning, these intuitions are reflected in abstract ideas like the principle of legality, as well as principles of the guilty mind and of proportionality. Particularly important to observe, however, is that the fidelity of criminal lawyers to a criminal justice system based on the idea of the rechtsstaat, or the rule of law, not only comes down to a fidelity to the principles just mentioned, but also appears to manifest itself in an equally strong scepticism as to the importance and function of restorative justice practices, whatever shape they might take.

I would like to step into the current discussion concerning restorative justice and its relation to the traditional criminal justice system, by articulating a *modest* and at the same time somewhat *hybrid* position.

The position is a hybrid one because on the one hand, it sees criminal justice through the eyes of the legal practitioner, by trying to understand the meaningfulness of his adherence to the rule of law. The ambition developed in this paper consists of exploring the *full potential* of a criminal justice system ruled by the law, and particularly, the *ethical credentials* of such a system. On the other hand, it takes interest in the point of view of many criminologists. I would like, indeed, to observe the criminal justice system, feeling and exploring its *limits* from the perspective of both victim and offender. Behind this somewhat ambiguous line of approach lies the conviction that a more refined insight into the vitality, and also into the inevitable vulnerability of the rule of law might help prepare the way for a well-considered debate regarding the future, if any, of restorative justice.

This conviction also explains why my stance in the debate should be considered as a *modest* one. The primary concern of this paper is not to present a full and substantial account of restorative justice –that will be the subject of the second part of this volume – but simply to mark out, as a sort of preliminary reflection, the space in which one could try to develop such an account. The position this paper offers is also modest, because, as has been suggested, it will demarcate the space for discussion on the future of restorative justice *only* in so far it examines the credentials and limits of the rule of law. What is not discussed in the paper is setting a stage for discussion on the fate of restorative justice, insofar as it is related to the strengths and vulnerabilities of punishment and penal practice. These kinds of reflections will be partly dealt with in the third part of this volume.

In addition, I have modestly narrowed my stage-setting ambitions by reducing my research on the potentials and limits of the rule of law to an enquiry into the credentials and vulnerabilities of one basic idea: the principle of *legality*. This option is not a complete coincidence: the principle of legality is not only taken to be essential to the idea of the rule of law, it is also recognised as a fully-fledged human right since it is enshrined in Article 7 of the European Convention on Human Rights.

The option, however, to select the ideal of legality as just one among other devices which constitute the arsenal of the rule of law, is not without consequences for the outcome of this paper. The reference points we will try to set out in order to establish a constructive discussion on the future of restorative justice will be inevitably incomplete, because they are completely subordinate to the fate of the principle of criminal legality.

1. WORRIES ABOUT LEGALITY AND THE RULE OF LAW

In the judgement of 5 January 1999, the magistrates' court of Brussels had to decide quite an interesting case.[1] According to her witness, the victim initially consented to sexual intercourse, but during sex she was forced without consent to acts of sodomy, resulting in considerable physical injury. The tribunal concluded that there was no absence of consent and, consequently, that the requirements were not met for qualifying the facts as an offence of rape. The court justified its decision by referring to an old doctrinal source asserting "qu'en matière de viol, il n'y a pas de degré dans le consentement".[2]

When in the case at hand, one might invite the court to argue its decision in a somewhat more elaborate way, one could foresee the court giving a standard account on the criminal justice system which embeds the behaviour of public officials in the idea of "the rule of law". According to this standard account the attitude of the tribunal finds its justification in the idea that the criminal judge, by virtue of his power to punish, has to submit his judicial process to rigorous restrictions. One of these restrictions is embodied in *the principle of legality* and constitutes, as the standard account goes, the essence of "the rule of law". A criminal judge may convict

[1] Magistrates' court of Brussels, 5 January 1999, *J.T. (Journal des Tribunaux)* 1999, 627.
[2] Magistrates' court of Brussels, 5 January 1999, *J.T. (Journal des Tribunaux)* 1999, 627.

an individual citizen and impose punishment on him if a double requirement is met: (a) the facts fall within the scope of a legal rule existing at the time of the facts and clearly define a criminal offence (nullum crimen, sine lege); (b) the penal sanction is defined in a previously existing legal provision. (nulla poena, sine lege). According to the standard account, the magistrates' judge, in the case mentioned above, is not allowed to creatively adapt the term "absence of consent", and consequently the content of the offence of rape, in the light of the circumstances of the case'. For, by virtue of the principle of legality criminal judges may not extend the scope of statutory offences. They are held to interpret criminal law in a strict way.

While in doctrinal writings this conventional justification of the exercise of coercive power by the criminal judge is still accepted in one version or another, most criminal lawyers, however, must have some notion of the fact that in our contemporary societies the credibility of this standard account has been subjected to critical scrutiny from different perspectives and for various reasons. Criminologists from their side base their criticism on the following observations: our criminal justice systems have a far-reaching effect on the individual lives of victims and offenders, but, at the same time, they appear to be indifferent to the manner in which citizens try to give meaning to their lives and their surroundings.

Look again, for example, at the somewhat odd decision of the Belgian judge. *On the one hand,* the present case shows clearly how far reaching the effects produced by the criminal judge's decision can be for the parties concerned. The answer to the question of whether the facts of the case constitute the criminal offence of rape will have an enormous impact on how victim and offender will face their lives in the future. If the decision works out badly for the victim, then she stands a chance of being deeply hurt for not being fully recognised in her feelings as a victim. If the judge's decision works out badly for the offender, he runs the risk of leading his life as a stigmatised person, bearing a destructive self-image of a rapist.

On the other hand, one does not need much imagination to see how difficult it must be for the victim to recognise the reasonableness of the decision made by the Belgian judge. The argument that in matters of rape there is no such thing as a degree in absence of consent, can hardly be matched with the way the victim has experienced her own feelings of humiliation and the debasing character of the offender's behaviour. She undoubtedly felt raped for being brutally subjected against her will to acts of sodomy. The fact of an initial consent in sexual intercourse does not erase her perceptions.

Where does the gap between criminal legal practice and the experiences of victims and offenders come from? According to criminologists – and here we are approaching the core of their criticism – this gap is due partly to the *abstract* character of criminal law and of criminal legal reasoning. A web of abstract concepts and principles together with a strong tendency to conceptualisation, at least in continental legal doctrine, is in fact responsible for citizens not being able to grasp the meaning of public official's legal habits in wielding their coercive power. If we take again the example of sodomy, one could argue that the alienating effect of criminal law is due to the abstract level at which the criminal judge, first, defines an essential element of the criminal offence of rape, and, second, verifies whether this element is applicable to the facts of the case.

Indeed, according to criminologists, it is quite misleading to assume that citizens understand each other's behaviour in the light of abstract and previously defined legal concepts. In daily life people do not understand the situations to which they respond and act by means of abstract rules and categories. They see immediately the point of what has been done and how to react meaningfully, guided by a tacit background understanding of a variety of concrete and context-specific practices in which they live and act.

In response to the criticism of criminologists, criminal lawyers in turn will likely conduct their defence by drawing on the normative credentials of the principles of legality and the rule of law, and consequently, by articulating the political ideals behind these principles. The judicial restraint of criminal judges with regard to the interpretation of legal norms embodying a criminal offence is in part inspired by the interest of citizens in making *foreseeable* the official's behaviour in the exercise of their power to punish. In determining the scope of a criminal offence from case to case and in the light of changing social circumstances, judges run the risk of surrendering citizens to a strong margin of judicial discretion. This could easily lead to a situation in which the latter will have lost their ability to determine precisely the limits between lawful and unlawful behaviour.

But criminologists will see this reply from lawyers and legal scientists more as an *affirmation* of their criticism. To justify the importance of the use of abstract definitions of terms like the absence of consent, criminal lawyers need to appeal to an *even more abstract* concept, the principle of *legality*, which would be applied at least in an equally context-indifferent manner. For a victim of violent and debasing sexual behaviour, it is even more difficult to understand that in virtue of the principle of legality the judge decided to put the facts, *her* facts, beyond the scope of the criminal offence of rape.

But there is more. Criminologists consider this adherence to legality and the rule of law also as a strengthening and broadening of their criticism. The aforementioned principle not only seems to generate indifference from public officials with regard to the concrete circumstances of the case and the concrete experiences of victims and offenders. It also seems to produce a perception of the case, which draws a highly reduced and distorted image of the conflict to be resolved. What the criminologist's observation of the *conflict-reducing* effect of legality is about, can be best explained by means of an example. I will use here a case borrowed from a recent publication of J. Braithwaite on restorative justice.[3]

The case involved the serious assault of one man by another. The victim, in the words of Braithwaite, "was left lying in a liter and a half of his own blood and required $ 3,000 in dental work". The offender risked prison time for committing a criminal offence. Criminologists will surely indicate here that by means of the principle of legality only those aspects of the conflict are presented that could possibly fall within the scope of the legal definition of assault and battery. Consequently, the penal sanction to be imposed will almost exclusively depend on these aspects of the conflict, which constitute only a fragment of a complex process and of complex human interactions. For B. Hudson, "what we presently call a crime, is a complex event, which will have a different meaning according to the circumstances of the offender, the victim and the community, and the relations between them".[4]

These observations have led criminologists to criticise the criminal justice system. For it would produce, through the conflict-reducing effect of legality, a completely inadequate response to criminal behaviour, thus intensifying the underlying conflict with a possibly dramatic outcome. In the present case, for instance, the offender just came out of prison and was about to return to prison for another offence. During his last detention the offender cultivated a spiral of rage against the victim of the assault. The former believed that the latter raped his fiancée. Victim and offender where thrown into regular contact because they purchased heroin from the same place. The victim feared that the offender's detention would generate even more anger, and that he would come out of prison and kill him next time he was released.

In addition to the conflict-reducing effect of criminal law criminologists could also argue that public officials, because of their adherence to legality, deprive themselves of the opportunity to take into account the desire of victims and offender to hear of and to communicate to each other their respective interpretations of the facts, their emotions and their reasons for acting as they did. By focussing considerably on the essential elements of the offence and by limiting their intervention only to these facts which fall under the scope of "assault and battery", the criminal judge fails to consider the desire of victim and offender to be taken seriously in their anger and

---

3 J. BRAITHWAITE, *Restorative Justice and Responsive Regulation*, Oxford, Oxford University Press, 2002, 83.

4 B. HUDSON, *Understanding Justice. An Introduction to Ideas, Perspectives and Controversies in Modern Penal Theory*, Buckingham, Open University Press, 1996, 145.

fears. He also fails to consider their desire to communicate to each other their stance in the conflict. Or, to put it another way: together with a conflict-reducing effect, legality also appears to generate a *depersonalising*-effect.

2. SOME PRELIMINARY REMARKS

When one tries, as a criminologist, to place oneself imaginatively in the position of the victim or the offender, one can easily come up with reasons explaining, at least "prima facie," why victims and offenders through their own experiences can hardly give sense to a criminal justice system guided by the principles and concepts of the rule of law. Victims and offenders, so runs the diagnosis of many criminologists, do not feel at home in such a criminal justice system because of its abstract and *context-indifferent* character, as well as its *conflict-reducing* and *depersonalising* effect. It is equally important to note here that these effects would have been generated by at least one of the very principles which helps to ground the criminal justice system in the rule of law, namely the *ideal of legality*. As already stated above, almost every legal practitioner will adopt the familiar account that public officials, in particular legislators and judges, in their exercise of coercive powershould define criminal wrongs in clearly defined legal provisions, and interpret the scope of these provisions in a strict manner.

In virtue of the criminologist's criticism this familiar account of a legality-based criminal justice system is inevitably the subject of fundamental questioning. A questioning of its *adequacy*, first, because this principle through its undeniable abstract character apparently fails to *fit* the concrete contexts in which victim and offender lives and acts. The ideal of legality is supposed to constrain the behaviour of public officials in the interest of every individual citizen. But where does this interest lie when it is too abstract, and accordingly, when it is not recognised as concrete, from the perspective of victim and offender in an actual case?

This issue is closely interwoven with another question concerning the *justifiability* of a criminal justice system grounded in the ideals of legality and the rule of law. As already pointed out, one of the normative credentials of a system in which public officials adhere to legality, is the predictability and the limited scope of their coercive actions. These ideas of predictability and limited realm of public intervention would enable legal subjects to regulate their own conduct, to mark off clearly rightful behaviour from legal wrongdoing, and to dispose of a large realm of free action. But these ideals of predictability and individual freedom, when respected and secured by public officials through their adherence to legality, appear to bring about distorted images of inter-individual conflicts (conflict-reducing effect). Moreover, these ideals would rule out in advance every consideration of victims and offenders as concrete human beings with concrete wants and desires (depersonalising effect). It seems then that the application of the principle of legality and its underlying ideals is not without sacrifice on the human side, which brings us necessarily to a questioning of the justifiability of legality, of its weight and importance in the administration of criminal justice.

Is there still a case for an adequate principle of legality, given the gap between its undeniably abstract character, on the one hand, and the context-related perspective of victim and offender, on the other? Is defence for a legality-based criminal justice system still justified, given the conflict reducing and depersonalising effect of this principle? These are at least two important intellectual challenges which must be addressed if a criminal justice system guided by legality and the rule of law, is to successfully answer the criticism of many criminologists. As already noted above, both challenges here will be subject to a somewhat hybrid approach.

On the one hand, this contribution aims to exhibit, like criminal lawyers, true fidelity to the ideals of legality and the rule of law. One of the basic motives behind this line of approach is the conviction that these ideals possess a conceptual and ethical potential which has not yet been fully exhausted.

On the other hand, an attempt will be made to address both problems of adequacy and justification as serious issues calling into question *from the outside*, like criminologists, the whole enterprise of a criminal justice system constrained and guided by the rule of law. But there is more to be added to it. In what follows, an inquiry will be pursued relating to the existence of some *internal* reasons and arguments by virtue of which criminal lawyers within their legal practice are forced to take positions with regard to adequacy and justifiability of the principle of legality. This inquiry reflects two underlying motives. First, contemporary developments in the criminal law of most of the Western legal traditions have launched a process of continual erosion of the basic conceptual arsenal of the rule of law. This erosion calls into existence a not yet fully recognised, but undeniably reflexive need for articulating, revitalising and reinvigorating this conceptual arsenal. Second, the uncovering of these reflexive needs existing somewhere deep in criminal law may actually provide interesting material so as to sharpen the focus of the aforementioned challenges of adequacy and justifiability.

3. IS LEGALITY STILL ADEQUATE ENOUGH FOR A SUCCESSFUL ADMINISTRATION OF CRIMINAL JUSTICE?

Does the practice of criminal law incite criminal lawyers to reflect on the seemingly unbridgeable gap between the abstract dimension of the principle of legality and the inevitable context-sensitivity of every case at hand?

Consider the judgement of 24 June 1993 in which the European Court of Human Rights had to decide the case Kokkinakis vs. Greece.[5] Two Jehovah's Witnesses, Mr Kokkinakis and his wife, called at the home of Mrs Kyriakaki in Sitia. She let them in because they said they had good news for her. As soon as they were inside Mr. Kokkinakis began to read and explain passages from the Holy Bible. He also tried to sell different kind of books. Mrs Kyriakaki did not understand much of what was said. Mrs Kyriakaki's husband, who was the cantor at a local Orthodox church, informed the police, who then arrested Mr and Mrs Kokkinakis and took them to the local police station. They were prosecuted and convicted under section 4 of Law no. 1363/1938 making proselytism an offence. The second paragraph of this section reads as follows: "By proselytism is meant, in particular, any direct or indirect attempt to intrude on the religious beliefs of a person of a different religious persuasion (eterodoxos), with the aim of undermining those beliefs, either by any kind of inducement or moral support or material assistance, or by fraudulent means or by taking advantage of his experience, trust, need, low intellect or naivety".[6]

Before the European Court the question arose whether the definition of proselytism, as mentioned in the previous paragraph, in virtue of its vague formulation would constitute a violation of Article 7 §1 E.C.H.R. This article states: "No one shall be held guilty of any criminal offence on account of any act or omission which did not constitute a criminal offence under national or international law at the time when it was committed. Nor shall a heavier penalty be imposed than the one that was applicable at the time the criminal offence was committed".

According to the applicant, Mr Kokkinakis, the aforementioned definition of proselytism was too vague, creating an inadmissible risk of unforeseeable and extensive applications by the law courts and, consequently, preventing legal subjects from knowing precisely which behaviour is lawful and which not. In its second paragraph, section 4 of Law no. 1363/1938 "had retained", in the words of the applicant, "all the "extendible, catch-all expressions", merely using a more concise but equally "pedantic style" designed to ensure that non-orthodox Christians were permanently gagged. Consequently, no citizen could regulate his conduct on the basis of this enactment".[7]

---

5 European Court of Human Rights (ECHR), 25 May 1993, Kokkinakis vs. Greece, *Publ. Eur. Court. H.R.*, Series A, nr. 260.

6 ECHR, 25 May 1993, Kokkinakis vs. Greece, *Publ. Eur. Court. H.R.*, Series A, nr. 260, 12.

7 ECHR, 25 May 1993, Kokkinakis vs. Greece, *Publ. Eur. Court. H.R.*, Series A, nr. 260, 22.

While considering the facts of the case, as a criminologist would do, one could note that the depth and complexity of the inter-individual conflict, underlying the case, had been considerably narrowed by the principle of legality. The focus is now mainly on the question whether the criminal offence of proselytism is too broadly defined in section 4, as well as whether the facts can be brought under the terms of this section, without extending its scope too far. From this seems to follow that in virtue of the principle of legality too great an abstraction would be made from the particular stance the victim and offender had originally taken in the conflict. Abstraction could also be made by questions such as how did victim and offender experience the conflict, what role did other persons, like Mrs Kyriakaki's husband, play in the genesis of the conflict.

It is quite interesting to see that similar critiques of a too rigid and too context-insensitive concept of legality have also been heard within the practice of criminal law itself. When one observes more attentively some evolutions and tendencies within the court law of contemporary legal systems, on the continent and in the UK, one would be surprised to see that judges in reality show a far more relaxed attitude towards the interpretation and application of legal norms than is dogmatically presupposed. It is of course not within the scope of this paper to present the facts of an extensive comparative legal study. Three observations should suffice. *First*, in interpreting statutes and legal norms establishing criminal offences, judicial decisions are often informed by context-specific considerations which are covered by traditional interpretation techniques like an inquiry into the semantic meaning of the terms of the law or a reconstruction of the intention of the legislator. Second, responsive to changing circumstances in society and responsive to the danger of excessive rigidity, legislators are forced to put criminal offences in vague and imprecise terms. In the case of Kokkinakis vs. Greece, for instance, the European Court of Human Rights states "that the wording of many statutes is not absolutely precise. The need to avoid excessive rigidity and to keep pace with changing circumstances means that many laws are inevitably couched in terms which, to a greater or lesser extent, are vague".[8] From this observation it follows that the law-making process of the judge, even in criminal matters, has been gradually recognised. In the wordings of the Court: "The interpretation and application of such enactment depend on practice".[9]

Third, legal practitioners have become more and more aware of the fact that the wordings of legal norms, including criminal statutes, contain an inevitable "open texture". This implies, at least in cases showing the open texture of a legal norm, that the judge's attention to the circumstances of the case is an inevitable ingredient of his interpretative practice. This

8 ECHR, 25 May 1993, Kokkinakis vs. Greece, *Publ. Eur. Court. H.R.*, Series A, nr. 260, 19.

9 ECHR, 25 May 1993, Kokkinakis vs. Greece, *Publ. Eur. Court. H.R.*, Series A, nr. 260, 19.

awareness can be evidenced in a striking way through another decision of the European Court of Human Rights. In its judgement of 22 November 1995 in the case S.W. vs. United Kingdom the Court argued: "However clearly drafted a legal provision may be, in any system of law, including criminal law, there is an inevitable element of judicial interpretation. There will always be a need for elucidation of doubtful points and for adaptation to changing circumstances".[10]

In the light of these observations one could easily conclude that criminal lawyers are invited from *within* their own legal practice to address at least one issue concerning legality and the rule of law, which is similar to those raised from the *outside* by criminologists: to what extent can a judge *adequately* uphold the abstract principle of legality if his interpretative practice is inevitably context-sensitive?

In order to refine what we called the questioning of the adequacy of legality, it is, however, important to draw attention to the fact that besides similarities between the criminologist's diagnosis and the reflexive need of the criminal lawyer, at least one essential difference has to be pointed out.

Indeed, we just need our intuitions to feel that the questioning of the adequacy of legality in the light of the very structure of judicial interpretation relates to a different type of context-sensitivity than the one criminologists have in mind when identifying themselves with the perspectives of victim and offender. The question is then: Where does the difference lie between these two types of context-sensitivity?

Consider again the judgement of the European Court of Human Right of 22 November 1995, mentioned above.[11] The applicant was a British citizen. His relationship with his wife was turbulent and came under great strain in 1990 when he became unemployed. In the early evening of 18 September 1990, she told him that for some weeks she had been thinking of leaving him and that she regarded the marriage as over. The applicant did not accept that his wife meant what she said and they had a row following which he ejected her from the house, bruising her arm. Later the same evening she re-entered the house and the applicant raped her at knifepoint. The British courts convicted the applicant for the criminal offence of rape as provided in section 1 (1) of the Sexual Offences Act 1956.

The European Court was to answer the question whether or not the conviction of the applicant by the British courts for the offence of rape

[10] ECHR, 22 November 1995, S.W./ United Kingdom, *Publ. Eur. Court H.R.*, Series B, nr. 335, 41.

[11] ECHR, 22 November 1995, S.W./ United Kingdom, *Publ. Eur. Court H.R.*, Series B, nr. 335, 41.

constituted a retrospective incrimination, and, consequently, was in breach of the principle of legality as couched in Article 7 of the Convention. Until 1976 the principle of marital immunity was unanimously part of the British law. This principle stated that a husband having sexual intercourse with his wife without her consent could not be charged with the criminal offence of rape. After 1976, though, case law was divided as to the continuing existence of this principle given the changing social attitudes concerning the institution of marriage. The European Court, in other words, was to decide whether the British courts were with regard to the principle of legality (Article7 E.C.H.R) in a legitimate position to determine the scope of the wordings of the criminal statute defining the offence of rape in the light of changing social circumstances. The European Court had to address a delicate issue. If the Court decided to adopt a strict conception of legality, then it risked losing its grip on the inevitable context-sensitivity of judicial reasoning. If the Court adopted a more lenient version of legality, then it threatened to deny the principle in its essence by eroding the prohibition of retrospective incrimination.

In order to elucidate the intuitively felt distinction between two types of context-sensitivity, it is important to note in the case at hand that the sensitivity of the British Courts for the circumstances of the case was not completely detached from the legal norm to be interpreted. In fact, changing social attitudes only obtained their relevance and meaningfulness after the case was confronted with the legal norm making rape a criminal offence. It is because the idea of placing the facts beyond the scope of the offence of rape sounds unreasonable for many judges today that interest is taken in the broader social background of the case. From this *norm-relativity* of the facts it follows that the relevance of certain circumstances is not confined to the case at hand, but can be extended to other similar cases. These facts, such as changing social attitudes towards marriage, retain a certain degree of a generality depending on the degree of abstraction contained in the related legal norm to be interpreted.

If the inevitable context-sensitivity of judges in their judicial reasoning proves to be related to legal norms, one could reasonably ask to what extent this would also apply to the type of context-sensitivity criminologists display when they place themselves in the position of victim and offender.

Take for example the already mentioned case borrowed from Braithwaite in which one person seriously assaulted another. From the point of view of criminologists attention is focussed on the concrete motives of the offender and the actual needs and desires of the victim, as well as on the complexity and the genesis of the conflict in which victim and offender are placed. In the case at hand a criminologist would be particularly sensitive to the fact that the offender in assaulting the victim was moved by the conviction that the latter had raped the former's fiancée. His attention would be also focussed on the victim, and in particular on his fears of being killed by the offender who, due to an eventual imprisonment, would develop still more frustrations and anger. Finally, criminologists would be sensitive to the secret wants of both offender and victim to communicate to each other their feelings and story in the case.

Characteristic of the sensitivity of these facts is that their meaning is not completely exhausted by a legal norm to be interpreted. In contrast to changing social attitudes concerning the institution of marriage in the case S.W. vs. United Kingdom, the anger of the offender and the fears of the victim have no role to play in the determination of the criminal offence of life threatening assault. For the criminologist who tries to grasp the conflict from the perspective of victim and offender, these feelings refer to the isolation in which they feel they have been placed, as well as to the respective desires of victim and offender to be recognised in those feelings as a fully-fledged person. In contrast to the type of facts and context-sensitivity, which was called *norm-relative* above, we will qualify the type of facts and context-sensitivity, which is at stake here, as *person-relative.*

Such a distinction is not without consequences for refining one of the two main issues this paper is addressing, namely the challenge of the *adequacy* of a legality-based criminal justice system. As is evidenced by the foregoing remarks, this challenge can only be met provided that (a) the concept of legality addresses adequately the context-sensitivity of the judge which in its nature is related to legal norms to be interpreted (norm-relativity); (b) the idea of legality can accommodate a type of context-sensitivity that brings to the fore victim and offender as individual persons (person-relativity).

4. DOES LEGALITY STILL CONTAIN ENOUGH JUSTIFYING POWER TO GUIDE AND CONSTRAIN THE ADMINISTRATION OF CRIMINAL JUSTICE?

So far an attempt has been made to sharpen the focus of our questioning on the adequacy of legality by placing this principle against the background of some tendencies in contemporary criminal law. A similar exercise can be made with regard to the questioning of legality in terms of its degree of *justifiability.*

As already stated above, criminal lawyers, in the capacity of magistrates or doctrinal writers, are faced with a rapidly changing society involving new problems to be regulated and new types of behaviour to be co-ordinated. It is not surprising, therefore, that contemporary states try to overcome these problems by deploying an impressive arsenal of openly formulated rules establishing very indeterminate standards of behaviour as criminal offences and, in doing so, allowing judges to concretise them with a wide margin of flexibility. Against this background, it is not surprising that criminal lawyers are almost forced to reflect on the underlying values of the principle of legality in such a rapidly changing society. One can in fact say that today, criminal lawyers are pushed into a somewhat ambiguous position regarding a legality-based criminal justice system. On the one hand, legal doctrine and the tradition of the rule of law tells them to affirm the ideal of legality as a "rempart de la liberté individuelle" and as an essential guarantee against the arbitrary use of coercive power by public officials. On the other hand, society tells them to establish new and mainly flexible habits in the administration of criminal justice, which are adapted to the needs of efficient and co-ordinated social interaction.

This ambiguity is surely located in the legal systems of many contemporary welfare states and a comparative study in this respect would be very welcome indeed. But the ambiguity is also in a striking way reflected in the case law of the European Court of Human Rights with regard to principle of legality enshrined in Article 7 of the European Convention on Human Rights.

Consider, for instance, again the case S.W. vs. United Kingdom of 22 November 1995. The European Court had to decide whether the British courts, by applying the offence of rape to a marital context, were in breach of Article 7 E.C.H.R. and, consequently, of their obligations to restrain themselves from extending the scope of criminal offences. The Court decided, without the support of a single-voiced case law on the matter at the time of the facts, that in the present case no breach of Article 7 could be established. Affirming the importance and value of the principle of legality as a fully-fledged human right, the Court stated that legality remains an essential element of the rule. This principle, in the words of the Court, "should be construed and applied, as follows from its object and purpose, in such a way as to provide effective safeguards against arbitrary prosecution conviction and punishment".[12] The Court – and here lies its ambiguity – argued that the principle of legality, in its application, does not prohibit the judge from adapting the scope of a criminal legal rule to changing social circumstances, provided the change was reasonably foreseeable at the moments of the facts.

It goes without saying that this ambiguity, especially as evidenced in S.W. vs. United Kingdom gives every criminal lawyer a good reason to reflect on the underlying values of legality, on the ideal of predictability of public officials using their coercive power, and in particular, on the question what makes a progressive explanation of the legal terms of criminal offence, in the words of the Court, to be reasonably (un)foreseen.

---

12 ECHR, 22 November 1995, S.W./ United Kingdom, *Publ. Eur. Court of H.R.*, Series B, nr. 335, 41.

It thus seems that the need to question the justifiability of legality presents itself from an *outer* criminologist's perspective as well as from an *inner* legal perspective. But as it was not sufficiently clear for the questioning of legality's adequacy to what extent these two perspectives can be compared with one another, so too for the questioning of legality's justifiability.

Consider for instance the case of marital rape. Being part of their ambiguous position, criminal lawyers might argue in the present case that the principle of legality is of importance, because it has to be traced back to the right of the defendant to be protected against judicial arbitrariness, combined with his/her right to privacy and individual freedom. In this respect the principle of legality seems to be somehow intuitively linked to the still more fundamental right of respect for *human dignity*.

It is paradoxical, though, that the idea of human dignity, which appears to present itself as the ultimate ground of legality, also appears to find its expression in the criminologist's remarks on the conflict-reducing and depersonalising effect of the very same principle of legality. For, a similar intuitive association can be made between respect for human dignity and attention to the personal fate of victim and offender, and their respective desires to communicate their perception of the conflict.

This paradox is in a need of clarification. For the time being it is actually far from clear which aspect of human dignity is attacked, when for instance the facts of the case would have proved a violation of legality. It is even less clear which dimension of human dignity is denied, when by the very impact of legality on the criminal justice system there is no space left for full attention to the personal perspective of both victim and offender. And, finally, uncertainty exists as to how these seemingly different faces of human dignity are related to each other. In particular, doubt is cast on the extent to which they are reconcilable or, even, cancel each other out.

In other words: one can reasonably hold that the questioning of the justifiability of a legality-based criminal justice system in fact focuses mainly on the complex nature of the idea of human dignity which seemingly inspires both friends and critics of the principle of legality.

Where are we? We have tried to show that both the issue of legality's adequacy and its justifiability do not exclusively flow from the criminologist's criticism with regard to the context-indifferent, conflict-reducing and depersonalising effect of a legality-based criminal justice system. It has been argued, first that the issue of *adequacy* finds it source also in the practical need of criminal lawyers to be provided with a principle of legality which fits the inevitable *context sensitivity* of judicial reasoning. It has been argued, secondly, that the issue of *justifiability* finds its roots in an equally practical need of criminal lawyers to free them from ambiguity with regard to legality. Criminal lawyers are invited here to reflect on the normative credentials of legality, if any, in their contemporary society the dynamics of which are determined by the claims of efficient and co-ordinated social interaction.

Following these insights, the comparison between an *outer* criminologist's perspective and an *inner* legal perspective led us at the same time to a refinement of our questioning of legality in its adequacy and justifiability.

Bringing us to a distinction between two types of context-sensitivity, the comparison just mentioned results, first, in a sharpening of the issue of *adequacy*, which comes down to this. How, if possible, to design a principle of legality fitting the judge's context sensitivity, which needs to be rule-relative, and at the same time, accommodating special circumstances of the case, the meaning of which needs to be person-relative, revealing a perspective from which victim and offender appear and express themselves as individual persons?

Revealing ambiguous intuitions concerning the idea of human dignity, the comparison between a criminologist's and a legal perspective, brings us, secondly, to a reformulating of the issue of *justifiability*, which reads now as follows. To what extent can there be made conceivable a coherent and justifiable conception of respect for human dignity that can provide for the ultimate ground of legality in an ever changing society, and accommodate the desire of victim and offender to express themselves as individual persons through their own perception and experience of the conflict?

In what follows I will address both issues in their full complexity by concentrating a bit more on the phenomenon of the principle of legality as enshrined in Article7 of the European Convention on Human Rights. In order to find a satisfying answer to the issue of adequacy, our inquiry will start off by asking what it actually means to recognise the principle of legality as a fully-fledged human right. An attempt will therefore be made, supported by the case-law of the European Court of Human Rights, to grasp the conceptual implications of legality having become part of the human rights discourse. An effort will thus be made to see what turns legality into *a rights-conception of legality*.

In order to find a satisfying answer to the issue of legality's *justifiability*, our inquiry will seek, again with the help of case-law of the Court, to uncover *these aspects of human dignity* which are secured/denied by respecting/denying a rights-conception of legality. This should lead us to an as accurate as possible comparison between the idea of human dignity insofar as it is reflected in a rights conception of legality and one which is reflected in the criminologist's criticism of legality.

We will first tackle the issue of legality's adequacy, after which we shall turn to the issue of legality's justifiability

5. THE IDEA OF A RIGHTS-CONCEPTION OF LEGALITY

One of the most important objections criminologists raise with regard to the principle of legality is related to its abstract, and therefore, they tell us, to its dogmatic, rigid and context-indifferent character. Criminologists assume here abstraction and context indifference to be identical. This criticism is compromised as soon as one becomes aware of what the recognition of legality as part of human rights fully implies. Characteristic of human rights is their abstract character, but this does not mean that they are essentially dogmatic in their application by judicial institutions, like the European Court of Human Rights. On the contrary.

Identifying legality as an abstract right implies, *first*, that it is recognised in its *underdetermined* structure, by which is meant that the principle is not applicable in an all-or-nothing fashion, but gives a certain direction to the assessment of a given case. So the concrete weight and content of the principle are not established in advance, but need to be induced from the circumstances of the case.[13]

A good example revealing the underdetermined structure of legality is the judgement, already familiar to us, of the European Court of Human Rights in the case of Kokkinakis. The decision of the Court, as well as the dissenting opinion of Judge Martens shows that it is misleading to assert that the applicant's right to clear and accessible rules and to strict interpretation of these rules can be made applicable in an all or nothing fashion. In its inquiry into a possible breach of Article 7 E.C.H.R, the Court determined the relative weight of legality by examining how much flexibility is needed for a legal rule expressing the criminal offence of proselytism. Similarly, Judge Martens, in his dissenting opinion, also tried to estimate the weight of legality. The latter underlined that in the case at hand the balancing of legality's weight must be informed by the particular context of Greek society. Religious minorities are vulnerable there and for them there is a considerable risk of a changing climate of cultural and religious intolerance. The right to a legal provision clearly defining a criminal offence, and the right to strict interpretation of such a rule, grows in importance to the extent that the vulnerability of religious minorities is increasing.

It must be clear by now, as is evidenced by the Kokkinakis case, that it is completely wrong to think, as some criminologists do, that the principle of legality because of its abstract character, is at the same time context-indifferent. The opposite is true the moment one adopts a rights conception of legality. From a rights perspective, the principle of legality is highly abstract, because it can only obtain its shape in a given case, after

---

13 See, in extenso, R. DWORKIN, *Taking Rights Seriously*, London, Duckworth, [1977] 1996, 14-49, 91 et seq.

determining its relative weight in the light of the concrete circumstances of the case.

However, from the undeniable fact that the principle of legality forces the judge to consider the specific context of the case, it does not follow that the content of legality and its resulting rights and duties differ from case to case. Beside their underdetermined structure, human rights, the principle of legality included, contain, *secondly*, an inevitable tendency to *generalisation*. To be protected by the principle of legality, it is not sufficient for a person to communicate before a court her own, context-related idea of what her concrete rights are. This person must also show that his context-related interpretation of the claims bound up with legality can at least justifiably be carried further in other similar cases. This duty of generalisation surely does not emerge from nowhere. It mainly flows from the fact that human rights are fundamental rights, by which is meant that they underpin the legal order as a whole. From this results inevitably that citizens aspiring for the protection of their personal interests by human rights provisions, are to offer convincing reasons that these interests, given their position in the conflict, indeed can be justifiably reconstructed as underlying the legal system as a whole.[14]

Surprising as it may be for pragmatic criminal lawyers, this requirement of generalisation is surely not an invention of philosophers. It fits legal reality and even plays a substantial role in the case-law of the European Court of Human Rights. Take for instance the already analysed judgement in the case S.W. vs. United Kingdom. The applicant, who forced his wife to have sex at knifepoint, did not succeed in getting the court to establish a breach of Article 7 of the Convention, simply by referring to the fact that British case law was subjected to change. As follows from the argumentation of the Court, the applicant also to show that, given his specific position in the conflict, his concrete interest in stable case law could be reasonably extended to cases in past and future in which the persons concerned would take a similar stance in the conflict. Furthermore, the applicant is under a kind of duty to demonstrate that *his* claim could reasonably underpin the legal order as a whole and could justifiably be conceived in a coherent scheme with other fundamental rights, like the right of every person, regardless of sex, to an equal respect for her sexual and physical integrity.

A *third* important feature of human rights, which will inevitably bear on the principle of legality, as laid down in Article 7 E.C.H.R., comes down to the fact that they call into existence correlative obligations and that, therefore, rights should be thought of as having *priority* over these kind of obligations. The underlying reason for this idea of priority is that rights, and thus

[14] See R. DWORKIN, *Law's Empire*, London, Fontana Press, 225-258.

human rights, refer to a kind of social practice which takes its specificity from the fact that the normative expectations underlying this practice are stated in terms of *claims*. These are claims of some *individualised* agent *to* something *against* someone, be it a contract-party, a third party or the government. This means that the kind of obligations related to these social practices and normative expectations finds its roots and is, therefore, wholly dependent on the claims of some individualised agent. For the principle of legality this is surely not without consequences. The connection between rights and claims and the idea of priority imply that the obligations of public officials to govern their behaviour by the law, is wholly dependent on claims that are at the disposal of every individualised agent. If, in our case of marital rape for example, the violent husband were ultimately able to prove hehad a concrete right to stable case law in his domestic legal order, then this would mean two things. It would mean, first, that the person concerned merits having an individualised claim against the British courts, thus undercutting an all too flexible kind of judicial practice undertaken by them. It would mean, secondly, that these British courts are, in virtue of the individualised claim of the violent husband, under a corresponding duty to refrain from unstable case law regarding to sexual violence in a marital context.

Closely related to the above-mentioned aspects of the concept of "rights", attention is finally drawn to a *fourth* feature, which will be called the *relational* dimension of rights. To clarify this unavoidably relational element, it might be useful to reconsider the judgement of the European Court of Human Rights in the case Kokkinakis vs. Greece, and more in particular the dissenting opinion of judge Martens. In contrast to the judgement of the Court, the latter held the opinion that the applicant, Mr Kokkinakis, in virtue of legality should indeed deserve protection with respect to the right to a clear legal rule defining the offence of proselytism and to foreseeable case-law. For, according to judge Martens, the specific position of the applicant in the conflict, in fact, revealed a duty on the state to define and to interpret the legal norm of proselytism in such a way as to protect religious minorities in their equal right to religious liberties.

If I understand the dissenting opinion well, then the right Mr Kokkinakis could draw upon in virtue of the principle of legality (Article 7 E.C.H.R.), is to be tailored according to the relation in which the former stands, with regard to the victim, but also with regard to his fellow citizens. On a more abstract level, this leads to a rights conception of legality containing an undeniable relational dimension. The right a person invokes to clear legal rules and foreseeable case-law depends in its scope and weight on the extent to which this person and her fellow citizens could draw from these rules and case-law reasonable expectations with regard to each other. The rights Mr Kokkinakis can draw from the principle of legality have an unmistakable relational dimension. The weight of these rights and correlative duties depends on to what degree Mr Kokkinakis and his fellow citizens (the victim included), could expect to be equally respected in their free exercise of religious freedom by virtue of the legal rule defining the offence of proselytism.

So far a rights perspective has offered us enough material to develop a conception of legality that fits the inevitable open texture of legal norms, including those which define criminal offences, as well as the context-sensitivity undeniably involved in judicial interpretation. From this, the objection of criminologists with respect to the abstract dimension of legality could be easily rebutted. In contrast to what criminologists assert in these matters, legality in its abstract form does not lead spontaneously to dogmatic application following which the very existence of an open norm and of judicial law making would be sufficient to establish a violation of the principle of legality. It will inevitably be so that, due to the underdetermined structure of human rights, the concrete content of the principle of legality will depend on the concrete circumstances of the case as well as on the concrete situation in which the person concerned will invoke it. It will also be so that, due to the relational dimension of rights, the concrete weight of legality and its claims will depend on the initial relation in which both the suspect and his fellow citizens (the victim included) have taken a stance towards each other.

6. CAN LEGALITY FIT PERSON-RELATIVE FACTS?

When taking the background of a human rights perspective into account, one must not be too pessimistic about the future of legality because it can be offered now to the criminal law and to its practitioners as a dynamic and flexible conception. This also means that the same perspective undercuts a great deal of criminologists' criticism regarding the context-indifference of legality. However, there is no reason to become too optimistic either. Having developed a rights conception of legality that fits the context-sensitivity of the judge, this still leaves us with the question of how this same conception of legality should be refined in order to fit the type of context-sensitivity criminologists have in mind. In contrast to the kind of facts judges focus on while interpreting a legal norm, we are dealing here, as has been noted previously, with facts and sensitivity which is person-relative, instead of norm-relative. These facts and sensibilities take their meaning not from a set of rules establishing a criminal offence, but from the particular perspective of victims and offenders in a given case. In the previous remarks we attempted to explain how the principle of legality in a case like marital rape need not be applied in a rigid all-or-nothing fashion. We have shown how this principle can easily accommodate the judge's sensibility for changing social attitudes with regard to marriage. But this leaves open the question of to what extent public officials in exhibiting their habits of legality can take into account the singular story of the violent husband, the particular way he experienced and is experiencing the conflict through his own frustrations, his social powerlessness and isolation. Moreover, it still remains unanswered to what extent legality is capable of offering space to the violent husband and his wife, both desiring to be recognised as persons in *their* story of the facts.

At first sight a rights-conception falls short in addressing the issue just raised. And this is to a considerable extent related to the dimension of generalisation contained in the very structure of human rights, the principle of legality included. Take for instance our violent husband who invokes the principle of legality on the grounds of unforeseeable judicial law making. The same person can only refer to these aspects of his situation insofar as these facts are also relevant with respect to other cases and only insofar as they can help to restate their rights in a way which can be reconstructed as underlying the legal system as a whole. But, and here lies the crux of the problem, the context-sensitivity many criminologists have in mind, like the despair and frustrations of the offender due to his employment, resist these dynamics of generalisation. Having become the focus of the criminologist's sensitivity, the despair and frustrations of the violent husband appears in its meaningfulness by referring to the particular life story of the person in question, and not through a rule or a right to be interpreted in the light of the legal system as a whole.

If these observations are correct, then our inquiry appears to encounter here what can be called an *irreducible deficit* of the principle of legality, and consequently, an unbridgeable gap between the concrete sphere of offender and victim on the one hand, and the sphere of a legality-based criminal justice system, on the other. To the extent that no conceptual route would be available for legality to be connected with a context-sensitivity which is person relative, and to the extent this kind of sensitivity inevitably slips out of legality's grip, one could conclude that the principle of legality has attained the limits of its impact, and thus of its adequacy.

Before drawing these conclusions all too hastily, the following matters have to be considered.

One has to keep in mind, *first*, the fairly restricted line of approach adopted in this paper. As already said above, the criminal justice system is only faced with the perspective of victim and offender, insofar as it is guided and constrained by the principle of legality. If from a certain point this principle proves to be incapable of accommodating the perspectives of both victims and offenders, these conclusions do not necessarily imply that this incapability accounts for the whole system. One can imagine that on the grounds of other concepts, principles and doctrines which constitute the arsenal of the rule of law in criminal affairs, possibilities could be found for the criminal justice system to integrate the point of view of both victim and offender. Of course, one can only weigh the importance of this remark after a full exploration of all these concepts and principles, which is beyond our current scope. Nevertheless, while claiming that the limits of legality have been reached, one cannot yet conclude that the limits of the rule of law have been attained.

A *second* remark to be made finds its starting point in focusing our attention a bit more on the position of victim and offender, and their desires to express their story of the conflict, to be heard in their subjective feelings through which the conflict is experienced. What retains our interest here is to find out what occurs when victim and offender are given a space in which they can communicate directly to each other their subjective account of the facts. If the observations of criminologists and victim-offender mediators are correct, then one of the most salient features of such an encounter comes down to an attempt made both by victim and offender to *redefine* what their stance is towards the conflict. The direct confrontation defies them to *relocate* their position within the space of the conflict and to find there the appropriate stance they can speak from and from which they can be answered. But this is only possible when they are capable of withdrawing from their initial position in the conflict. Take for instance our violent husband. To enable his telling his wife his story of the facts through his own powerlessness, and to give him a chance to be recognised, requires at the same time an appropriate distance from his initial stance in the conflict. But this is difficult when there is no minimal institutionalised practice providing the necessary strategies to mark off the conflict from the person concerned. What is needed is a system capable of translating the position of both parties in the conflict in fair procedural relations, reconstructing the conflict in terms of legitimate expectations and in corresponding rights and obligations. Only on these conditions, victim and offender are brought in a position of relocating their stance in the conflict as persons with a life story of their own.[15]

These observations, if correct, lead us to a tempering of the idea that a legality-based criminal justice system fails to fit person-relative facts revealing a perspective of both victims and offenders from which they appear as individual persons. If the existence of an institutionalised practice proves to be necessary for reconstructing inter-individual conflicts in fair procedural relations, we cannot assert that no connection exists between legality and the desire of both victim and offender to affirm themselves as individual persons in redefining their stance in the conflict. So there might still be something to be said for the claim that the desire of victims and offenders, just mentioned, finds its starting point as well as its condition

[15] Compare L. VAN GARSSE, "Op zoek naar herstelrecht: overwegingen na jaren bemiddelingswerk", (2001) *Panopticon* 436.

of possibility in a legality-based criminal justice system. But, of course, this claim, to be a fully attractive one, calls for further elaboration, which is not possible here.

Finally, a short remark should be made regarding the importance of the kind of context-sensitivity and context-related facts revealing the perspective of both victim and offender in their particularity. Before discussing seriously the idea that legality shows an inevitable deficit when faced with this kind of context-sensitivity, one has to deepen the intuition we all have that the sensibility to these person-relative facts have a crucial moral importance and that no criminal justice system can deny these facts and sensibilities. One also needs to raise the question to what extent these kinds of facts and sensibility, when not accounted for by the criminal justice system, are capable, because of their unmistakable moral force, to drive the system into serious problems of legitimacy. To address this question, however, we have to tackle the second main issue of our contribution, namely the challenge of the *justifiability* of legality. In particular, we have to examine whether a concept of human dignity can be developed to help indicate the normative credentials of the principle of legality, and at the same time valorise attention for the perspective of victim and offender appearing as individual persons in their desire to affirm and redefine (to each other) their particular stance in the conflict.

7. LEGALITY, PREDICTABILITY AND HUMAN DIGNITY

Which aspects of human dignity make the existence of legality so indispensable, thereby justifying why it deserves to be upgraded to the status of a human right? How do these aspects relate to an ever-changing society focussed on efficiency and flexibility? To what extent do these same aspects of respect for human dignity underpin the special attention of criminologists to the particular perspective of victim and offender?

Let us concentrate again on the case S.W. vs. United Kingdom. The European Court of Human Rights had to decide whether the British courts, by bringing forced sexual relations within a marital context under the legal terms of the offence of rape, violated Article 7 of the E.C.H.R. (principle of legality). The Court upheld the decision that there was no breach of Article 7 of the Convention. It argued that the principle of legality does not imply a prohibition of judicial law-making, "provided that the resultant development is consistent with the essence of the offence and could reasonably be foreseen".[16] According to the Court the principle of legality appeared to be bound up with the right of every citizen to a kind of judicial interpretation that respects the essence of the criminal offence and could

---

[16] ECHR, 22 November 1995, S.W./ United Kingdom, *Publ. Eur. Court of H.R.*, Series B, nr. 335, 42.

be reasonably foreseen. This right is guaranteed under Article 7 of the Convention in order to secure individual citizens against arbitrary prosecution and conviction. What is remarkable here is that the Court in its argumentation also referred to the underlying purpose of the European Convention itself. It held that "the abandonment of the unacceptable idea of a husband being immune against prosecution for rape of his wife was in conformity not only with a civilised concept of marriage but also, and above all, with the fundamental objectives of the Convention, the very essence of which is respect for human dignity and human freedom".[17]

One could put this argument in another way here. With the European Court's argument, one could say that there is no violation by the law courts of their obligations flowing from the principle of legality, provided that judicial interpretation, if progressive, accommodates the rights of the victim, and, accordingly, the values of human dignity and human freedom which constitute the underlying purpose of the European Convention on Human Rights.

It is of course interesting to see here that the European Court, as in the Kokkinakis case, tried to mould legality into a more flexible conception, which would fit the inevitable law-making part of judicial interpretation. But still, the question remains as to the justifiability of such a flexible notion. Reacting to the Court's decision in the case of marital rape, a considerable number of continental doctrinal authors cast their doubts on this very lenient conception of legality. In response to the various nuances the Court made to the ideal of predictability, the question was raised as to the extent to which these nuances still safeguard the basic values underpinning the principle of legality.[18]

Additionally, it is of equal importance to note that by qualifying the ideal of predictability the Court invites criminal lawyers to examine the weight and value of this ideal of predictability as well as the requirements needed for that ideal to deserve human rights protection. Moreover, the Court provides some interesting material which could help us in elucidating the underlying normative point of legality. There is, first, the principle that national law courts have the competence to interpret legal provisions defining criminal offences progressively if the process of judicial law-making can be reasonably foreseen. And, second, there is the principle asserted that the concrete content of the duty to make judicial interpretation foreseeable in a reasonable manner, is to be construed in the light of

---

17 ECHR, 22 November 1995, S.W./ United Kingdom, Series B, *Publ. Eur. Court of H.R.*, Series B, nr. 335, 42.

18 See R. KOERING-JOULIN, "Pour un retour à une interprétation stricte du principe de la légalité criminelle (A propos de l'article 7, 1° de la Convention européenne des droits de l'homme)", in *Liber Amicorum M.A. Eissen*, Brussels, Bruylant, 1995; F. TULKENS and M. VAN DE KERCHOVE, *Introduction au droit pénal*, Diegem, Story-Scientia, 1998, 189.

the purpose of the European Convention on Human Rights, namely respect for human dignity and human freedom.

If both principles are read together somewhat creatively, then the principle of legality could be split into a twofold duty to be complied with by public officials. There is, first, the *negative* duty to refrain for the sake of human dignity from a kind of judicial law-making containing a degree of unpredictability which is utterly unreasonable. Second, there is the *positive* duty to interpret the scope of a criminal offence in such a way that could be reasonable foreseen, whereas the concrete content of this duty is again connected with the idea of (respect for) human dignity.

If, subsequently, these two types of duties are linked to the general concern of this paper to examine more closely the connection between human dignity and legality, then two important questions need to be raised here. First, for what reason does the breach of duty to withdraw from a completely unforeseeable interpretation of a rule of criminal law constitute a radically flouting of the value of human dignity? Second, where exactly does the connection between the positive duty to interpret the scope of a legal norm establishing a criminal offence in a way which could be reasonably foreseen and the respect for another's human dignity lie?

To answer the *first* question with respect to the relation between the *negative* duty of predictability and respect for human dignity, it could be useful to imagine a criminal justice system in which the principle of legality would be completely absent. Public officials would be able to prosecute, convict and punish their citizens without having to take into account a system of legal rules defined in advance that act or whose omission constitutes a criminal offence. The impact of such a system on the lives of individuals would be that every citizen would gradually lose his confidence in the legitimacy of his own actions, and consequently in himself. For, by virtue of a total absence of legal provisions defining criminal offences every act risks being qualified as criminal behaviour. Through such a pervasive lack of confidence citizens would be completely deprived of their capacity to act. In the end individuals stop seeing themselves as centres of agency.

This imaginary scene helps us to perceive how legality and the corresponding negative duty of predictability derive its deeper foundation from the idea of human dignity. Human dignity reveals itself here as the capacity of every person to act under minimal conditions of confidence, which comes down to the capacity of every person to discover in the rules of law a minimal regulatory force with regard to her own conduct and those of others. At the same time it becomes clear on what grounds the principle of legality, insofar as it is related to the ideal of *minimal predictability* of judicial law-making, deserves to be recognised as a human right. Indeed, every individual citizen, by virtue of respect for his human dignity deserves to be offered a position which enables him to call public officials, in particular the judge, on their duty to create minimal conditions under which one could act in a climate of self confidence. Without such a position, and thus without such a right, citizens lack all guarantees that their capacity to act will be assured.

Let us consider, next, the *second* question involving the relation between human dignity and the *positive* duty of predictability. Following the line of approach of the European Court of Human Rights in the case S.W. vs. United Kingdom, – mentioned above – one could state the following principle. Public officials, and more in particular national courts, while concretising their duty to judicial interpretation which could be reasonable foreseen, are to ensure that in adapting the offence of rape to changing circumstances, they act upon reasons inspired by the idea of human dignity and freedom.

Or, to move a little bit further from the Court's position and to define the principle in a more radical way, courts are violating their positive duty to make their interpretation of criminal law reasonably foreseeable, if they fail to show that the adaptation of the scope of the legal rule defining the criminal offence is informed by considerations construed in terms of human dignity and freedom. Courts do not comply with their positive duty either, when they fail to show that their context-sensitive considerations are reconcilable with these values of human dignity and freedom. So, national courts, when giving content to their duty of predictable conduct, must show that they have determined the scope of the statutory definition of rape in the light of a well-balanced scheme of rights, taking into account respect for the human dignity of both offender and victim.

This principle, in its restated form, seems also to underpin the above-mentioned dissenting opinion of judge Martens in the case Kokkinakis. The general vein of the opinion, indeed, was that the Greek State did not comply with its obligation to draft clear legal provisions and to make judicial interpretation foreseeable. For, according the judge, no sufficient safeguards existed assuring that Greek courts, in giving content to the statutory definition of proselytism, would equally respect the right to free exercise of religious freedom. By such means, Mr Kokkinakis, as a member of a religious minority, was provided with insufficient guarantees to be equally respected by the Greek orthodox majority in his religious freedom.

While considering again the relation between legality and human dignity, the following issue needs to be addressed here, namely a further examination of the reasons explaining why by virtue of the idea of human dignity this positive duty of predictability deserves to be protected by a human rights provision. Additionally, citizens, in particular in their potential capacity of suspects in a criminal procedure, must be able to be confident that public officials both in their adjudicative and legislative function, define and interpret the scope of a criminal offence in such a way that it can accommodate the citizen's fundamental rights. Another part of the answer could reasonably be that citizens, in particular, in their potential capacity of a suspect, must be able to be *confident* that public officials make sure that citizens act and deliberate on their choices in the light of an equal concern for each other's fundamental *rights*.

From this legitimate trust and corresponding expectations, citizens, in their turn, deserve, again by virtue of their dignity, to draw on a fundamental right which constitutes an essential part of legality. It is the claim-right that public officials through a variety of actions should enable, reaffirm and protect this trust and confidence, or, at least, refrain from breaking this confidence. For, it is self-evident that a person is affected in her dignity and self-respect, when it is evidenced that the courts in interpreting the law defining a criminal offence manifestly refuse to put in balance the relative weight of her "prima facie" rights which are at stake in the normative standards underlying the legal definition of the criminal offence. The dignity of a person is also affected when the judge in interpreting the law falls short in affirming and reassuring this person in her confidence that her fellow-citizens will act on reasons which express an equal concern for each other's fundamental rights. This person threatens to be violated in her self-respect when a procedural position is not available that enables her to call both legislators and law-courts on the above-mentioned feelings of trust and corresponding set of expectations.

So far, departing from the questioning of legality in its justifiability some insights have been gained with regard to the intuitions of human dignity that underpin the principle of legality. Respect for human dignity involves (a) enabling and assuring the capability of every person to deliberate, choose and act within a minimal climate of (self) confidence, and corresponding climate of trust in the rule-guided habits of public officials and fellow-citizens; (b) enabling and assuring the capability of every person to deliberate, choose and act within a climate of trust in the rights-guided habits of public officials and fellow-citizens.

These insights on the concept of human dignity help us to see why the principle of legality is especially precious in modern societies that are governed, in part, by efficiency and flexibility. In light of every person's trust in the rule- and rights-guided behaviour of public officials and fellow-citizens, criminal judges do not to give equal weight to every contextual consideration, which expresses society's concern for change or efficiency. Against the background of this kind of trust, adjudicative reasoning and interpreting inevitably contains the responsibility of judges to reconstruct these contextual considerations in terms of fundamental rights underlying the legal system as a whole. This amounts, at the least, to responsibility for examination of the extent to which these considerations are reconcilable with every citizen's trust in rule-and rights-guided behaviour.

However, while gaining insight into the relation between human dignity and the principle of legality, we have not yet demonstrated how our insights concerning human dignity might be bound up with the desire of both victim and offender to feel recognised in their account of the facts. In what follows we will cast a light on this issue, by concentrating on a case we will borrow from the restorative justice-literature and which is known as a successful example of victim-offender mediation.[19]

8. TWO FACES OF (RESPECT FOR) HUMAN DIGNITY

Bob and Anne Northrup, a couple in their forties, were victims of residential burglary for the second time in a few years. Jim Albright was arrested within several weeks of this second burglary. He admitted to the facts. During the sentence hearing in court, as a condition for probation, Jim was referred to the local victim offender mediation programme. The mediator succeeded in convincing both offender and victim of the possibilities such a mediation programme might offer. To the offender he told that a confrontation with his victims would enable him to tell his story of the facts to them and to hear how they experienced what happened to them. To the victims, to Bob and Anne, the mediator pointed out that they could let the offender know how angry they were and how this crime affected them. During the joint session Bob was invited to tell to the offender, Jim, what happened from his perspective and how it affected him. Because Bob was expressing a high level of anger and indignation, saying he was fed up with kids who violated other people's property, Jim was so shocked that he was ready to leave the session. The mediator decided at that moment to intervene. He talked to Jim telling him he fully understood how difficult it was listening to the anger expressed by Bob, but affirming that Bob was still interested in working out a settlement.

When Bob completed his statement, the mediator turned to Jim and asked him if he could tell them *his* story of the facts, to unfold what happened that evening from *his* perspective, what drove him to commit the offence.

After Jim completed his version of the facts, Bob and Anne began to ask numerous questions. Why us? Were you watching our movements? Jim indicated that he did not have a premeditated intention to burglarise Bob and Anne's home. Suddenly, and quite unexpectedly, Anne asked Jim if he knew her daughter Carol. She mentioned that Carol had been living on the streets for the past year, ever since she had left a drug treatment centre. Jim said he knew that. At this time of the session the conflict began to develop within a different framework. The participants interacted on

19 M.S. UMBREIT, *The Handbook of Victim Offender Mediation. An Essential Guide to Practice and Research*, San Francisco, Jossey-Bass, 2001, 85 et seq.

a level from which they expressed their concern about issues beyond the criminal event.

From this report of a successful mediation session, it could easily be concluded that the communication between victim and offender, when constructively guided by the mediator is somehow related to a growing acknowledgement of the human dignity both of victim and offender. But why is this so and which intuitions about human dignity are at stake here?

It is remarkable to note here that the type of respect shown by the mediator for both parties is quite different to that displayed by the criminal judge when interpreting the law in full accordance with the principle of legality. The most obvious reason for this difference in style of respect could lie in the simple fact that the mediator, in guiding the session, and the criminal judge, in interpreting the law, are each operating in a different stage of the criminal procedure. In the case of the judge, the human dignity of the offender is at stake, insofar as the facts still have to be qualified and insofar as the scope of a legal provision defining the criminal offence has not yet been fully determined. In the case of the mediator, the dignity of victim and offender is at stake insofar as it concerns the finding of an appropriate response to certain facts, which undoubtedly constitute a criminal offence and are admitted by the offender. Or, in other words, the kind of respect of dignity involved in the mediation session can not just be identified with the kind of trust underpinning the principle of legality which proves to be constitutive for every citizen's dignity and which relates to the rule-and rights-guided behaviour of public officials and fellow-citizens. The kind of trust involved in the case of the criminal judge interpreting the scope of a legal offence appears to be far less at stake in the case of mediation. This is due to the fact that the session took place at a stage of the procedure where the offender had admitted to the facts and been found guilty.

But this is not all that needs to be said here. The type of respect victim and offender show each other in the mediation session also resists fitting their desire into a legal framework in which they would count on the rule- and rights-guided behaviour of public officials, of each other and their fellow-citizens. The greater the distance taken by the victims of the residential burglary from their claim-rights, the greater the space left for recognising the dignity of the offender. The more Bob and Anne have become sensitive to Jim as a person with his own life-story, beyond the conflict in which they are involved, the more they have distanced themselves from their injured feelings of privacy as well as their violated trust that their property would be respected.

To summarise, in this case, respect of the mediator for both victim and offender, as well as the growing respect of victim and offender for each other, seems to point to another aspect of human dignity than the one underlying the principle of legality. The question is of course what aspect of human dignity and kind of respect are we dealing with.

Consider again the type of respect that is paid by the mediator to Bob, Anne (the victims) and Jim (the offender). In contrast to the criminal judge respecting the principle of legality, the mediator's attention is not focussed on *norm-relative* facts (the marital context, changing social attitudes) evidencing the need to interpret the scope of standards of behaviour (with regard to the offence of rape) and corresponding rights. The focus of the mediator's respectful attention is directed to *person-relative* facts. It is directed to the body language of Bob, the silences of Anne, their suddenly emerging questions. In this respect, the attitude of the mediator to Bob, for instance, is radically different from the one displayed by the British courts in the case of marital rape. The latter saw the frustration and indignation of the humiliated wife as the expression of new standards concerning sexual mores in marital relations. The mediator, on the contrary, tries to give Bob his dignity back in quite a different way. He does not see Bob's frustration and indignation towards Jim as an expression of his legitimate trust in being respected in his own property, but as a kind of emotion where Bob manifests himself as a unique and separate human being. For the mediator, Bob's indignation has become a very special point of attention belonging to Bob, singularising him from others, and at the same time serving as a kind of vehicle by means of which Bob is trying to express himself, and to be recognised, in his unique distinctness.[20]

The case at hand shows us how a similar kind of respect for human dignity is nestling in the relation between the victims and the offender, between Anne, Bob and Jim. Here too, the growing respect between both parties has taken the form of an evolving attention and sensibility for the words, questions, silences and gestures in which Anne, Bob and Jim are appearing in their uniqueness and are trying to express their distinctness to each other. Characteristic of this face of human dignity is that the kind of respect, sensibility and respect through which the affirmation of each other's dignity takes place, does not start off from a growing sense of responsibility for each other's claims that victims and offender dispose of. Jim develops an appropriate sensibility for the humanity of Anne from the moment he is *touched* by *her* question whether he knew *her* daughter. Through this unexpected question, revealing itself somewhat exterior to the conflict, Jim feels obliged to do justice to the humanity of Anne, but this obligation does not flow from a kind of claim Anne possesses to obtain information from Jim. This implies at the same time that Anne can only

---

[20] For the philosophical elucidation of the human interactions in the case at hand, I'm indebted here to H. Arendt's phenomenology of action, in H. ARENDT, *The Human Condition*, Chicago/London, University of Chicago Press, [1958] 1984 176 et seq.

be fully recognised as a unique and distinct human being, when she *vulnerably delivers* herself to the attention of Jim without laying a claim on him.

In what preceded we have tried to extract two faces of respect for human dignity from both the principle of legality and the acknowledgement of the perspective of victim and offender.

The type of respect that underpins the principle of legality, I would like to call the *generalist face of respect for human dignity*, because this kind of respect is bound up with desires and capabilities which deserve to be awarded to all persons in an equal way and which are equally at their disposal in the form of individual rights. Indeed, fidelity to the principle of legality refers to the respect of every person's equal capacity to act against a background of overall trust in the rule- and rights guided behaviour of public officials and fellow-citizens. To prevent arbitrary and discriminating treatment, legislators, magistrates, but citizens as well, have to prove that their determining of the concrete content of the rights and duties, involved in the application of legality, can be justifiably generalised in similar cases and circumstances. Circumstances of the case are only relevant insofar as they are meaningful for the interpretation of these rights and duties and insofar as their meaning can be extended to other cases.

The type of respect that is connected with the desire of victim and offender to be heard in their perception of the conflict, in their feelings and motivations, I would like to name the *particularistic* face of respect for human dignity. Here respectful attention is not in the first place directed to capabilities, needs and desires attributable to every person, but focussed on concrete details (gestures, facial expressions, silences, etc) in which a person appears as singularised from others, in which he appears in his uniqueness and through which that same person is trying to express himself in his distinctness from others. The dignity of a person does not refer to a quality that can be ascribed to that person at all times and in every situation. The kind of dignity we are talking about here cannot but be sensed together with the appearance of a person in her uniqueness. The dignity of a person can only be sensed at a particular time, through certain points of attention and in the eyes of another concrete human being who is touched by the singularity of that person. It follows that the kind of respect which is at stake here, resists being the focus of rights and obligations. The appearance of a person in her singularity, and thus her dignity, is something that to a large extent overcomes her in an almost equally unique relation with another person. So the type of dignity involved here resists being something that, like a right, can be disposed of at another moment and on other occasions. The kind of dignity encountered here is given with a person's appearance before another person and can only persist when it is rendered *gratuitously* by that other person.

The distinction just made between a generalist and particularistic face of respect for human dignity, is not without consequence for our questioning of legality in its degree of justifiability. It can clarify a great deal why the conceptual refinement of legality can no longer help us to integrate the criminal lawyer's fidelity towards the law with the criminologist's empathy for the perspective of both victim and offender. Both perspectives now seem to be informed by two faces of human dignity which structurally are so different that the issue immediately arises how to attune them.

In the case of Bob, Anne and Jim, the relation between these two faces of human dignity does not pose a problem. Both types of respect hardly interfered with each other, because they were at stake in different stages of the criminal procedure. But this observation cannot undo the fact that surely situations are conceivable where these two faces of human dignity *do* interfere, and in such a way that the affirmation of the particularistic face of human dignity threatens to suppress the generalist face, and vice versa.

Take again the example of proselytism in the Kokkinakis case. On the one hand, one could reasonably imagine here a situation in which Mr Kokkinakis (the alleged offender), Mrs Kyriakaki (the victim) and his husband harbour a deep and sincere desire to express to each other their particular stance in the conflict. It is also conceivable that they have the possibility of attaining a level of mutual understanding as regards their distinctness as unique beings, and able to render gratuitously their human dignity to each other. The type of respect for human dignity that is involved here, I have called *particularistic.*

But on the other hand, it is also a fact that Mr Kokkinakis harbours an equally sincere desire to know which kind of conduct he can undertake in his free exercise of religion as a Jehovah's Witness. As a member of a religious minority living in a society which is mainly orthodox, Mr Kokkinakis is harmed in his confidence that the government and his fellow-citizens, Mrs Kyriakaki and her husband included, would guide their behaviour by rules and by a well-balanced scheme of rights. The kind of human dignity which is involved here and which underpins the principle of legality, we have portrayed as a *generalist* one.

The case of Kokkinakis vs. Greece, when considered with a zest of literary imagination, shows that both the particularistic and generalist face of human dignity might possibly emerge in one and the same context, and, consequently, might interfere with each other, at risk of suppressing each other.

Imagine that our attention is primarily informed by the generalist face of human dignity. We would, as magistrates and lawyers would do, be inclined to construe the situation in terms of rights and duties, and more in particular a right to be confident with regard to the rule and rights-guided behaviour of public officials and fellow citizens. Such an attitude, albeit incorporating quite perfectly our common habits of legality and albeit completely justified in the light of a generalist kind of respect for human dignity, would in fact be characterised by an undeniable deficit in legitimacy. It would fall short of offering space for the acknowledgement of deep wants and desires which are inspired by a particularistic kind of respect for human dignity.

In the case of Kokkinakis for example, our inclination to interpret the present conflict in terms of rights and duties, would force us easily to neglect these aspects of the case revealing the singularity of the participants in the conflict. And the same applies to the participants themselves. By interpreting their relation in terms of rights and duties, Mr Kokkinakis and Mrs Kyriakaki would risk losing their capacity to deliver themselves to each other's recognition without trying to enforce it from the other as a kind of claim. Both parties would have narrowed their focus on what has been called previously norm-relative facts (for example the dominance of the Orthodox-Christian church in Greece), the meaning of which will prove to be exclusively relevant as regardsthe final weight of their rights and claims. And, consequently, Mr Kokkinakis and Mrs Kyriakaki would have cut off their capacity to be affected spontaneously by particular points of attention (questions, emotions, gestures, silences), through which they appear to each other as singular persons trying to express themselves in their distinctness.

This suppressive power however is not confined to a generalist type of respect for human dignity. It can also occur when we, like criminologists are inclined to do, imagine our attention to be dominated by respect for a *particularistic* type of respect for human dignity. In the light of this kind of attention we would be almost solely motivated by the concern of bringing about a situation in which Mr Kokkinakis and Mrs Kyriakaki would render gratuitously each other's dignity moved as they would be by the appearance of their respective uniqueness.

But this attitude too, albeit perfectly justified against the background of a particularistic face of human dignity, would be marked by a deficit of legitimacy. For there would not be enough space left for the participants to be reaffirmed in their confidence with regard to their rights and duties. Mr Kokkinakis might feel restored in his dignity through a touching encounter with Mrs Kyriakaki and her husband. But by such means he still would not feel restored in his confidence that, when proclaiming his religious convictions in other situations, he would be equally respected in his religious freedom by public officials and his Greek fellow citizens. In such a hypothetical situation, which would be dominated by a particularistic concern for human dignity, we would lose sight of particular circumstances, like the risk of religious oppression. We would lose sight of these facts which are relevant to the content of Mr Kokkinakis' rights and which are important for articulating standards of behaviour exceeding the context of the case. Denied of his legitimate trust in the rights-guided action of public officials and fellow-citizens, Mr Kokkinakis' dignity would be easily affected.

Moreover, too much attention for a particularistic face of human dignity would easily lead to too strong a stressing of the spontaneous gratuitous character of mutual recognition seemingly without feeling the necessity of the existence of claim-rights and duties. Such an emphasis would disable Mr Kokkinakis' access to the claim-rights he deserves from the perspective of a generalist face of human dignity. From this perspective Mr Kokkinakis merits a feeling of trust with regard to the way public officials and his fellow-citizens define and interpret his legitimate expectations underlying his free exercise of religious convictions. A violation of this trust would give him, again, in the light of a generalist face of human dignity, the claim-right to respect his religious freedom enforceable against the Greek government, against Mrs Kyriakaki and against other fellow-citizens in similar situations.

In our hypothetical situation in which Mrs and Mr Kyriakaki would only be given the space to confer gratuitously to Mr Kokkinakis' dignity as a unique human being, we would risk losing sight of the legitimate trust of the latter deserving to be protected by enforceable claims and duties.

The possibility of a struggle between two faces of human dignity, as it is actualised in our example above, has important consequences for the examination of the question how far the principle of legality has enough justifying force to guide and constrain the administration of criminal justice. It seems, indeed, that a legality-based criminal justice system that is grounded in a generalist type of respect for human dignity, only displays enough legitimacy when being able to accommodate in a balanced way the kinds of attitudes, desires and modes of interaction which are inspired by a particularistic type of respect for human dignity. But can we ever conceive of such a legality-based criminal justice system?

9. THE IDEA OF A "CAPABILITY"-CONCEPTION OF LEGALITY

A possible way out of the issue just mentioned may be a conceptual one and consists of having a closer look at the little examined connection between the concept of "rights" and the notion of "claims". Both criminologists and criminal lawyers are inclined to think that while drawing on a right, a person immediately has a claim on another, commanding her to comply with duties flowing from this right. Consequently, a person who waives her claim, we are told, necessarily waives her right.

The point of our argument is that this assumed assimilation of rights with claims, seriously misrepresents the very essence of what rights are all about. For an interest, a need or a value to be recognised as a right, it is crucial that the holder of the right acknowledges the fact that he *can* call others to display respect for the special importance of these needs and interest from *his* perspective.[21] Essential for the exercise of rights is thus not in the first place the practice of claiming itself, it is being in a *position* to make a claim. Or, to put in another way, the very nature of rights involves a person being *capable* of taking actively, freely and consciously a stance towards certain claims flowing from his rights.

From this it follows that a person, when waiving her claims in a concrete situation, does not automatically waive her rights as such. Quite on the contrary, a holder of a right, while releasing a particular person from her corresponding duty in a particular situation, does something that is essential for the exercise of rights, namely using his *capability* to determine actively, freely and consciously his position before one's rights. In addition, it has to be said that a holder of a right, waiving his claims to a particular person, continues to have a right against other persons in other situations. Faced with these persons the holder of a right retains his *capability* to claim and to plead before the law courts the compliance of the duties related to his right.

One should not be surprised here to find many reasons for portraying this idea of "rights", this *capability-conception of rights*, as an attractive one.

One of the most interesting implications of the capability-approach, which concerns us here, is that it allows developing a *capability-conception of legality* that, at least, conceptually, could succeed in establishing an equilibrium between a particularistic and generalist type of respect for human dignity.

Legality involves then the capability of every person to take a stance towards her right to be protected in her confidence in the rule- and rights-guided behaviour of public officials and her fellow-citizens. A person who is suspected of the criminal offence of proselytism disposes, if considered desirable, of the opportunity to suspend the alleged victim of the instant claim to respect her confidence in an equal concern for her religious freedom as a member of religious minority. By giving the suspect a free margin of discretion and making him capable of taking his own stance towards the principle of legality, a space can be opened for suspect and victim to a kind of respect of human dignity we portrayed as particularistic. By building into the very structure of legality a margin of appreciation, a minimal framework, or at least a conceptual one, is set out in which the

21 J. FEINBERG, "The Nature and Value of Rights", in J. FEINBERG, *Rights, Justice and the Bounds of Liberty. Essays in Social Philosophy*, Princeton, Princeton University Press, 1980, 151 et seq.

spontaneous and gratuitous dimension of this kind of particularistic respect of human dignity can be fully valorised.

While accommodating a space for this gratuitous dimension, a capability-conception of legality at the same time continues to be linked intrinsically with a *generalist* kind of respect for human dignity. A person who waives her claims in a concrete case and with regard to a concrete person, must be recognised in her trust in the rule-and rights guided behaviour of public officials and her fellow-citizens. Imagine the case in which the suspect of the offence of proselytism and the victim of the alleged offence would happen to remain unaffected by each other's story of the facts, and consequently, fail to rediscover each other as unique human beings. In this case a capability-conception of legality furnishes the suspect with the ability to fall back on his fundamental enforceable right to be protected in his confidence in the rule- and rights-guided actions of the state, of the victim, but also of other fellow-citizens on other occasions.

CONCLUSION

I would like to conclude by revisiting the point of departure of this contribution. It involved the ambition to indicate some reference-points which could set a stage for a well-balanced and constructive discussion on the future of restorative justice with regard to the criminal justice system and to its classic form of legal and penal reasoning. This ambition, as already anticipated in the introductory remarks, has been realised only partially. The fate of restorative justice has been made wholly dependent on the future to be assigned to the principle of legality in our contemporary criminal justice systems.

This future is not unproblematic. A legality-based criminal law will face at least two intellectual challenges that concern the adequacy and the justifiability of the principle of legality. The challenge of *adequacy* requires that public officials a.) should take seriously the open texture of legal provisions defining criminal offences as well as the inevitable context-sensitivity of the judge involved in judicial interpretation, (b) are to accommodate a person-related context-sensitivity which is revealed in (the identification with) the perspective both of victim and offender.

The challenge of *justifiability* referred in this contribution to the requirement of conceiving a conception of human dignity (a) which can justify why the principle of legality ought to guide and constrain the habits of both legislator and law-courts, (b) that can deepen our intuitive respect for needs of both victims and offenders to express and communicate themselves (to each other) in redefining their stance in the conflict.

As to the challenge of *adequacy*, this contribution has extensively demonstrated that the principle of legality, despite and by virtue of its abstractness, is perfectly able to fit the judge's context-sensitivity in judicial interpretation, provided the legality is conceived from a *rights perspective*. Legality refers then to the right of every person who, given her concrete relation with her fellow citizens, is in a position to call both legislator and judge on their duties the concrete content of which is to be generalised in a way that fits a scheme of fundamental rights underpinning the legal system as a whole. Insofar as a rights perspective involves a relational perspective, legality can also accommodate to a certain extent the perspective of the offender and the victim and their respective stance in the conflict. With the help of case law from the European Court of Human Rights we have shown that, in virtue of this relational perspective, the concrete content of the rights flowing from the principle of legality is determined by the stance of the suspect towards the victim and his fellow-citizens.

The ability of legality to fit the position of victim and offender, however, is not unlimited. Indeed, the issue persists of matching legality to facts and sensitivities which reveal the perspective of victims and offenders affirming themselves as individual persons *(person-relativity)*. This issue has brought us close to the *limits* of a legality-based criminal justice system. Here, even a rights perspective fails to remedy the principle of legality. In contrast to the context-sensitivity of the judge the meaning of which is mediated by the legal rule to be interpreted and applied *(norm-relativity)*, the kind of facts and sensitivities we are dealing with here resist generalisation. This requirement of generalisation, unfortunately, is an essential requirement for facts and circumstances of the case to be accommodated by a rights-conception of legality.

Which repercussions could these conclusions have on the future of restorative justice? Starting from our insights regarding both credentials and limits of a rights-conception of legality, one should take into account at least three reference-points to enable a well-balanced discussion on the future of restorative justice with regard to the criminal justice system.

First reference-point. While evidenced that the principle of legality, conceived from a rights-perspective, perfectly fits the context-sensitivity of judges in determining the scope of a criminal offence, and insofar as this context-sensitivity includes an examination of the position of victims and offender in the conflict, it is *superfluous* to present restorative justice practices as a fully-fledged alternative to the principle of legality. Such a presentation denies the full potentials of legality-based criminal justice system and will, therefore, destabilise from the start a well-balanced discussion on the future to play of restorative justice in such a system.

Second reference-point. Restorative justice, without, of course, exhausting its meaning with regard to criminal law, can serve a complementary function in relation to a rights conception of legality. This is insofar as legality cannot pay sufficient attention to the facts and sensibilities that are not mediated by legal norms and that reveal an attention to the perspective of victim and offender through which they appear as individual persons with their own life story. This second reference-point can help us further to examine the optimal conditions under which restorative justice practices can create a framework in which such facts and sensibilities can be taken seriously. But before steering the discussion in this direction, other reference points will be marked after summing up a few insights we acquired with regard to the question of legality and its justifiability.

As to the challenge of justifiability, we have tried to show that criminal lawyers' adherence to the principle of legality and the attention of many criminologists to the perspective of victims and offenders are, to a great extent, informed by two different kinds of respect for human dignity which, if interfering, tend to suppress each other.

We have portrayed the ultimate ground of legality and of criminal lawyers' fidelity to legality, as a generalist type of respect for human dignity. This comes down to respect for every one's ability to act in a climate of trust or confidence, confidence in the rule-guided and rights-guided behaviour of both public officials and fellow-citizens. This essential trust justifies why legality ought to guide and constrain the context sensitivity of criminal judges when interpreting legal provisions defining a criminal offence. Reasons of flexibility are, indeed, not enough to justify an adaptation of the scope of legal provisions to new social circumstances. Law courts must prevent these reasons and the corresponding judicial interventions from violating the kind of trust just mentioned.

This generalist idea of human dignity, along with the idea of trust, underlying the principle of legality, also justifies why the concrete content of a right flowing from the principle of legality should pass the test of generalisation. It also justifies, at least to an important extent, why this right as part of a whole scheme of rights should underpin the legal system as a whole. The capacity to be confident in the rule and rights guided behaviour of public officials and citizens concerns every person and deserves to be distributed equally to everyone. Therefore, it is essential that a person, who feels violated in that confidence, should make the concrete content of her claim also acceptable for similar cases.

In this paper we have also painted another face of respect for human dignity, grounding the concern for the perspective of both victim and offender and their desire to be recognised in their story of the facts. It was called a *particularistic* type of respect, because it is closely linked to a spontaneous, direct and gratuitous attention for concrete details through which victim and offender appear as unique and separate human beings trying to express themselves in their distinctness.

The difference as well as the tension between these two faces of respect for human dignity enabled us to see how the principle of legality, when grounded in the idea of confidence in the rule- and rights-guided behaviour of both officials and citizens, will inevitably run against a fundamental deficit, for it fails to offer a space in which victims and offenders can express themselves in their unique distinctness. So the justifiability of the principle of legality, in the end, depends on the extent to which this principle can mark its own limits, but also on the extent to which, at least conceptually, it can create an opening for a more particularistic kind of respect for human dignity.

To answer this last issue, we sketched in the last section of our contribution what has been called a *"capability"- conception of legality*. Legality refers there to the capability of every individual citizen to define actively, consciously and freely his own stance towards the right to be protected, and affirmed in his confidence in the rule-and rights-guided behaviour of public officials and their fellow-citizens. This capability-approach gives every person who draws on legality a margin of discretion towards this principle, thus creating an opening to a particularistic type of respect for human dignity. Legality offers here, at least conceptually, a framework to a person (the suspect), to grow sensitive to these points of attention (silences, gestures) which reveal the other (the alleged victim) in his singularity.

Here again we can ask how far these results could set the stage for a well-balanced debate concerning the future of restorative justice in relation to the criminal justice system. Two further points can be made here.

Third reference-point. Insofar as a rights-conception of legality finds a firm foundation in respect for everyone's ability to act in a climate of trust in the rule-and rights-guided behaviour of public officials and fellow-citizens (generalist type of respect for human dignity), it can no longer be justifiable to see restorative justice as a kind of alternative for the principle of legality and for a legality-based criminal justice system. Advocating such an option would mean denying the undoubtedly strong normative credentials of the principle of legality and the rule if law. It would also undercut in part a meaningful discussion between criminal lawyers and criminologists on the role restorative justice can play in the criminal justice system.

Fourth reference-point. Insofar as a rights-conception of legality falls short in leaving victim and offender enough space to appear as distinct human beings and give back each other's dignity gratuitously (particularistic type of respect for human dignity), restorative justice practices present themselves as a kind of necessary complement to a legality-based criminal justice system. Within the limits of the stage set by this reference-point criminal lawyers and criminologists might examine a bit further which aspects would and would not make restorative practices *complementary* to the principle of legality, and this in virtue of a particularistic respect for human dignity. They could also discuss which procedural framework should be constructed to enable restorative justice to serve this complementary function. Finally, they could reflect on how to translate procedurally the idea of a capability-conception of legality. They could examine here which procedural safeguards should be built into the criminal justice system, ensuring thereby a generalist kind of respect for human dignity, a kind of respect which is shown to inspire one of the criminal lawyers' basic attachments: fidelity to legality and to the rule of law.

2. PUNISHMENT, HUMAN DIGNITY, AND THE SOCIOLOGICAL IMAGINATION: A REPLY TO CLAES

TOM DAEMS

In his paper "Criminal Justice, Legality and Human Dignity" (see pp. 17-56 in this volume) Claes' main aim is to defend the principle of legality as the cornerstone of the penal system. This is done through a revalorisation of the principle of legality from the perspective of respect for human dignity which, so he argues, is predominantly about the issue of trust. Although I have the impression that the concept of human dignity is to figure as the core concept of a future theory of punishment Claes does not, as yet, offer such a theory.[1] However, in another publication he justifies punishment by means of the same concept of human dignity as which is assigned the role of protagonist in the paper in this collection.[2]

Since Claes' work is still in progress, and far from finished, his thoughts on punishment are, as they stand, utterly fragile and can serve as a mere legitimation of the status quo. In the end, the mere rethinking of the principle of legality, a core principle on which Western penal systems *already* claim to rely, and the justification of punishment by means of the concept of human dignity, does not call for much reform. Conservatives can rub their hands. The message they can read into Claes' discussion of legality and punishment may serve their purposes extremely well: pay respect to the principle of legality and the penal system will be turned into a "just" mechanism for dealing with law breaking since it will enhance people's confidence that the behaviour of public officials and fellow citizens is guided by rules and rights and it will deliver them scope for action.

Claes' observations on legality and human dignity, however, can also be interpreted as a first step towards a more fundamental questioning and rethinking of current penal systems. This is the way I have approached Claes' thought experiment in this paper. The concept of human dignity,

---

1 According to J.G. MURPHY, five questions need to be addressed in order to have a philosophical theory of punishment: (1) What is the nature of crime and punishment?; (2) What is the moral justification of punishment?; (3) What is the political justification of punishment?; (4) What are the proper principles of criminal liability?; (5) What are the appropriate punishments? See J.G. MURPHY, "Does Kant Have a Theory of Punishment?", (1987) *Columbia Law Review* 510-512. Claes answers none of these questions in his paper.

2 See E. CLAES, "Punitieve rechtshandhaving, herstelrecht en menselijke waardigheid", in B. VAN STOKKOM (ed), *Straf en herstel. Ethische reflecties over strafdoeleinden*, Den Haag, Boom Juridische Uitgevers, 229-253. In this paper Claes does address MURPHY'S second question.

the space opened up for restorative justice initiatives within the existing penal system, and his strong adherence to a human rights perspective, may form the starting point for a real theory of punishment which, in the end, will need to be placed within a broader political philosophy. However, in order to get the most out of the concept of human dignity, some important potential pitfalls need to be taken into account. My critique, therefore, is not meant to dismiss Claes' discussion as yet another attempt to legitimise the penal status quo. Rather it aims to be a constructive contribution to (my interpretation of) Claes' project by pointing to some intricate issues that follow from the steps he has taken thus far.

The structure of the paper will be as follows. In a first paragraph I will outline three challenges which need be taken into account by any penal theory which aims to be "critical": the challenge of punishment, the challenge of context / viability, and the challenge of victims. In the second paragraph I enter into discussion with Claes and aim to assess to what extent his thinking on legality and punishment, as it stands at this moment, is able to formulate an answer to these challenges. Throughout my discussion I try to remain sensitive to the "public" side of the problem because there is a tendency in Claes' paper to treat the question of punishment and human dignity predominantly in terms of "private troubles".

1. THE CHALLENGE FOR NORMATIVE THEORY

Sociologists of punishment have often been sceptical of attempts of philosophers to justify punishment, arguing that we first need to understand what punishment is in order to think what it can and should be.[3] This scepticism flows from a well-documented and, by now, thoroughly analysed observation that penal theory often does little more than gloss over practices that are light-years away from the principles and values they ought to embody according to the theories that support and legitimise them. Yet, in recent years the need for normative theorising has once again penetrated the agenda of sociologists of punishment and control.[4] The "rise in

3 D. GARLAND, "Philosophical Argument and Ideological Effect: An Essay Review", (1983) *Contemporary Crises* 79-85; D. GARLAND, *Punishment and Modern Society. Study in Social Theory*, Oxford, Clarendon Press, 1990, 9-10.

4 In her latest book Barbara Hudson reflects on her own experience in this respect in the following words: "(...) so much of my work is about things I dislike – race discrimination in punishment, for example – and it was good to be writing something positive and idealistic, what justice should and could be like", B. HUDSON, *Justice in the Risk Society. Challenging and Re-affirming Justice in Late Modernity*, Sage, London, 2003, ix. For other examples, see B. HUDSON, "Punishment, Rights and Difference: Defending Justice in the Risk Society", in K. STENSON and R.R. SULLIVAN (eds), *Crime, Risk and Justice. The Politics of Crime Control in Liberal Democracies*, Cullompton, Willan, 2001, 144-172; I. LOADER and N. WALKER, "Policing as a Public Good. Reconstituting the Connections Between Policing and the State", (2001)

punishment", which according to Jock Young[5] has become the focus for contemporary criminological analysis, has incited penal observers to reconnect the explanatory / interpretive question of what punishment *is* to the normative question of what it *ought* to be. Such a normative theory of punishment must offer us a critical standard: "an ideal conception of what punishment ought to be, in whose light we can evaluate (and no doubt find seriously wanting) our existing practices."[6]

This task of reconnection, however, is not an easy one. Any normative theory of punishment which aims to be critical[7] will have to face up to at least three "practical" challenges which are well-documented within the sociology of punishment:

- *Punishment*: The challenge of the *quantity* (the rising amounts of deviance processed by current penal systems) and the *quality* (deteriorating prison conditions, overcrowding, high caseloads, huge delays, etc.) of punishment;
- *Context and viability*: The challenge of a socio-political context in which growing feelings of uncertainty, caused by broader structural transformations, are *translated* into problems of unsafety. This development goes hand in hand with the rise of the "public" as a key actor in the shaping of penal policy, and a concomitant tendency toward "populist punitiveness".[8] A normative theory has to be sensitive to these transformations and has to assess its own viability under contemporary conditions;
- *Victims*: The challenge of the recent entrance of the victim, with his *private* feelings and worries, in a penal setting which is meant to serve the *public* interest.[9]

Theoretical Criminology 9-35; L. ZEDNER, "Dangers of Dystopias in Penal Theory", (2002) *Oxford Journal of Legal Studies* 341-366.

5 J. YOUNG, "In Praise of Dangerous Thoughts", (2003) *Punishment and Society* 99.

6 R. A. DUFF, *Punishment, Communication, and Community*, Oxford, Oxford University Press, 2001, xv.

7 According to DUFF a normative theory of punishment *must* be a critical theory: "We must be open to the possibility that what punishment ought to be – what it must be if it is to be adequately justified – will be radically different from what it actually now is", R. A. DUFF, *Punishment, Communication, and Community*, Oxford, Oxford University Press, 2001, xv.

8 The phrase "populist punitiveness" was coined by Anthony BOTTOMS and refers to "the notion of politicians tapping into, and using for their own purposes, what they believe to be the public's generally punitive stance", A. BOTTOMS, "The Philosophy and Politics of Punishment and Sentencing", in C.M.V. CLARKSON and R. MORGAN (eds), *The Politics of Sentencing Reform*, Oxford, Clarendon Press, 1995, 40; on the changing stance of the "public" from "indifference" to "involvement", see J. PRATT, *Punishment and Civilization*, London, Sage, 2002, 213p. and A. FREIBERG, "The Four Pillars of Justice: A Review Essay", (2003) *The Australian and New Zealand Journal of Criminology* 223-230.

9 T. DAEMS, "Is It All Right for You to Talk? Restorative Justice and the Social Analysis of Penal Developments", (2004) *European Journal of Crime, Criminal Law and Criminal Justice* 132-149.

In the next paragraph I will discuss some aspects of Claes' paper, thereby focusing on the ways in which his thinking, as it stands at the moment, deals with the challenges that I have outlined in this paragraph.

2. PUNISHMENT, HUMAN DIGNITY, AND MODERNITY

In his latest book *Wasted Lives*[10] Zygmunt Bauman argues that the story of modernity can be told in more than one way. The story he presents in that particular book, however, paints a rather grim picture of the modern project. The production of "human waste", so he argues, is an inevitable outcome of modernisation, an inescapable side-effect of order-building. It reminds him of Michelangelo's famous answer when he was asked how he obtained the beautiful harmony of his sculptures: "Simple. You just take a slab of marble and cut out all the superfluous bits." This implies that "For something to be created, something else must be consigned to waste". Waste, then, is an indispensable ingredient of the creative process.

Bauman's story of modernity offers a thought-provoking framework to approach the question of punishment. Penal systems, on might argue, form part of the modern "waste disposal industry": they recycle or dispose of those "wasted humans" who deviate from the norms of a particular design for order. If we imagine the question of punishment from this perspective, then it becomes clear that punishment cannot be seen in isolation, neither from other mechanisms of "waste disposal" (e.g. welfare provisions, immigration policies, asylum regulations, etc), nor from the particular design of order to which it is attached, and which it aims to preserve. In my discussion of how Claes has dealt with the three challenges that I outlined above, I will try to remain sensitive to the role of punishment within a broader "industry of waste disposal". This is necessary, it seems to me, because there is a tendency in Claes' paper to treat the question of punishment and human dignity too much in terms of "private troubles" rather than in terms of "public issues".[11] The first subparagraph will address the challenge of punishment. The second will deal with the challenge of context / viability and victims.

2.1. The Other Crisis: Punishment as a Public Issue

Claes opens his paper with a brief discussion of "the penal crisis" which, in his opinion, has two aspects: on the one hand, the practice of punish-

10 Z. BAUMAN, *Wasted Lives. Modernity and its Outcasts*, Cambridge, Polity Press, 2004, 140 p.

11 The distinction between "private troubles" and "public issues" was coined by the great C. WRIGHT MILLS and has to be seen against the backdrop of his famous plea for a "sociological imagination" which aims to grasp the interplay between "private troubles" and "public issues", See C. WRIGHT MILLS, *The Sociological Imagination. Fortieth Anniversary Edition*, Oxford, Oxford University Press, 2000, 3-24.

ment, the very idea of criminal punishment itself; on the other hand, the abstract and alienating character of the legal framework of criminal law. It should not come as a surprise that he stresses these aspects of the crisis since the challenge of restorative justice for criminal justice systems based on the principle of legality runs as a red thread throughout his discussion. Indeed, the deliberate infliction of pain, and the numbing impact of traditional criminal justice processes on the morale of victims and offenders are at the heart of restorative criticism.

However, this depiction of the penal crisis tends to treat the question of punishment too much in terms of "private troubles": the infliction of pain on *particular* offenders, and the alienating effects for *particular* victims and offenders are stressed as core aspects of the crisis thereby obscuring the "rise in punishment" which for many years has been (and still is) high on the criminological agenda. This "public" part of the penal crisis will not be solved by addressing the private worries of victims and offenders, whatever the beneficial consequences of new initiatives may be for those caught up in the judicial system.[12] I assume that Claes is aware of this "public" aspect of the penal crisis, and that he will address the difficult question of punishment's place within broader strategies of governing deviance as his project progresses. Yet the question remains whether a discussion of legality can *überhaupt* be separated from an analysis of subsidiarity.

In his discussion of the "generalist face of respect for human dignity" Claes argues that "(...) fidelity to the principle of legality refers to the respect of every person's equal capacity to act against a background of overall trust in the rule- and rights guided behaviour of public officials and fellow-citizens" (see p. 47 in this volume). People need this "confidence" in order to be able to continue seeing themselves as "centres of agency". I cannot but agree with this argument. However, I doubt whether this aspect of the principle of legality can ever be valued positively without *at the same time* knowing what the *content* is of the rules and rights that need to be subjected to the principle of legality. In this respect one can, with a little imagination, give a twist to his thought experiment of "a criminal justice system without a principle of legality" (see p. 41 in this volume) and devise a thought experiment of "a criminal justice system *with* a principle of legality but *without* a principle of subsidiarity". Imagine, for example,

12 As Stan COHEN has put it in a landmark essay: "(...) in the long run – as they say – social control is in the interests of the collective, not the individual. It could hardly be otherwise", S. COHEN, "The Punitive City: Notes on the Dispersal of Social Control", (1979) *Contemporary Crise* 360; More recently Tim HOPE made a similar comment with respect to the proliferation of private security: "What is of interest, though, are the collective consequences of these individual actions, not only for the level but also for the distribution of private security", T. HOPE, "Crime, Victimisation and Inequality in Risk Society", in R. MATTHEWS and J. PITTS (eds), *Crime, Disorder and Community Safety*, London, Routledge, 2000, 195.

a society where excessively large amounts of deviance are criminalised – let us say from murdering a king to being left-handed or redheaded.[13] At the same time public officials happily abide by the principle of legality. Why should they do not? In the end, they are respecting their *own* criminal code. Yet it can hardly be argued that people (not least the left-handed and redheaded ones) will live "confidently" and see themselves as "centres of agency".

His argument, as it stands, pays insufficient attention to this power game, that is, to modern law as a powerful instrument of "human engineering" in the service of a particular design for order. Claes' underlying vision of the connections between criminal law and society is too Durkheimian, as if legal norms reflect and emerge, so to speak, automatically from a *conscience collective*. The potentially oppressive and interest-based character of legal norms is therefore lost out of sight and this anomaly will not be remedied by a mere respect for the principle of legality. The question to be asked, then, becomes: To what extent can Claes' core concept of human dignity inform decisions on where to draw the boundaries between the regulation of deviance by means of criminal law on the one hand, and its tolerance or regulation by other means, on the other hand? Without a doubt this will be one of the toughest nuts to crack in Claes' project.

I was pleased to see the question of legitimation being treated in an utterly *dynamic* way.[14] Indeed, it is not fixed throughout times and places but may pose itself in different ways when new challenges need to be addressed. For Claes the issue of legitimation is being reshaped in the light of restorative developments and concomitant accusations of alienation that are directed at traditional criminal justice systems based on the principle of legality. Yet in the light of punishment's place within Bauman's broader "waste disposal industry": Is the answer he provides satisfactory? Above it was already argued that, until this moment, the issue of subsidiarity has hardly been touched upon in Claes' project. There are, however, some indications that the direction he is heading towards may not lead to the "critical" theory of punishment one may legitimately expect[15] or vigorously hope for. Indeed, at this moment he has succeeded in re-legitimising both

---

13 Just to avoid any confusion: I have nothing against left-handed and redheaded people! These examples are borrowed and adopted from Howard BECKER's classical study on the sociology of deviance, H. S. BECKER, *Outsiders. Studies in the Sociology of Deviance*, New York, Free Press, 1991 (original: 1963), 4.

14 See also: "Dit heeft tot gevolg dat het klassieke strafrecht, indien het geen plaats kan bieden aan deze aspecten van de menselijke bestaansconditie, met een ernstig legitimiteitstekort *wordt opgezadeld*" (Translation: "This implies that if classical criminal law is not able to address these aspects of the human condition, then it *will be confronted* with a serious deficit in legitimation") (my italics), E. CLAES, "Punitieve rechtshandhaving, herstelrecht, en menselijke gelijkwaardigheid", in B. VAN STOKKOM (ed), *Straf en herstel. Ethische reflecties over sanctie-doeleinden*, Den Haag, Boom Juridische Uitgevers, 239.

15 See footnote 7.

the principle of legality and the deliberate infliction of pain[16] through a creative rethinking of the concept of "human dignity". In addition, he has argued that restorative initiatives *can* be an important *addition* to a criminal justice system based on punishment as the infliction of pain.[17] The penal system one *can* imagine from these achievements does not have to be that different from the penal system we *already* have at the moment. Moreover, since restorative justice is assigned a secondary role, and since the potential number of cases amenable to restorative treatment is limited, one cannot but conclude that his developing theory, as it stands at the moment, does not promise to be very ambitious in terms of penal reform. Again, much will depend on how he will treat the tricky issue of "drawing boundaries": What forms of deviance can be regulated *outside* the criminal justice system? And where will those forms of deviance that are judged as being in need of regulation *inside* the criminal justice system be located on the penal continuum (intensity and choice of sanctions / depth of penetration in the penal system)?

Lastly, should we not ask ourselves whether the project of a theory of *punishment* is too limited in scope and that it may divert our attention from other developments which are in urgent need of normative theorizing? On the one hand, a theory of punishment is not able to cover all those intrusive and exclusionary developments that are happening *outside* the criminal law. In a recent book David Lyon paints a disturbing picture of surveillance developments that have occurred after September 11. Technological measures that are concerned with monitoring behaviours and identifying individuals such as biometrics, "smart cards", Closed Circuit Television, and a broad range of communicational measures (e.g. wiretaps, message interception methods, Web-based surveillance, etc), have been proposed and implemented after the attacks. Yet it would be wrong to argue that everything changed after 9/11. As Lyon puts it: "9/11 may be viewed as both *revealing* and actually *constituting* major social change (my italics)".[18] Surveillance societies emerge, so he argues, "(...) wherever such practices begin to touch daily life at every point – whether we are working, shopping, voting, travelling, being entertained, or communicating with others".[19] These developments were already under way well *before* 9/11, and not only in the United States. In this respect it is not a coincidence that David

---

16 The legitimation of the deliberate infliction of pain was developed in E. CLAES, "Punitieve rechtshandhaving, herstelrecht en menselijke gelijkwaardigheid", in B. VAN STOKKOM (ed), *Straf en herstel. Ethische reflecties over sanctiedoeleinden*, Den Haag, Boom Juridische Uitgevers, 244 et seq.

17 E. CLAES, "Punitieve rechtshandhaving, herstelrecht en menselijke gelijkwaardigheid" in B. VAN STOKKOM (ed), *Straf en herstel. Ethische reflecties over sanctiedoeleinden*, Den Haag, Boom Juridische Uitgevers, 244 et seq.

18 D. LYON, *Surveillance after September 11*, Cambridge, Polity Press, 2003, 4.

19 D. LYON, *Surveillance after September 11*, Cambridge, Polity Press, 2003, 5.

Garland's latest book is entitled *The Culture of Control* and not *The Culture of Punishment*. Indeed, one of the most significant developments Garland points out is exactly those new forms of control and surveillance (often subsumed under the heading of situational crime prevention) that proliferate in the "fight against crime" and that have profound social and cultural consequences.[20]

On the other hand, a mere consideration of the question of punishment, independent of broader control developments, may leave us complacent and divert our attention from some tricky normative issues that arise with these developments. In a recent paper Lucia Zedner has stressed the urgent need for special justification of security developments thereby drawing attention to six paradoxes in the pursuit of security: "namely that security pursues risk reduction but presumes the persistence of crime; that the expansion of security has enlarged not diminished the penal state; that security promises reassurance but in fact increases anxiety; that security is posited as a universal good but presumes social exclusion; that security promises freedom but erodes civil liberties; and finally that security is posited as a public good but its pursuit is inimical to the good society".[21] These developments are not abiding by any principles whatsoever. Moreover, they agilely transgress the public-private divide which is still at the heart of penal theory. Indeed, these control developments, which are often stimulated by state agencies, proliferate predominantly in shopping malls, workplaces, parking lots, airports, etc, that is, at places which largely escape public scrutiny. I do not mean to downplay the tremendous importance of justifying the state's power to punish. Yet it has to be recognised that these developments pose important challenges for normative theorising[22], not only because of their *individual* consequences (i.e. the threat to privacy), but also, and foremost, because of their *social* consequences (i.e. what Lyon calls "social sorting": the classification of groups which profoundly affects their choices and chances in life). It might be interesting to explore to what extent Claes' concept of human dignity can open up potential avenues to arrive at a broad normative theory, not merely of punishment, but of control *tout court*.

---

20 D. GARLAND, *The Culture of Control. Crime and Social Order in Contemporary Society*, Oxford, Oxford University Press, 2001, 307 p.

21 L. ZEDNER, "Too Much Security?", (2003) *International Journal of the Sociology of Law* 157-158.

22 As LYON puts it: "Normative approaches, already implicitly present in analysis and theory, need to be highlighted. It is one thing to be made aware of situations where freedoms are being constrained, human rights neglected, and people are suffering needlessly for things they have not done and for deeds they never contemplated; it is another to suggest what to look out for as warning signs as new measures are proposed, what sorts of alternatives are appropriate, and why some kinds of response are preferable to others", D. LYON, *Surveillance after September 11*, Cambridge, Polity Press, 2003, 148.

2.2. Respect for Human Dignity: "Private Trouble" or "Public Issue"?

What is "human dignity"? This is a tricky question, and Claes is well aware of this: "(...) one can reasonably hold that the questioning of the justifiability of a legality-based criminal justice system in fact focuses mainly on the *complex nature of the idea of human dignity* which seemingly simultaneously inspires friends and critics of the principle of legality" (see in this volume p. 31, my italics). Indeed, there seems to be a strange paradox at work. On the one hand, "friends" of the principle stress its importance by invoking Article 7 of the European Convention of Human Rights which, ultimately, refers to respect for human dignity. On the other hand, "enemies" abhor the alienating and numbing impact of criminal justice processes driven by the principle of legality. And, so it seems, also the "enemies" tend to rely on a notion of "respect for human dignity" to provide themselves with ammunition.[23] How to reconcile these competing perspectives on human dignity? Claes proposes the following solution: the type of respect that flows from the principle of legality is called the *generalist* face of respect for human dignity; the one that underpins the critics' argument is called the *particularistic* face. But is the ambivalence resolved by the mere introduction of this, admittedly, imaginative construction? Should one "face" be given priority over the other? And, if so, on what grounds should this decision be made? Moreover, do we have to understand *human* dignity differently in conflicts which involve *non-humans* or *humans-at-a-distance*, as there are massive amounts of ecological, corporate and fiscal deviance, and rule transgressions in the field of road traffic?

I merely raise these questions to highlight the complexities that surround the concept of human dignity. There is, however, one question I want to dwell on in the remainder of this paper: To what extent is the principle of legality *really* able to secure an overall climate of trust in which people can see themselves as "centres of agency"? The idea that people can act "against a background of overall trust in the rule- and rights guided behaviour of public officials and fellow citizens", as Claes argues, is important. Yet it tends to treat the issue of trust (and thus human dignity) too much in terms of "private troubles": the *one-on-one* relationship between a *particular* citizen on the one hand, and the penal machinery / his fellow citizens on the other hand, dominates the scene. His discussion therefore lacks "sociological imagination" and needs to be supplemented by a consideration of human dignity as a "public issue".

Indeed, Claes tends to give trust an a-historical content, as if its meaning would be the same for people living in 19th Century liberal states, 20th Century post-war welfare states, or 21st Century post-welfare states (at war).

[23] E. CLAES, "Legaliteit, herstelrecht en menselijke waardigheid", (2004) *Delikt en Delinkwent* 14.

However, the *experience* of trust is always, and inevitably, mediated by the prevailing societal context. To put it simply: How do we have to understand the idea of "trust" that supposedly flows from a criminal justice system based on the principle of legality in an uncertain and suspicious society? This question relates to the challenge of context / viability that was discussed above and is vital for any theory which aims to be "critical". Trust, then, is no longer a timeless and abstract concept related to respect for the principle of legality, but emerges from a particular way of "human togetherness" or social solidarity. With respect to this last issue recent sociology has a lot to offer. Themes such as the return of uncertainty, ontological insecurity, new forms of anxiety, etc., are at the heart of sociological reflections on the social transformations that have shaken and reshaped Western societies since the 1970s.[24] If human dignity is to figure as the core concept of a future penal theory then its societal underpinnings, apart from protection against unjustified state intervention, need to be explored. In fact, this would imply nothing more (but also nothing less) than the incorporation of some basic insights from the sociology of punishment into philosophy. Indeed, the interrelatedness of the "social" and the "penal" has been stressed time and time again by criminologists working in this field.[25] A closer engagement with sociology may be necessary if Claes wants to avoid being accused of using grand, and potentially hollow, notions.

A last question concerns the issue of "ownership": Whose human dignity is at stake? Claes' discussion reveals a clear and well-articulated preference for a balanced approach in this respect: people in general (in the case of the *generalist* face of human dignity), and victims and offenders (in the case of the *particularistic* face of human dignity) are all put on equal footing. With respect to "ownership" I only want to highlight the issue of "emotional correctness"[26], that is, an attitude of sympathy and compassion towards the victim in order to conform to social expectations. The importance of

24 See e.g. A. GIDDENS, *The Consequences of Modernity*, Stanford University Press, Stanford, 1990, 186 p. (on ontological insecurity); P. WAGNER, *A Sociology of Modernity. Liberty and Discipline*, London, Routledge, 1994, 267 p. (on the crisis of "organized modernity"); R. CASTEL, *L'insécurité sociale. Qu'est-ce qu'être protégé?*, Paris, Edition du Seuil, 2003, 95 p. (on the crisis of socialised risk management and the return of uncertainty).

25 See e.g. D. GARLAND, *Punishment and Welfare. A History of Penal Strategies*, Aldershot, Gower, 1985, 297 p. (on the emergence of a *penal-welfare* complex in Britain in the period 1895-1914) and his book *The Culture of Control, Crime and Social Order in Contemporary Society*, Oxford, Oxford University Press, 2001, (on the decline of, and shifts of emphasis within, that *penal-welfare* complex); P. MARY, *Délinquant, délinquance et insécurité. Un demi-siècle de traitement en Belgique (1944-1997)*, Brussels, Bruylant, 1998, 784 p. (Part Three, Title II, Chapter III: developing the hypothesis of the "penalisation of the social" in the Belgian context).

26 I borrow and adopt this nice phrase from Z. BAUMAN who has used it to characterise the remarkable silencing of critical voices in the USA in the aftermath of 9/11, Z. BAUMAN, *Society under Siege*, Cambridge, Polity Press, 2002, 7.

"emotional correctness" will probably increase as penal systems progressively open their gates for victims and their private worries. The potential implications for a balanced understanding of human dignity are quite obvious, and will need to be taken into account by Claes as his developing theory aims to give more weight to the *particularistic* face (which includes the victim's face) of human dignity.

CONCLUSION

In this paper I have stressed some of the issues which need be taken into account by Claes if he aims to develop a penal theory that can be "critical" and "viable" under present societal conditions. Subsidiarity; the power play of legal norms; control developments *outside* the realm of criminal law which tend to escape public scrutiny; the refinement and further clarification of the concept of human dignity; and the ever present danger of "the struggle for ownership" have been singled out as themes that are in need for further reflection. Above all, I have the impression that his project, as it stands, lacks "sociological imagination". If Claes wants to convince sociologists of punishment, who have very legitimate reasons to be sceptical about attempts to justify penal interventions, then he needs to pay more attention to the societal context in which penal systems process criminalized forms of deviance. On the other hand, his argument contains interesting elements such as an explicit attention for human rights and restorative developments which may turn his project, which is still in an early phase of development, in the direction of a "critical" and "viable" theory. Much will depend on how the issues that have been raised in this paper will find their way into his theory.

3. BACK TO BASICS: A REPLY TO CLAES

SANDRA MARSHALL

The challenge that the ideals of restorative justice throw up for our familiar systems of criminal justice[1] can be taken in two ways. It would be hard to deny that in various ways these systems may fail to do justice to victims of crime and/or the perpetrators of crime. Victims may sometimes be so ignored in the process of trial and conviction, for example, that they are not even informed either of the date of trial or indeed the outcome of trials.

Many of those accused of crimes come from the most deprived areas of our society, are badly educated and have little understanding of the process of trial to which they are subjected. Once convicted they undergo a period imprisonment in overcrowded prisons, separated by distance from their families and with little or no hope of employment once they have served their sentence and are released. For a host of such reasons victims and offenders have reason to feel that they have not been justly treated. The upsurge in victims' rights campaigns, well documented and discussed by David Garland amongst others[2], attest to the strength of the dissatisfaction felt. In this context then the claims of restorative justice can be seen as providing an alternative way of doing things which could in theory be met by changes in the way the existing criminal justice systems in fact operate whilst the basic features of those systems remain the same. It should be clear, however, that the findings of criminologists do not lead *directly* to the ideals of restorative justice. Many of the demands of the victims' rights movement are punitive in ways that would be inimical to those values. The changes necessary to remedy the failures to include victims more fully in the process of trial and sentencing might require no more than that they be kept informed about how the case is going and the harm they have suffered more carefully addressed when it comes to deciding on sentences. It could also mean that they are compensated for the harms they have suffered to a greater extent than they currently are. Similarly, there are many quite obvious ways in which the treatment of offenders could be reformed within the criminal justice system. In this way then the challenge

1 By this I mean simply the legal systems of western democracies and those other jurisdictions that have been influenced by such traditions.

2 Cf. D. GARLAND, *The Culture of Control, Crime and Social Order in Contemporary Society* Oxford, Oxford University Press, 2001; M. D. DUBBER, *Victims in the War on Crime*, New York, New York University Press, 2002.

is to be understood as a practical one which does not undermine the fundamental concepts of the criminal justice system itself. However, in his paper Erik Claes quite rightly takes the challenge of restorative justice practices to be rather more radical. He takes it that what underlies the "critical diagnosis of the criminal justice system made by criminologists" (pp.19-24 in this volume) is a claim to the effect that the failures that they identify – those of conflict reduction, context indifference and depersonalisation – are not merely accidental features of particular systems but flow necessarily from some of the fundamental principles of the criminal law system itself. These are not simply empirical claims, therefore, but claims at the level of principle. The very ideals of the rule of law which inform the criminal justice system are inimical to the aspirations of victims and offenders to be heard, primarily by one another. What victims and offenders want, (or perhaps need, it is not always clear) according to this view is "to be taken seriously in their anger and fears and to communicate to each other their stance in the conflict" (p. 22 in this volume). The legal norms which inform criminal justice are then both too abstract and too narrowly interpreted, when seen through the lens of rule-of-law values, to meet these aspirations. Restorative justice, some may argue, is not just a challenge to criminal justice but also an alternative to it.

The first task then that Claes sets himself is to rebut these charges of abstraction and context insensitivity and in doing so he brings to the fore one of the familiar philosophical problems about the nature of legal reasoning. To say that this is a familiar issue is not a criticism of the argument; to the contrary, one of the values of the paper is indeed that it precisely does relate the arguments about punishment and restorative justice to such a fundamental philosophical debate. The point is that it is in the nature of rules, legal or otherwise, that they stand in need of interpretation. The question which Claes' discussion opens up is precisely that of what constraints there can or must be on the kinds of consideration that are to weigh in interpreting the law. What features of the agents' context should be influential in deciding what the law is in the particular case and what not. These questions could not be settled without some further discussion of the political theory that underpins the whole conception of law itself, as Dworkin might be seen as arguing in some of his early writings. I shall take it that Claes' own arguments about the centrality of the idea of human rights in a proper understanding of the nature of legality is a move in that direction. If this is so then more will need to be said to fill out the political values which are at the core of the argument. It should be clear here that I am using the term "political" in its broadest sense, i.e. the sense in which theories of Aristotle, Kant, Rawls might all be called moral as well as political theories. One criticism of the "restorative justice movement" (if we suppose that there is such a thing) is that it often fails to engage sufficiently with the arguments at this level.

At the core of the debate about the ideals of legality and restorative justice ideals must be a discussion of such values as liberty, autonomy, human dignity and so on. It is one of the virtues of Claes' paper that he opens this engagement, though whether the rapprochement he seeks is possible is another matter.

One important claim from the criminologists, as he sets it out, is that the law cannot take into account the particularity of the victim and offender, what he refers to as *person-relativity* in interpreting the law. How far this is so depends on how one interprets this idea. That the victims of crime are individuals (I leave aside the vexed question of corporate victims here and) is surely not something that the law ignores, nor does it ignore their particular features or circumstances and these may sometimes make a considerable difference to the nature of the crime committed against them. Thus what might appear to be a simple case of assault becomes a case of manslaughter where the victim turns out to have a thin skull and dies as a result of the attack. No doubt there is a good deal of argument to be had about what range of particularities ought to be relevant. The law on provocation provides a good example of the kind of such a debate: how far for instance should such a law reflect the fact of ethnic differences? How far, that is to say, should the law reflect the fact that what may be counted as a grievous insult in one cultural context may not in another? Clearly the person-relativity at stake in Claes' paper is broader and more contentious than that. It is a matter not just of the individual victims or offender's circumstances or context but also of their *perspective*. What is crucial here is that it is a *subjective* notion, that is to say it has to do with how it *seems* to the agent, what their feelings and judgments about the situation are. So, he says "From the point of view of criminologists' attention is focussed on the concrete motives of the offender and the actual needs and desires of the victim, as well as on the complexity and the genesis of the conflict in which the victim and offender are placed... Finally, criminologists would be sensitive to the secret wants of both offender and victim to communicate to each other their feelings and their story in the case. ....Characteristic of the sensitivity for these facts is that their meaning is not completely exhausted by a legal norm to be interpreted" (pp.28-29 in this volume). The problem surely is then of what the status of these feelings and judgements ought to have in the criminal process. Insofar as Claes seeks some rapprochement between rule-of-law values and restorative-justice values then his account of the fundamental principles of legality should provide some answer to this question. What may not be clear is how far the restorative-justice perspective requires us to take the victim's and/or the accused's subjective views as dispositive, either of how the law ought to be interpreted or what the outcome of the criminal process ought to be. Here Claes' appeal to the value of human dignity is crucial for it provides a standard against which the claims of individuals must be judged.

The way that Claes develops his argument might call to mind the idea of the *inner* morality of law elaborated by Lon Fuller[3], by which I do not mean that Claes would agree with the content of much of what Fuller argues. The crucial point is however, that what he does argue is for an *internal* connection between human dignity and legality. The extent to which a system exhibits fidelity to the value of human dignity is the extent to which it can properly be called law. The reason for this has to do with the way in which law functions as a system of rules capable of guiding conduct in a liberal polity. If this is the argument then we need a clear account of what human dignity comes to. This is most certainly a notoriously complex notion and much more needs to be said by way of filling it out the detail than Claes has been able to set out in his paper.[4] The core of the idea comes at the point where he outlines the consequences that would flow from a legal system which did not respect human dignity insofar as the outcomes of its procedures were unpredictable and the interpretations of law reasonable. If citizens are to guide their conduct and relations with one another as *citizens* by rules that they can all accept then these are necessary features of those rules. Without this the citizen would, Claes says, "lose his confidence in the legitimacy of his own actions, and consequently in himself." (p. 41 in this volume) Now this is a strong claim to make and perhaps needs more argument than is given here. For one thing we need to see in a more developed way just how this connects to the idea of *human dignity*. Certainly, it might be argued, laws, which are unclear, and procedures, which are unreasonable in their outcomes, make life very difficult but that is someway from an affront to human dignity. What is needed is an argument that will connect more explicitly with an appropriate conception of rational agency and autonomy, the latter itself being a notoriously slippery concept. As it stands it might look as if the claim Claes makes is simply a psychological and contestable one. Not everyone needs to respond to confused law in the way he describes. It is perfectly possible to imagine people whose disregard for the law is such that they do not expect to govern their behaviour in accordance with it. They live by their own rules and their sense of what is required without relating this to publicly sanctioned values. Social and moral rules are not identical with law, so it is perfectly possible to imagine social life going on even in a context of inadequate law such as the one Claes imagines. Indeed, some of the practices of restorative justice might seem to presuppose just such an informal structure of rules. However, this might be missing the point Claes makes when he says "Through such a pervasive lack of confidence

---

3 L. FULLER, *The Morality of Law*, Yale, Yale University Press, 1964.

4 This is, of course, no more than should be expected since he makes clear at the outset that his intention is the modest one of setting out a general line of argument rather than a fully developed legal theory (p. 18 in this volume).

citizens would be completely deprived of their capacity to act" (p. 41 in this volume), this should surely be understood as a claim not about their capacity to act *simpliciter* but their capacity to act as *citizens*. This brings into the picture the public dimension, which might seem to be lacking from the restorative-justice perspective. The conflict, (though I am not convinced that this is the best way to characterise it) between the victim of crime and the offender is not simply a private disagreement. If we were to see it in that way then it would be hard to see why we need speak of crime at all, rather than seeing it as a civil matter to be dealt with through a civil law process and it is no doubt the case that some proponents of restorative justice would indeed argue that the concept of crime is one that should be abandoned. Crimes need to be understood as public wrongs for which an offender needs to answer not just to the victim but also to the whole community of citizens of which they both are members. This I take it is one of the motivations for Claus' argument concerning generality.

Where then does this leave the person-relative perspective that appears to be at the heart of the criminologist's criticisms of the rule-of-law perspective? Should Claes be at all optimistic that his position can accommodate it sufficiently to deflect the criticisms? It is in this context that his emphasis on the importance of the foreseeability of judicial interpretation as an aspect of the way legality respects, or should respect human dignity, comes into play. I am not sure, however, that *foreseeability* is quite what is at stake here. If we think, for instance, of the "hard cases" where judicial interpretation is called for then is it not obvious that what we ought to expect is that we can *foresee* the outcome, since if we were able to do that then it would not be a "hard case". Rather we might say that whatever the decision a court comes to in such cases it should be such that citizens, both victims and offenders, *should* see it as *reasonable*. I emphasise that they *should* see it so to make it clear that its being so is not simply a matter of their subjective judgements. Individual citizens, like judges, may in fact be as rational or irrational as you like, the point here is not that the requirement of reasonableness is designed to give them what they happen to *want*, rather one might say, drawing on a conception of human dignity and human rights in the way that Claes does, it should give them what they ought to want.

The kind of reflection on the role of human dignity and human rights that Claes' paper invites us to carry out might indeed lead us to think that one outcome of the criminal process should be that victims and offenders should achieve the kind of reconciliation that Bob and Anne and Jim achieve in his last example. (p. 44 in this volume) Yet, if we take this example as exhibiting some of the core features of restorative justice then it raises some questions for any compatibilist approach. One thing that should be noticed is that the view that we are told the victims, Ann and Bob came to, is not the only one possible. Other victims faced with the same offender might well respond to Jim and his circumstances quite differently. It might be that everything they learn about him confirms their belief that he, the offender, is nothing more than an idle waster. It need not be the case that all victims of crime make judgements that are sympathetic or indeed rational. Nor need it be the case that offenders come to adopt a more sympathetic attitude to the victims. This, of course, says no more than that mediation might fail but that can hardly be a knockdown criticism since the same can be said for criminal justice. It cannot guarantee that it always succeeds in its aims. Of course, it need not be the case that victims who do not respond in such a sympathetic way need themselves feel that the process has failed, they might be perfectly happy to have had their chance to express their anger, to have had their judgements confirmed. This might mean, though it need not, that they did not enter into the process in the right spirit in the first place.

What is of more concern is the way in which, as Claes puts it, "At this time of the session the conflict began to develop within a different framework. The participants interacted on a level where they expressed their concern about issues beyond the criminal event" (p. 45 in this volume). This propensity to move beyond the confines of the initial "conflict", i.e. the crime of which the offender was found guilty, involves a degree of intrusiveness which may itself conflict with human dignity. It may conflict, that is, with the right to a degree of privacy not just for the victims and offenders but for others who may become the subject of these mediating discussions and who are not there to give their side of the story too. The "story" has the potential to grow to include much that is no longer directly related to the original offence, which one might think conflicts with a rule-of-law conception of justice. One might also argue, though I shall not expand upon it here, that the extent to which victims demand more by way of explanation than that given through the criminal justice process conflicts with the right to privacy of thoughts and feelings on the part of the offender. The very constraints of rule of law processes which were criticised for being too abstract, for having a de-personalising and distancing effect might be seen here as a positive virtue for they depend upon a conception of the citizen, and thus the accused, which draws a clear distinction between the public and the private. In defence of the restorative justice process it could be argued that a mediator properly trained to the task will be sensitive to the issue of privacy and that in any case the process itself is voluntary and offenders may simply refuse to engage in the discussion. This, however, is less than convincing if restorative justice claims to be an alternative to criminal justice, for then it cannot be left up to victims and offenders to choose whether to engage in the process or not, unless we are to suppose that crime is to be seen as a private matter and thus subject to something more like a civil law process. It is undoubtedly the case that some proponents of restorative justice do wish to be quite radical and argue for the abandonment of the concept of crime, which focuses on the idea of a wrong against the victim and prefer to speak only of harms that need to be addressed.

It seems prima facie implausible that the rule-of-law position argued by Claes could readily accommodate such a position, resting as it does on a strong conception of fundamental human rights which go to the core of a citizen's identity.

So, seeing the extent to which it is possible to bring restorative justice values and practices to bear upon a criminal justice process, which is founded on the values of legality as identified by Claes, requires a more detailed examination of those values and processes. One of these values, one might think is equality: the requirement that like cases be treated alike for instance. If this is to be achieved, restorative justice practices will need to be rather more coercive than its current practitioners seem to avow, for example. Indeed, this is so even if we do not envisage a rapprochement with criminal justice processes, for how else are victims to get what they want and need? Similarly, to what extent will offenders get equal justice? This is where the discussion would take a new turn for we need to ask what equity *means* in this context. Criminal justice does not necessarily measure up to its own standards and it is certainly true that what much of criminological evidence shows that as a matter of hard fact our criminal justice regimes do not achieve equality of treatment or outcomes for either victims or offenders. If as Claes suggests restorative justice "can serve a complementary function in relation to a rights-conception of legality" (p. 55 in this volume), then we might suppose that the parties have a right to a process of mediation and the chance of reconciliation that this brings. One consequence of this then is surely that victims have some obligation to meet those who have offended against them and listen to them. Yet many victims, rape victims for example, might feel that the last thing they need is any personal engagement with the person who so wronged them. On the other hand, those who have had their cars vandalised might be quite happy to meet the vandal and to see whether they can come to some understanding. How are the different offenders to be given equal treatment here, or rather perhaps we should ask *what* exactly would count as equal treatment. This is not simply a matter of whether it would be difficult to require rape victims to face those who have offended against them, either through the criminal justice process itself, by being prepared to give evidence in court for example, or through the complementary process of a restorative justice kind but of what assumptions we are now making about the responsibilities of citizens to one another. In other cases there may be a question of *who* should be regarded as victims for the purposes of restorative justice, in homicides for example. Clearly engagement with the immediate victim is not a possibility but who else then might have a legitimate interest? Is this something that can be settled by appealing to the person-relative perspectives? The whole point about such a perspective is that it is person specific and sensitive to the different ways in which individuals respond to their circumstances. It is perfectly possible for the impact of an offender's actions to have a differential impact on the victims.

Supposing that my car has been stolen, I may view this as something of an inconvenience and certainly believe that it is a crime but have no interest at all in the perpetrator of that crime, in his story or future, beyond expecting that justice will be done if he is caught and brought before the law, i.e. that due process is followed, the evidence is sound and the sentence fair. My neighbour, for whom her car is an object of great pride (and perhaps love of sorts), reacts quite differently and for her it is important to confront the offender and let him know how much she has suffered as a result of his actions. Can offenders here be subject to equal treatment? Clearly "equal treatment" does not have to be "same treatment" but then what would constitute equal treatment? Note also that victim responses to crime may vary not just in terms of the degree to which they have been affected but in the ways they are affected. It does not follow that these subjective reactions to crime have to be entirely rational. To what extent is this something that can or should be taken into account when considering whether offenders should be confronted with their victims? In the course of the criminal justice process the claims made victims about themselves may to be subject to scrutiny, not always a comfortable process to be sure. Moreover, there is no doubt a great deal of insensitivity displayed by those who are involved in that process, none of which is necessary. What is not clear is the extent to which restorative justice processes can sustain a commitment to equal treatment unless the subjective perspectives are subject to scrutiny. The point here is not to rule out the kind of rapprochement Claes argues for, but suggest that it raises interesting questions which are worth pursuing if we are to make progress on what seems an eminently worthwhile enterprise.

PART TWO.
RESTORATIVE JUSTICE AND THE MORALITY OF LAW

4. RESTORATIVE JUSTICE AND THE MORALITY OF LAW

SERGE BROCHU

The commission of an offence constitutes a violation of a statutory value that aims at protecting the law. While reacting to the offence, courts reaffirm the standard which this violation could have weakened.[1]

I am not a specialist of restorative justice. My field of expertise has more to do with criminal issues related to drug abuse. If there is a field that restorative justice did not penetrate in North America, it is the one of drugs. Indeed, in this field, the procedures that approach most the concepts of restorative justice are the establishment of Drug Courts, which supports the treatment of drug addicts. Thus, an approach that aims at the rehabilitation of the offender rather than reconciliation with society or with certain potential victims (not always easy to define with drug offences).

The International Center for Comparative Criminology counts many specialists in restorative justice; these include, among others, Mylène Jaccoud, Jean Trépanier and Jo-Anne Wemmers. However, as I have been asked to present a lecture at this conference of restorative justice and morality of the law, I understand that the conference organisers of this 10th Aquinas Conference seek an independent and candid point of view on the topic. Anyway this is all I can offer you, especially here in Belgium where we have the best specialist on restorative justice in the world.

I will divide my presentation into four sections. I will begin by briefly discussing what I understand by "Morality" and what large principles could guide a justice that is moral. Then, I will discuss recent evolution of the punitive justice doctrine. Thereafter, I will try to define what I understand of restorative justice, and finally discuss restorative justice and the Morality of justicial practices.

1. MORALITY

Morality is a question of culture, epoch and point of view! The war between the coalition US/Great Britain and Iraq is a good example while each of

---

[1] J. TREPANIER, *La justice réparatrice et les philosophes de l'intervention pénale sur les jeunes*, Montréal, 2000. Récupéré le 6 février 2003 de http//www.rojaq.qc.ca.documents/trepan.html.

the parties involved have the tendency to describe their aggressive measures in terms of good actions against Evil. What is moral and what is not moral in this war is sometimes very hard to define. A few decades ago, morality was relatively easy to define. In Quebec, it was based on Catholic principles. Moral quality, rightness and wrongness, standards of right conduct, as well as virtue were guided by moral instructions or lessons delivered by the Catholic Church. Catholic principles had a strong influence on the definition of crime (e.g. attempted suicide, homosexuality and abortion were both sins and crimes). Catholic principles were also influential in the ways we were dealing with offenders: censure, condemnation, punishment and pardon.

In the middle of the twentieth-century, Quebec had to face two relatively new phenomena: 1) immigration from non-Catholic countries that brought different moral philosophies often in accord with Catholic principles but sometimes in divergence; and 2) the gradual loss of influence of the Church on the population and their civil behaviour (birth control, sexual practices, etc.). These two important factors contributed, each in its way, to decriminalised behaviour like suicide and homosexuality that are still not accepted by the Catholic Church.

What else could replace religious principles to assure that justice is based on appropriate values, that treats citizens with respect in a responsible manner? On which principles should we hold a citizen responsible for the wrong he/she committed? And more importantly, how do we define an equitable measure to impose on an offender? How to resolve the conflict introduced by the so-called "wrong doing"?

I propose that we use three basic concepts which are essential to our contemporary western culture: every citizen, offender or victim, should be treated with *bien-être* (well-being); *dignité* (dignity); and *sécurité* (security).

Keeping in mind these three principles, a moral justice system should: 1) take care of the victim and his/her suffering/needs; 2) take care of the offender and protect their fundamental human rights; 3) take care of society and prevent recidivism.

2. RECENT EVOLUTION OF THE DOCTRINE OF PUNITIVE JUSTICE

During the 20th century, there was an important increase in the use of imprisonment and penal control. In North America, and in several other so-called civilized countries, the penal justice system became THE means "to control" certain social problems, such as drug-addiction and domestic violence. However, this movement in favour of imprisonment as a means of controlling offenders was accompanied by various other, sometimes conflicting, ideas. These included issues of offender rehabilitation, victims' right and decriminalisation or depenalisation of certain acts. Moreover, the need to reduce public expenditure had a strong influence towards controlling the number of offenders being imprisoned.

It was in this context that the resurgence of restorative justice appeared.[2] We speak of resurgence here because this form of justice was most common before the development of a centralised system of control, the emergence of prison institutions and the professionalisation of certain experts.[3] However, it is only recently that interest in this system reappeared.

The question is whether this ideology could live together with the reinforcement of the "punitive justice mode" that manifested itself through the increase of minimal statutory sentences, the emergence of "intensive probation programmes", the additional criteria imposed on inmates for release on parole, and the intensification of the monitoring system for dangerous delinquents.

Well, it seems both types of measure could live together since many Criminal Codes have been modified to allow the use of replacement measures. Similarly, the use of mediation programmes has increased during this same period. Moreover, in scientific circles, the topic of restorative justice has become impossible to ignore.[4]

3. RESTORATIVE JUSTICE

In modern society, restorative justice constitutes a new paradigm parallel to the traditional duel between repression and the rehabilitation. Cario would say that it positively transcends the punitive and rehabilitative models.[5] This paradigm presents new priorities (i.e. conflict relations rather than crimes) and guidelines for our justice system.

The sought objective is no longer a moral rebalance nor the expiation of the offender's infraction (retribution) nor prevention and rehabilitation (dissuasion). Rather, through restoration it aims to empower and conciliate; to relocate the lost goods; to restore a state of safety lost; to reinstate a vanished dignity; to repair a feeling of equity damaged; to rebuild a sense of social belonging. Crime is viewed primarily as a conflict between

---

2 N. ADMO, *La justice réparatrice vue par les personnes contrevenantes et les personnes lésées, Mémoire de maîtrise inédit*, Université de Montréal, 2001.

3 S. COHEN, *Vision of Social Control*, Cambridge, Cambridge Polity Press, 1985.

4 M. JACCOUD, *Justice punitive et justice réparatrice: cohabitation paradoxale ou complémentaire?* 68ième Congrès de l'Association Canadienne Française pour l'Avancement des Sciences, 2002. Texte récupré de http://rojaq.qc.ca/Textemylene.html le 6 février 2003.

5 R. CARIO, "De la reconnaissance des droits des victims à la justice restaurative", in F. Fatah and S. PARMENTIER (eds) *Victim Policies and Criminal Justice on the Road to Restorative Justice*, Leuven, Leuven University Press, 2001.

individuals that results in injuries and secondly, as a violation against the Law.

Mediation, negotiation and reparation then constitute the measures most commonly used. However, the initiatives of restorative justice are found on a continuum. Some strategies are completely independent of the traditional penal justice system, some are juxtaposed strategies, and others are measures additional to the regular penal procedures. So, it is not excluded that people taking part in a process of mediation are also the object of probation; are referred towards treatment services or have already purged an incarceration period.[6]

However, the principles driving these measures are based on: 1) the offender-victim relation in the community and 2) on the process allowing reconciliation. The offender, the injured person and society[7] constitute the three key actors of the judicial process. They agree to be in disagreement but pursue the negotiation in order to gradually reach a consensus. Thus, these key actors must participate actively in dialogue and negotiation to settle the conflict situation. The dialogue mainly aims to create peace in the community, and the resolution of conflicts.[8] Thus it is an empowerment and repair process. This repair process allows for negotiation between the actors concerned, taking their needs and limits into account. For example, monetary compensation or refunding of material losses by work; symbolic remedy; agreement on future behaviours; contribution to a assistance's victims funds; etc. In other words, it is a consensual approach in which the parties admit their participation in a conflict situation after which the repair process may begin. This process entails levels of a psychological, social and/or symbolic nature for the implied actors. Each party must assume its responsibilities in order to succeed. The offender must accept his share of responsibility; make excuses, and be open to compensate for the wrongful acts. On the other side, the victim must accept the apologies and be ready to forgive. Lastly, the community must provide the support as well as the incentives necessary to proceed in an optimal way and without losers.

---

6 M. JACCOUD, *Justice punitive et justice réparatrice: cohabitation paradoxale ou complémentaire?* 68ième Congrès de l'Association Canadienne Française pour l'Avancement des Sciences, 2000. Texte récupré de *http://rojaq.qc.ca/Textemylene.html* le 6 février 2003; D. MIERS, M. MAGUIRE, S. GOLDIE, K. SHARPE, A. NETTEN, S. UGLOW, K. DOLIN, A. HALLAM, J. ENTERKIN, T. NEWBURN (eds), "An explanatory Evaluation of Restorative Justice Schemes", *Crime Reduction Research Series Papers 9*, London, Home Office, 2001.

7 Though the society as a key actor in this process does not really reach the unanimity.

8 N. ADMO, *La justice réparatrice vue par les personnes contrevenantes et les personnes lésées, Mémoire de maîtrise inédit*, Université de Montréal, 2001; J. BRAITHWAITE, "Restorative Justice and a Better Future", (1996) 76 *Dalhousie Review* 9-13; L. WALGRAVE, "La justice restaurative", (1999) 32 *Criminologie* 7-29.

4. RESTORATIVE JUSTICE AND THE MORALITY OF JUSTICE PROCESS

4.1. Taking Care of the Victim

Let us return to the three principles I have mentioned that should rule a moral justice. As I have said before, moral justice should first base its action on harm and suffering caused to the victim. Restorative justice, being centred on the process of reparation, provides a clear message about the importance (worth) of each party implied in the conflict. It is a normalisation process of the relations broken by the conflict. Thus, rather than being centred on the culpability of the delinquent and on the sanction that will be imposed in a confrontational process between the parties, it emphasises the analysis of the damage caused by the conflict in order to propose a reparation in a consensual manner. As such, it gives back to the victim a significant place. The victim appears important not only to the service of justice in the pronouncement of culpability, they become the principal actors in the whole process. The victim often occupies a central role in these negotiation procedures.

4.2. Taking Care of the Offender

If we grant too much significance to the place to the victim, do we not risk introducing an additional punitive element to the penal process already in place? According to Admo the restorative approach, for the Quebec victims she interviewed, "falls under the current penal system; i.e. the punishment (or imprisonment) represents a complementary measure or, even sometimes, a preceding step for reparation".[9] In the absence of punishment, it appears that victims have the impression that there was no justice. Therefore, we are faced with the problem of creating a balance between listening to the contravener and the victim.:"As we see it, the principles governing the philosophy of restorative justice are diverted and orchestrated in a punitive logic. The latter is primarily aiming at satisfying the lobbies of the promotion of the rights and interests of the victims".[10]

Thus, participation in a restorative process does not exclude incarceration or other penal measures. On the contrary, it appears, according to Jaccoud, that the latter is becoming a condition for the acceptance from

---

9 N. ADMO, *La justice réparatrice vue par les personnes contrevenantes et les personnes lésées, Mémoire de maîtrise inédit*, Université de Montréal, 2001, 138.

10 M. JACCOUD, *Justice punitive et justice réparatrice: cohabitation paradoxale ou complémentaire?* 68ième Congrès de l'Association Canadienne Française pour l'Avancement des Sciences, 2002. Texte récupré de *http://rojaq.qc.ca/Textemylene.html* le 6 février 2003.

the victims to undertake a restorative process. In Quebec, with an adult population, when the principles of reparation are not accompanied by retribution or dissuasion, very often, the same files would have simply been closed by the police officers.[11] Too often within American standards, restorative justice is an additional measure to traditional retributive justice. A moral justice should not be too punitive to please the victims. However, a study conducted by Wemmers does not include punishment among the needs of victims. Rather, these needs are: information; compensation; psychological support; participation in the justice process; security and other practical needs.[12]

4.3. Taking Care of Society

Being from Canada, where ¼ of citizens are afraid to walk in their neighbourhood at night, prevention of recidivism is crucial for acceptance of new penal measures.

Restorative justice researchers seem more interested in conducting process evaluation on negotiation, mediation and conciliation between the actors implied in a conflict rather than conducting impact studies in terms of recidivism. Process studies indicate that restorative justice works well. For example, a 15-month study of restorative justice schemes across England revealed that: "Victims who had experienced some form of restorative justice were broadly favourable towards the concept. They appreciated the opportunity to "have their say", and some were pleased and even moved to receive letters of apology. Those who had not previously known their offenders often welcomed the provision of information about them, commenting that this gave them peace of mind. About two-thirds believed that the intervention had had some beneficial impact on the offender. On the other hand, some victims were sceptical about their offender's motives or found direct personal contact with them unsettling an even intimidating. The most frequently cited negative aspect of involvement with the schemes was the time taken to complete the process".[13]

---

11 M. JACCOUD, *Justice punitive et justice réparatrice: cohabitation paradoxale ou complémentaire?* 68ième Congrès de l'Association Canadienne Française pour l'Avancement des Sciences, 2002. Texte récupré de *http://rojaq.qc.ca/Textemylene.html* le 6 février 2003.

12 J.A. WEMMERS, "Les victimes et la justice réparatrice", in J.A. WEMMERS and K. CYR (eds), *La Justice réparatrice et les victims d'actes criminels. Les cahiers de recherche criminologiques n° 37*, Montréal, Centre international de criminologie comparée, 2002.

13 D. MIERS et al. (eds), "An explanatory Evaluation of Restorative Justice Schemes", *Crime Reduction Research Series Papers 9*, London, Home Office, 2001, IX.

We found many studies about positive effect reports by victims. Generally, the victims who agreed to take part in a mediation process reached a state of well-being. On the other side, offenders seemed to better accept responsibility and to acquire better self-esteem. Results lead us to believe that restorative justice strategies have a greater potential than classical Retributive Justice to meet the needs of each party.

However, doesn't the justice system also have the social responsibility to prevent recidivism? The great satisfaction of people involved in the restorative justice process does not comment on the recidivism of offenders who participate in this process. However, is restorative justice better, equal or worst than the usual alternatives in terms of impacting recidivism rates? Prevention of recidivism constitutes an objective of every element of the justice system and more efforts should be devoted to document the impact of restorative justice on recidivism. Strang, who produced a more exhaustive literature review than I did, confirmed this impression when she wrote: "Even in relation to programmes in the justice setting, where most of the evaluative research has taken place, we do not know very much yet about how effective the restorative approach may prove to be in reducing re-offending; this is especially difficult to estimate when programmes are mostly directed at a population of offenders whose offences are minor and criminal careers briefs. Large claims of "success" among those who may never have re-offended anyway confuse and distract policymakers".[14]

So we urgently need more methodologically sound impact studies.

CONCLUSION

In the twentieth century, dissuasive and retributive justice was based on a conflict relation between two parties. The process itself does little to resolve the conflict, however. Alltoo often it exacerbates it. Its result consists in the proclamation of a person found guilty and a sentence proportional to the unlawful act. In order to ensure the objectivity of the imposed penalty and to reduce the risks of revenge, we rely on a list of regulations promulgated in a Criminal code. An objective referee, a judge or sometimes a jury, is then called to cope with the heavy task, full of significant moral issues, of convicting and sentencing the offender. The victim is then relatively isolated from the process if he/she only testifies about the undergone misdeeds and identifies the aggressor. This situation is seldom satisfactory for the victim who sometimes ends up suffering from a new form of victimisation from the justice process.

---

[14] H. STRANG, 2001, 38.

The idea of restorative justice, which is based on old concepts, constitutes an interesting alternative approach for filling in the gaps of the modern justice system. The restorative justice process proposes an alternative paradigm to the penal justice format, which up to now has been the subject of retributive or dissuasive procedures. Restorative justice considers that crime constitutes a conflict between an injured person and an offender. Reparation strategies therefore imply the active participation of the victim and the delinquent and, if required, members of the community (i.e. family, friends, neighbours, etc.) in a consensual process. The objective is then to reach equity and greater comfort for each one. This new paradigm forces criminologists to ask a fundamental question: whom must the justice system serve?

To satisfy the principles of restorative justice, we will use mediation strategies of negotiation, of amicable settlement, compensation and reparation. In other words, we seek to fulfil the requirement of reparation for the victims, the need for re-establising the social bonds of the contravener and addressing society's claims for justice. To some extent, the process resembles psycho-social therapy that makes it possible to reach greater comfort; but a greater comfort for whom? In my opinion, the answer to this question is crucial for the development of restorative justice. In theory, it is easy to affirm that all the parties in question must be treated in an equitable way. But in reality, what is the main objective of restorative justice; compensating[15] the victim or normalising social links with the offender? Which interest will prevail? Or rather, which interest will society favour?

Restorative justice is neither punitive, nor cut-rate justice. In theory, it has enormous merit in terms of morality and justice. In practice, too often in North America, restorative justice seems to be regarded as a justice of second order: good for young offenders or for minor crimes. When it is possible to penetrate the level of adult justice, it is complementary to retributive or dissuasive justice. Following Jaccoud's studies, we could believe that this is probably due to the fact that it does not sufficiently emphasise punishment to seem equitable to some victims. Moreover, it probably does not sufficiently emphasise the reality of recidivism to a society that has come to fear increasingly the presence of criminals within the community. With this in mind, restorative justice is extremely likely to complement the penal panoply rather than becoming an alternative to the latter in North America.

[15] Even the idea of compensating the victim is not without problems since it is not easy to determine the natureof adequate compensation for each party, especially when a good lost was of great value to the victim, and the offender comes from a more economically deprived living environment than the injured person.

This is unfortunate because, as Cario maintains, to "restore" is to recognise the other one as a person having rights and feelings; as a step towards reconciliation by a person who has offended us; and, it is the recognition of both parties as worthy of the society in which they live.[16] Restorative justice is certainly a better way to achieve the goals of a moral, astute and ethical justice than punishment and exclusion.

But first researchers in this field must reconcile their point of view about the victim's place in the process and conduct more systematic studies about recidivism in order to offer strong opposition to zero tolerance penal policies and demonstrate that punishing offenders is not the only way to go forward.

[16] R. CARIO, "De la reconnaissance des droits des victims à la justice restaurative", in F. FATAH and S. PARMENTIER (eds) *Victim Policies and Criminal Justice on the Road to Restorative Justice*, Leuven, Leuven University Press, 2001.

5. RESTORATIVE JUSTICE AND THE MORALITY OF THE FAIR TRIAL: A REPLY TO BROCHU

Mireille Hildebrandt

INTRODUCTION

In this paper I will look into restorative justice from the perspective of the fair trial, as it developed over the past 200 years. For those who take the fair trial for granted this might seem a redundant exercise, that can only lead to a meaningless comparison based on the refusal to take restorative justice serious on its own merits. My aim is, however, to acknowledge the particular and fragile character of the fair trial as a means to build checks and balances in the power-relationships between governments and their citizens. On top of that the fair trial is meant to assure publicity and transparency in a way that is instrumental for the goals of punishment, such as prevention and retribution that constitute the (re)establishment of the authority of the violated legal norm. To be instrumental in this sense both prevention and retribution depend on publicity and transparency. While the rise of restorative practices might elucidate the shortcomings of the fair trial (and/or of the way it is practiced today) this should not prevent us from a critical evaluation of certain aspects of mediation in penal matters.

In the following text we start from a historical perspective on the fair trial, linking this to a discussion of the legal norm as conceived by lawyers and social scientists. I will propose a third way to look at legal norms that might provide common ground for lawyers and criminologists. From this groundwork we can proceed to discuss the public context of restorative justice in relation to the morality of law. This public context leads to questions about the primacy of the victim as legitimisation of the criminal justice system. I will reformulate this legitimisation by claiming that the criminal justice system is constructed to protect citizens in their capacity as both *potential* victim and *potential* suspect. In the next paragraph I will analyse the procedural construction of our criminal justice system by examining the two aspects that constitute a fair trial: (1) (re)establishment of the allegedly violated legal norm, (2) in such a way that the suspect is protected against the abuse of state powers. These two aspects are related to the effectiveness of restorative and criminal justice that cannot be separated from their justification or moral evaluation. Referring to Claes' distinction between person- and norm-relative facts I continue by pleading that while this distinction is pertinent it should not be interpreted as a separation because legal norms and actions are mutually constitutive; a legally relevant fact always entails both a person- and a norm-relative aspect. In the concluding remarks we will summarise the consequences of our findings for the morality of restorative justice.

1. HISTORICAL PERSPECTIVE ON MEDIATION AND FAIR TRIAL IN PENAL MATTERS

In my doctoral research I investigated the consensual process model for punishment from the perspective of criminal law and legal philosophy.[1] I combined historical and anthropological findings on punitive actions in non-state societies and used these findings to describe the emergence of punishment in correlation with the emergence of the state, ending the exercise with a comprehensive analysis of our "fair trial" in counterpoint to both the mediative process-model of non-state societies and the inquisitorial process-model of the absolute state.[2] One of my conclusions was that mediation in the shadow of criminal codes should not be confused with the mediative practices of a society without a state. The looming powers of government control, implicating the state's monopoly on violence and the prohibition to take the law in one's own hands, change the nature of any attempt to "revert back" to mediation in criminal matters. In a society without a state punitive action is not only a right of every free person but a duty that is woven into a very complicated fabric of family, lineage and tribal interrelations. In a society without a state freedom equals independence from authority (the unfree being those that work within the ambience of their lord or pater familias) and this independence implies a continuous threat of war, revenge and feud. Punitive actions can thus endanger the fragile coherence of the society while they are also the means to confirm it. Mediation is a matter of life and death, not only for the persons directly concerned, the parties never being just persons but always families, lineages or the entire tribe. With the rise of the state this all changes and while this is not the moment to analyse the profound change of perspective that occurs, I do think it is of the utmost importance not to be romantic about mediation in non-state societies. In the setting of a

1 M. HILDEBRANDT, *Straf(begrip) en procesbeginsel*, Deventer, Kluwer 2002.

2 See for instance D. SALAS, *Du procès pénal. Eléments pour une théorie interdisciplinaire du procès*, Paris, Presses Universitaires de France, 1992; H.J. BERMAN, *Law and Revolution. The Formation of the Western Legal Tradition*, Cambridge Massachusetts, Harvard University Press, 1983, J. CHEVALLIER, *L'Etat de droit*, Paris, Montchrestien, 1994.

society without a state mediation always occurs when society itself is at stake, on the verge of war, while in the realm of the modern state, mediation is an uneasy side-show that is tolerated but – up until now – fits badly with state-organised criminal responsibility.

2. THE PUBLIC CONTEXT OF RESTORATIVE JUSTICE AND THE CONCEPT OF THE LEGAL NORM

To understand law in non-state societies – as well as law in the modern state – it is important to develop an understanding of legal norms that goes well beyond the formal and positivist conception of law that emerged within the civil law tradition, together with the emergence of the modern state.[3] One of the reasons why criminologists are surprised at the blind spots of lawyers when the realities of the law are at stake, is precisely this normativistic concept of legal norms as rules that seem to exist in another world, independent of the way people (inter)act. To a social scientist a legal norm can only be relevant if is it actually followed by legal subjects. However, to understand the relationship between rules and actions we should not confuse following a rule with the regularity of behaviour.[4] After drinking coffee in the evening I might not be able to sleep, but this does not imply that I am following a rule, which says that I should not sleep after drinking coffee. So to find out which are the legal norms of a society we can neither limit ourselves to the formal rules enumerated in codes, statutes, casebooks or law-reports, nor to a simple counting of regular behaviour patterns.

Legal norms are best perceived as rules that hold together the ever-changing fabric of a society. The relationship between legal norms and the actions of those that live within the same jurisdiction is, in this view, mutually constitutive: a rule that does not actually constrain the way people behave, in the end loses its authority as a legal norm. Punishment is the most direct way of restoring the authority of a legal norm, but to accomplish this task it must be understood as such. It cannot afford arbitrary interventions, because in that case people cannot attune their actions to the rule, simply because the rule is no longer clear.

This text is a contribution to the topic of restorative justice and the morality of law. Brochu has rightly observed that both morality and law are a matter

[3] A salient description of this emergence can be found in: H. P. GLENN, *Legal Traditions of the World. Sustainable Diversity in Law*, Oxford, Oxford University Press, 2000.

[4] This insight has been extensively demonstrated by L WITTGENSTEIN in his *Philosophische Untersuchungen*, see on this point Hans-Johann GLOCK, "rule-following", in *A Wittgenstein Dictionary*, Blackwell, Oxford, 1999, 323-330 and C. TAYLOR, "To Follow a Rule" in his *Philosophical Arguments*, Cambridge Massachusetts, Harvard University Press, 1995, 165-181.

of culture. It is interesting to investigate the relevance of this observation. If by culture we mean some kind of coherent set of values that holds together the fragile fabric of society, then the role of criminal law could be that it organises the rejection of actions that reject these values. Punishment – in terms of Anthony Duff: hard treatment – is a painful way to censure behaviour that denies crucial values of the culture that is at stake. In Hegelian terms: it negates the negation of shared norms. This is also the motto of Brochu's paper: "The commission of an offence constitutes a violation of a statutory value that aims at protecting the law. While reacting to the offence, courts reaffirm the standard which this violation could have weakened" (see p. 79 in this volume). This citation of J. Trépanier confirms an important intuition about punitive actions: these are never the business of offender and victim only; they always indicate a wider context and a public interest. A crime is not only a person-relative fact, that harms a victim and perhaps morally degrades the offender, it is also an *act* that brings to the fore the fragile character of the norm that is transgressed. It threatens to destabilise the interrelations between not only victim and offender but beyond that between others who are no longer sure what to expect of their fellow citizens – if this transgression is not dealt with adequately. From this perspective – and here I would agree with Duff – retribution and prevention are two sides of the same coin.[5] Re-affirmation of the violated legal norm is not a theoretical or purely moral endeavour, as some would perhaps have it, but the condition of possibility for citizens to base their actions on this norm. While retribution seems to look at the past and prevention at the future, they presume each other – if they are to have an impact on the interactions between citizens.[6]

---

5 Duff speaks of a "unitary justification of punishment rather than (...) a retributivist notion of censure and (...) a consequentialist concern for crime-prevention which will undercut the traditional opposition between retributivist or backward-looking and consequentialist or forward-looking theories". R.A. DUFF, *Punishment, Communication, and Community*, Oxford, Oxford University Press, 2001, 89.

6 In Dutch legal theory this conception of legal norms is sometimes termed an expectancy-theory of (legal) norms, because of the crucial role played by anticipation in the constitution of norms. This conception does not preclude the acknowledgement of another, more instrumental aspect of legal norms, which emphasizes their imperative character. My inspiration comes from J.F. GLASTRA VAN LOON, *Norm en Handeling. Bijdrage tot een kentheoretische fundering van de sociale wetenschappen*, Groningen, Wolters-Noordhoff, 1987, see also J.F. GLASTRA VAN LOON, "Rules and Commands", (1958) *Mind* 514-521 and P. RICOEUR, *Du Texte a l'action. Essais d'herméneutique II*, Paris, Editions du Seuil, 1986 and G. H. MEAD, (edited, with introduction by C. W. MORRIS), *Mind, Self & Society. From the standpoint of a social behaviorist*, Chicago, Illinois, The University of Chicago Press, 1959.

3. PRIMACY OF THE VICTIM?

This brings me to Brochu's three principles of a moral justice system: (1) it should be centred on the victim and his suffering, (2) it should be punitive in proportion and (3) it should be directed towards prevention. The first principle (primacy of the victim and his or her suffering) reminds me of Mill's and Feinberg's harm principle (only those actions should be punished that cause harm to others) and of Shklar's idea that the only value that is widely shared in our post-modern society is the horror of suffering.[7] While I do not have any problems with proportionate punishment or with the preventive aspect of punishment, I do wonder if the victim is really at the centre of a moral justice system. I would rather say that the citizen, both as potential victim *and* as potential offender is at the centre of a moral justice system (keeping in mind the fact that certain categories of citizens turn out to be more prone than others to become victim as well as offender, a fact that is common knowledge for criminologists but maybe less so for legal scholars). While decentring the victim, I would not rule out the possibility that mediation in penal matters could facilitate a type of meeting between victim and offender for which our "traditional" "fair trial" has no room. The point is rather, whether we can institutionalise such a meeting without facilitating a process in which psychological techniques like shaming are used as instruments to enforce apologies and forgiveness that are *caused* by humiliation instead of *brought forward* by a respectful appeal to reason. I would therefore agree with Duff when he rejects such techniques, which can easily be used as a means of what he calls prudential deterrence. In that case "what dissuades the person from crime is the discomfort that shame brings, not the thought that such conduct would be wrong".[8] Though – other than Duff – I do not think we can or should discard instrumental deterrence as a means to re-establish the authority of a violated legal norm, I also think that instrumental deterrence should appeal to human reason instead of humiliation. The problem with reintegrative shaming is that it is so closely related to stigmatic shaming and humiliation that for that reason alone it should not be used as a technique to manipulate the feelings of a victim and offender, let alone behind closed

---

7 J.S. Mill, *On liberty* (edited and with an introduction by G. Himmelfarb), London, Penguin, 1974 (first published 1859), 68. J. Feinberg, *The Moral Limits of the Criminal Law*, New York, Oxford University Press, 1990. J. Shklar, *The faces of injustice*, New Haven, Yale University Press, 1988.

8 R. A. Duff, *Punishment, Communication, and Community*, Oxford, Oxford University Press, 2001, 118.

doors.[9] Apart from that, the problem with instrumental deterrence is that it may only establish the authority of the violated legal norm during the time that the potential offender expects to be checked, persecuted and convicted. The legal norm itself might not mean anything to the possible offender and this problem cannot be solved by an instrumentalist use of shaming-techniques. An appeal to the offender's sensitivity and reason, on the other hand, might indeed reintegrate her into the fabric of legal norms that forms part of the construction of our society. The question is whether it is possible to organise this appeal to a reasonable sensitivity in such a way as to prevent pseudo-therapeutic sessions while still moving beyond the constraints of the fair trial. In the next paragraph I endeavour to clarify the constraints of our fair trial and to explain why they should be a source of inspiration for the processes of restorative justice.

4. THE MORALITY AND EFFECTIVENESS OF FAIR TRIAL AND RESTORATIVE PUNISHMENT

Historically the emergence of the "fair trial" integrates the horizontal perspective of the equality of arms for defence and prosecution, with the vertical perspective of the unilateral verdict pronounced by a judge in accordance with a pre-established law. In this way the fair trial is intricately bound up with the principle of legality. I would dare to advance the proposition that the principle of legality loses its meaning outside the fair trial: especially the independence of the judge is a condition of possibility for the realisation of a legality that is not at the mercy of the executive. This is precisely the meaning of Montesquieu's famous prescription that the *judge* should be "bouche de la loi", instead of the then prevailing adage that the *king* should speak the law (*iudex est lex loquens* instead of *rex est lex loquens*).[10]

The specific integration of horizontal and vertical aspects within the procedural setting of the fair trial constitutes a set of checks and balances that is absent from the process of restorative justice. The most prominent of these checks and balances is the publicity (external publicity to the public and the judge of appeal, and internal publicity between defence and prosecution which is part of the equality of arms). This constitutive feature

9 J. BRAITHWAITE, *Crime, Shame and Reintegration*, Cambridge, Cambridge University Press, 1989. Braithwaite differentiates between reintegrative and stigmatic shaming, rejecting the second and advocating the first. Point is that humiliation and shame are so closely related that it seems nearly impossible to prevent the one when trying to cause the other.

10 For this unconventional but well-documented interpretation see K.M. SCHÖNFELD, *Montesquieu en "La bouche de la loi"*, Leiden, New Rhine Publishers, 1979, 40-57.

of the "fair trial" works two ways: on the one hand it guaranties control, supervision, check upon the way the process develops and upon the coming about of the verdict (due process), on the other hand it publicly demonstrates the confirmation of the presumably violated legal norm. This means that the "fair trial" organises protection against abuse of state power while it is instrumental in a non-causal sense to (re)establishment of violated legal norms. These are moral matters in the sense that the "fair trial" is not only an instrument to fight crime but at the same time puts the legal subject in a position to defend herself against dominant codes of interpretation. Public debate in court provides the legal subject with a position from where she can suggest a redefinition of her incriminated actions in non-criminal terms. This type of debate is crucial for a complex society like ours, because it establishes legal certainty by publicly discussing and then deciding which actions fall within the scope of the allegedly violated legal norm. The interdependent character of the relationship between norms and actions as mentioned above implies that short cutting this type of discussion or keeping it behind closed doors is problematic. Public debate in court about the scope of an allegedly violated legal norm is decisive for the meaning of this norm in everyday life: to know which actions fall within its scope provides legal security that the rule itself cannot give. This is again the reason why the principle of legality (closely tied up with the principle of legal security) depends on what happens in court, because only in court – in the light of the case at hand – the meaning of an enacted rule can be determined. The underdetermined character of legal norms demands a serious discussion of what actually happened, of what must be the meaning of the incriminated action of the defendant – in the light of the supposedly violated norm, and what must be the meaning of the legal norm – in the light of the action of the defendant. After this discussion the judge determines the meaning of the legal norm by deciding whether the action of the defendant forms a violation.

As regards restorative punishment, questions arise as to how we will know what goes on in the confidentiality of mediation practices. The discussions that take place cannot determine the meaning of an allegedly violated legal norm and therefore cannot provide any legal certainty. Because they are not public and not registered they cannot demonstrate to the legal community that the authority of legal norms is re-established. Confidentiality also raises the question how we can be sure that secondary victimisation is avoided or that an offender is not humiliated into an apology he does not care for. This seems to be one of the major problems of restorative justice. Elsewhere I have suggested that it might be interesting to make the constitutive principles of the "fair trial" operational for the mediative trial of restorative justice.[11] In the original presentation of Brochu I missed an awareness of the procedural weaknesses of the restorative process, and I miss this awareness in the writings of many criminologists. It could be very interesting for social scientists to study the historical and fragile character of our "rechtsstaat" and the way our fair trial embodies countervailing powers to combine protection with effectiveness.[12] This is why I agree with Duff's plea that restorative justice should be understood as punishment, as an alternative but still punitive means to censure the offender.[13] The pertinence of understanding mediation as punishment (or rather as punitive) regards both the re-establishment of violated legal norms and the protection of victim and offender as legal subjects whose person may not be invaded by state officials. By denying the punitive aspects of mediative practice in criminal matters, the intrusive and painful character thereof is hidden under the veil of consensus and the protection of both victim and offender is thereby short-circuited.

Brochu poses the question whether restorative justice is effective. This immediately evokes interesting questions about effectiveness: are we speaking of the effect of the procedure on the well-being (empowerment) of the parties concerned, or are we speaking of the effect on recidivism (of the offender himself and other – potential – offenders). Since the individual well-being of victim and offender in individual cases may well have little or nothing to do with confirmation of legal norms at all, restorative punishment has little effect in the public context that is part and parcel of criminal offences. Not living in a face-to-face society the question becomes if and how we can sustain trust, confidence, (legal) security, safety between "strangers" (most citizens do not – want to – know each other) in such consensual activities as mediative practices?

These questions are all the more provocative if restorative justice is regarded as an alternative for punishment. As I don't think Claes or Brochu advocate abolitionism, let us presume that restorative justice contributes something extra, net widening perhaps, but not in competition with the present justice system. With Claes I agree that the kind of reparation that restorative justice seems to advocate lies way beyond financial compensation

---

11 M. HILDEBRANDT, "Mediation in strafzaken: afdoening buiten recht? Over de meerwaarde van het juridische", (2003) *Delikt en Delinkwent* 353-375.

12 Just as lawyers should allow themselves to be well informed about mediative practices: it confronts them with the deficits of the "fair trial" (perhaps not so much the deficits of its ideal type, but of its practice as it evolves under the pressures of efficiency and managerial control).

13 R.A. DUFF, *Punishment, Communication, and Community*, Oxford, Oxford University Press, 2001, 96-99.

as enabled by private law. It is aimed not so much at reparation of damage but first of all at restoring the dignity of both victim and offender (see p. 45 in this volume). It seems that both the sole payment of compensation and attempts to shame offenders into the "right" kind of behaviour fall outside the scope of this interpretation of restorative justice. In this conception neither retributive nor restorative punishment implies humiliation. I again refer to Duff for an extensive defence of hard treatment as a means of censuring a person's actions without intending in any way to humiliate or degrade her (see p. 139 in this volume).

5. PERSON- AND NORM-RELATIVE SENSITIVITIES

This brings me to Claes' opposition – and even incompatibility – of norm- and person-relative facts.[14] I think it would be a very fruitful challenge to legal professionals, legal scholars *and* criminologists to attend to these different angles. I have my doubts about the idea that criminologists in general have such a personalist perspective of the social realities they deal with. I suppose many criminologists have a causalistic conception of reality which is opposed to the normative conception of lawyers: while one looks for causes the other looks for reasons. And I believe that both the underdetermined conception of norm-relative facts and the particularistic conception of person-relative facts go well beyond causalistic and normativistic accounts of reality. However, I should think that the mediators that work within a restorative practice have a keen eye for the singularity of the persons and the cases they facilitate, and I would not rule out judges and other legal professionals in this respect. I would even suggest that the "fair trial" itself is constituted to create a position from where the defendant can put forward his personal and particular story in opposition to the attempts of the prosecution to reduce this story to one fitting a codified offence. But of course the victim seems left out and after the offender tells his story, a unilateral judgement is pronounced. I do not think the difference between mediation and the "fair trial" is to be found in the one being centred on the person-relative context and the other being centred on the norm-relative context, though the emphasis might be different in each case. The difference can indeed best be located in the quasi absence of the victim in the "fair trial", and I think many good arguments can be found for this quasi absence (not the least argument being that the victim should not be given the false impression that his pain can be undone by punishing the offender). But if this is the case, it could be an important reason to plead for restorative justice as a complementary

14 See his profound exposition of this point elsewhere in this book, pp.36-38.

part of a moral justice system. Not because the victim should be in the centre, but because both victim and offender should be given the opportunity to restore their self-confidence, to demand respect for their person – which means that an offender who joins the programme will have to face the suffering she caused and must be invited to acknowledge her wrongdoing and to offer some apology (without this ever being enough to compensate the harm done). As Duff articulates, restorative justice is a "confrontation of offenders with the effects of their offending [..] helping them to face up to the need for changes in their attitudes and behaviour".[15] Nevertheless, to change one's attitude and behaviour one cannot stick to a person-relative perspective: to evaluate one's actions and to choose a new line of behaviour, these actions cannot be looked upon as only singular. From the perspective of a conception of legal norms as developed above, the opposition between generality and singularity does not hold: a norm is constituted by actions that are understood in terms of the norm, while actions as such can only be meaningful in the light of a norm that constitutes their meaning. So the generality of the norm is dependant on the singularity of the actions that demonstrate its validity and meaning. To get to grips with a specific norm, one has to look around how it is enacted, confirmed and even changed. To respect and understand the particular action of a person, one has to listen to the biography in which it fits, the ethics that it demonstrates and this implies generality in precisely the underdetermined way Claes has so beautifully expounded. In other words, we could say that a norm as a token of generality and the action of a person as a token of singularity are mutually constitutive. This implicates a particular sensitivity to the continuity or discontinuity of human action as rule-guided behaviour, in which memory and anticipation play a crucial role.

This brings me to Brochu's claim, that restorative justice entails an "able-responsibility", while the "fair trial" is based upon "culpable-responsibility", the first looking into the future, opening up a new choice of actions – setting the offender free to choose another pattern of behaviour; the second looking back at the past, censuring past behaviour, never getting beyond what has already been Here again I plead for an integrated perspective: punishment looks forward to the past to bring us back in the future.[16] If norms depend on actions demonstrating them, and if actions

---

[15] R.A. Duff, *Punishment, Communication, and Community*, Oxford, Oxford University Press, 2001, 101.

[16] This may seem a rather esoteric position, since we usually have a linear sense of time. In other cultures as well as contemporary philosophical analysis we see a keen awareness of the fact that our presence is made up of pastness that integrates our anticipation of the future.

depend on norms to understand them, past and future behaviour are intimately linked in the expectations people develop of each other. Transgressions of fundamental norms destabilise these expectations and create general feelings of unsafety: to re-establish the violated norm this transgression may have to be met with "hard treatment". The focus is not only on the particular victim involved, but also on every citizen that perceives himself as a potential victim. The "culpable-responsibility" attributed to the offender in a "fair trial" is perhaps the condition of possibility of the "able-responsibility" of offender, victim and every other citizen that perceives re-establishment of the violated norm.

CONCLUDING REMARKS

The morality of law is closely tied up with the checks and balances of the "rule of law". Perhaps restorative justice comes closer to a "rule of man". To me the essence of the "rule of law" is the "fair trial", together with the principle of legality. Without a "fair trial" we do not know whether the principle of legality is respected, and without the principle of legality we would be at the mercy of a government of judges (or mediators?). But a fair trial implies more than legality, it creates a space for discussing the merits of the case, guarantees an independent and impartial judge, "equality of arms", external and internal publicity, contradictory proceedings and gives flesh and blood to the presumption of innocence. Our "fair trial" is effective in two ways: it publicly re-establishes the violated norm and protects citizens against arbitrary use of state powers. So, while I think legal scholars and professionals could learn a lot from restorative justice practices because maybe they have integrated some of the principles of the "fair trial" in a way that is better suited to the person-relative aspect of legal norms, I also think restorative justice could learn a lot from the historical evolution of the "fair trial" and the countervailing powers it integrates.

Without a memory we cannot find our way in the future, while without a future our memories may loose their sense. H.P. GLENN, *Legal Tradition of the World. Sustainable Tradition in the Law*, Oxford, Oxford University Press, 2000, 21-25; S. ODIN, "Existential and Ontological Dimensions of Time in Heidegger and Dogen by Steven Heine", (1987) 14 *Journal of Chinese Philosophy* 249-257. This concept of time is constitutive for the expectancy theory of (legal) norms as developed in par. 3 above.

6. RESTORATIVE JUSTICE AND THE MORALITY OF LAW: A REPLY TO BROCHU

IVO AERTSEN and KRISTEL BEYENS

INTRODUCTION

Restorative justice is a phenomenon with many faces. Its implementation is still rather marginal compared to the dominance of retributive approaches in criminal justice. Referring to the numerous academic publications, the different modes of restorative justice implementation in the field and the growing number of political initiatives both at national and supranational level, we can observe that restorative justice ideas are gaining interest worldwide. In some countries, such as Belgium, restorative justice has gained a definite place in the criminal justice discourse. However, there is still a large gap between official claims and daily criminal justice practice.

In this paper we would like to look at restorative justice from a sociological, penological and moral point of view. First we try to understand how the growing attention for restorative justice can be understood in contemporary social and penal context. The second part of the paper focuses on how restorative and classical retributive principles in contemporary sentencing practice can be integrated. We will end with a brief outline of some proposals of Belgian sentencing reform which go in this direction.

1. RESTORATIVE JUSTICE IN CONTEMPORARY CONTEXT

1.1. Contemporary Punishment

Contemporary penality is characterised by a persistent growth of the total penal population. In the last fifteen years, the number of prisoners has risen constantly in most countries. Also community penalties, such as electronic monitoring, probation and community service orders are being used more extensively. The net of criminal justice is widening constantly.

In his leading book *The Culture of Control*, David Garland indicates the following transformations of current penality in the US and GB: the decline of the rehabilitative ideal, the re-emergence of punitive sanctions and expressive justice, changes in the emotional tone of crime policy, the politisation of crime control and new populism in criminal justice policy, the reinvention of the prison and ... the return of the victim.[1] Although his analysis cannot always be applied to a continental European context[2], Garland describes a kind of penality that diverges radically from restorative justice ideas and practices. This penality focuses rather on control, risk management and incapacitation of offenders, and can be defined as a form of "cold justice". This kind of justice has been described by Feeley and Simon[3] as "new penology", "actuarialism" or "managerialism"[4]. These penal transformations should be situated in contemporary social transformations, which have been described as risk society or late modernity. The main characteristics of late modern society are globalisation, immigration and multiculturalisation, increasing influence of the media on political agenda-setting, individualisation and rising feelings of insecurity and unease.

1.2. Restorative Justice in Contemporary Society

Bottoms[5] notices that the above described developments seem rather remote from the preoccupations of restorative justice, remaining predominantly small scale and with very little interest in the issues of managerialism and risk in relation to criminal justice. Restorative justice seems to operate on a very different set of assumptions. This raises the question whether the growth of restorative justice could be interpreted as "anomalous". Bottoms gives five sociological reasons for the rapid growth of restorative justice in recent decades. In the light of this paper only three will be considered.[6]

1.2.1. The Appeal of the "Gemeinschaft" in Late Modern Societies

Bottoms links ways of dealing with crime, such as reconciliatory/restitutive processes, with a particular macro-structural and meso-structural context

---

1 D. GARLAND, *The Culture of Control. Crime and Social Order in Contemporary Society*, Oxford, Oxford University Press, 2002.

2 J. YOUNG, "Searching for a New Criminology of Everyday Life: A Review of the 'Culture of Control'", (2002) 42 *British Journal of Criminology* 223-261.

3 M. FEELY and J. SIMON, "The New Penology: Notes on the Emerging Strategy of Corrections and its Implications", (1992) 30(4) *Criminology* 452-474.; "Actuarial justice: the Emerging New Criminal Law", in D. NELKEN (ed) *The Futures of Criminology*, New Delhi, Sage, 1994, 173-201.

4 A.E. BOTTOMS, "The Philosophy and Politics of Punishment and Sentencing" in C.M.V. CLARKSON and R. MORGAN (eds), *The Politics of Sentencing Reform*, Oxford, Clarendon Press, 1995, 17-50.

5 A.E. BOTTOMS, "Some Sociological Reflections on Restorative Justice" in A. VON HIRSCH, A.J. ROBERTS, A.E. BOTTOMS, K. ROACH and M. SCHIFF (eds) *Restorative Justice and Criminal Justice. Competing or Reconcilable Paradigms?*, Oxford, Hart Publishing, 2003, 79-113.

6 A.E. BOTTOMS, "Some Sociological Reflections on Restorative Justice" in A. VON HIRSCH, A.J. ROBERTS, A.E. BOTTOMS, K. ROACH and M. SCHIFF (eds) *Restorative Justice and Criminal Justice. Competing or Reconcilable Paradigms?*, Oxford, Hart Publishing, 2003, 99-110.

of a given society. He points out that examples of restorative justice from pre-modern societies[7] are explicitly linked to a particular kind of macro-social organisation which is fairly clearly of a *Gemeinschaft* character. Restorative justice practices take place in a society which is characterised rather by mechanical than by organic solidarity. From anthropological literature we learn that in such societies the group is all-important. *Gemeinschaft*-societies also have a particular meso-social structural context, with an emphasis and trust upon kinship relationships, upon the "thick" relationships of people who live closely together and know many aspects of one another's business, and upon tradition. Elders dominate the proceedings and mostly take up the role of mediator. From a more critical point of view, Sally Merry points out the very important role of coercion and power that was linked to the meso-structural context in these pre-modern societies.[8] Reconciliation is especially important when the contesting parties have to necessarily continue sharing the same economic sources, which is typical for pre-modern societies.

Kamenka and Tay identify three types of law, viz. "*Gemeinschaft*"-type law, "*Gesellschaft*"-type law and "bureaucratic-administrative" law.[9] A *Gemeinschaft* society is characterised by a *Gemeinschaft*-type law, "which takes for its fundamental presupposition and concern the organic community".[10] Modern- and late-modern societies are ruled by *Gesellschaft*-type law (cf. the importance of legal rights and rights for individuals) and the bureaucratic-administrative law (cf. risk-based decision-making). Bottoms' main argument is that modern legal arrangements create "something of a hunger for Gemeinschaft-type approaches, as policies that could help to provide,

7 Referring to authors such as S.E. MERRY and G. JOHNSTONE, A.E. BOTTOMS ("Some Sociological Reflections on Restorative Justice" in A. VON HIRSCH, A.J. ROBERTS, A.E. BOTTOMS, K. ROACH and M. SCHIFF (eds) *Restorative Justice and Criminal Justice. Competing or Reconcilable Paradigms?*, Oxford, Hart Publishing, 2003, 88) points to the kind of foundational myth about the naturalness of restorative justice in pre-modern societies. Pre-modern societies are significantly more varied in their dispute-resolution procedures and sanctions than some restorative justice advocates have suggested. From the anthropological literature we learn that also in pre-modern society, restorative justice practices are sometimes set within a range of other procedures and sanctions that are much less restorative.

8 S.E. MERRY, "The Social Organization of Mediation in Non-industrial Societies: Implications for Informal Community Justice in America", in R.L. ABEL (ed), *The Politics of Informal Justice: vol 2, Comparative Studies*, New York, Academic Press, 1982.

9 E. KAMENKA and A.E.S. TAY, "Beyond Bourgeois Individualism: The Contemporary Crisis in Law and Legal Ideology", in E. KAMENKA and R. NEALE (eds), *Feudalism, Capitalism and Beyond*, London, Edward Arnold, 1980.

10 E. KAMENKA and A.E.S. TAY, "Beyond Bourgeois Individualism: The Contemporary Crisis in Law and Legal Ideology", in E. KAMENKA and R. NEALE (eds), *Feudalism, Capitalism and Beyond*, London, Edward Arnold, 1980, 19.

at a minimum, 'a certain humanising cosmetic for bureaucratic practice'".[11] It should be noted that restorative justice is most popular in youth justice, because juveniles are a group of offenders who many people would wish to see treated within a *Gemeinschaft*, rather than a bureaucratic-administrative policy approach.[12]

1.2.2. Victims and Moral Clarifications

Without any doubt, the success of restorative justice is, to a large extent, a result of increased attention for the victim in criminal justice.[13] Since the nineties, in Belgium as in many other countries, numerous initiatives have been taken to improve the position of the victim in the criminal justice process.[14] But also from a macro level, the rising success of a more victim-oriented approach can be understood. Boutellier[15], who looked for mechanisms of solidarity in our post-modern, fragmented society, defines the victim as a contemporary motor for solidarity, and the recognition of each other's suffering as a new legitimation of penal law. In a society with an organic solidarity, a crime is less often seen as an offence against the state or collectivity, and more often against the individual victim (cf. Durkheim). In such a social context, the victim and his suffering can and does tend to become the organising focus for a new moral code. It gives a hold in a context of moral relativism in a morally changing society. The suffering of the victim defines the morality of our culture and has become the source of a solidarity based on the recognition of each other's suffering.[16] Boutellier's thesis of the "victimalisation" of morality gains credibility in the Belgian Post-Dutroux era.

---

11 A.E. Bottoms, "Some Sociological Reflections on Restorative Justice" in A. von Hirsch, A.J. Roberts, A.E. Bottoms, K. Roach and M. Schiff (eds) *Restorative Justice and Criminal Justice. Competing or reconcilable paradigms?*, Oxford, Hart Publishing, 2003, 99-110.

12 A.E. Bottoms, "Some Sociological Reflections on Restorative Justice" in A. von Hirsch, A.J. Roberts, A.E. Bottoms, K. Roach and M. Schiff (eds) *Restorative Justice and Criminal Justice. Competing or reconcilable paradigms?*, Oxford, Hart Publishing, 2003, 103.

13 T. Peters and I. Aertsen, "Towards 'restorative justice': Victimization, Victim Support and Trends in Criminal Justice", in X., *Crime and Criminal Justice in Europe*, Strasbourg, Council of Europe Publishing, 2000, 35-46.

14 M.E.I. Brienen and E.H. Hoenen, *Victims of Crime in 22 European Criminal Justice Systems. The Implementation of Recommendation (85) 11 of the Council of Europe on the Position of the Victim in the Framework of Criminal Law and Procedure*, Nijmegen, WLP, 2000.

15 H. Boutellier, *Crime and morality: the significance of criminal justice in post-modern culture*, Dordrecht, Kluwer, 2000.

16 H. Bouttelier, *Crime and morality: the significance of criminal justice in post-modern culture*, Dordrecht, Kluwer, 2000.

1.2.3. The Questionable Legitimacy of Courts

Originally, restorative justice is also rooted in informal dispute settlement mechanisms. Its development can be interpreted in the light of a critique on the formally, inhuman, degrading and strongly routinised functioning of the courts and of the perceived deficiencies of the criminal justice system in general. Bottoms points out that a consumer led economy has cultural consequences too, viz. that consumers have realised they can make demands (cf. client-oriented culture) also in public sector organisations.[17] Moreover, Bottoms indicates the rising demands for lay participation in decision-making and a growing suspicion towards professionals (cf. demands for enhanced accountability of professionals). This demand for participation and accountability is considered as a contributory factor in the rapid development of restorative justice.

1.2.4. Is there a Place for Restorative Justice Mechanisms in Contemporary Advanced-Urban Societies?

Because of the importance of the macro-social organisation and meso-structural context, many scholars have warned against a simple transplantation of restorative justice practices from one social context to another. A lot of scepticism exists as to whether the social mechanisms of restorative justice can work in contemporary urban societies. Bottoms argues that restorative justice acts in some way as a "generative social mechanism"[18] to restore prior relationships in communities. An important condition for a successful reconciling process is however that both victim and offender belong to the same social/moral community and that a minimal interdependence between the parties involved exists. These social mechanisms work less well in contemporary than in traditional societies, because of the different social-structural context (cf. globalisation, multiculturalism, individualisation and fragmented morality). Although it is extremely unlikely that in contemporary societies restorative justice will replace quickly the existing criminal justice system, it seems defensible to accept and to encourage the growth of restorative justice principles in contemporary penality. Empirical evidence on the effects of victim-offender media-

---

17 A.E. BOTTOMS, "Some Sociological Reflections on Restorative Justice" in A. VON HIRSCH, A.J. ROBERTS, A.E. BOTTOMS, K. ROACH and M. SCHIFF (eds) *Restorative Justice and Criminal Justice. Competing or reconcilable paradigms?*, Oxford, Hart Publishing, 2003, 104

18 Bottoms extensively describes the apology as a generative social mechanism that can potentially lead to the restoration of prior social relationships in a community. A.E. BOTTOMS, "Some Sociological Reflections on Restorative Justice" in A. VON HIRSCH, A.J. ROBERTS, A.E. BOTTOMS, K. ROACH and M. SCHIFF (eds) *Restorative Justice and Criminal Justice. Competing or reconcilable paradigms?*, Oxford, Hart Publishing, 2003, 94.

tion and conferencing, as summarised in several meta-analyses, supports this point of view.[19] In the following parts of the paper we will examine how a restorative justice approach could be developed more particularly in sentencing.

2. RESTORATIVE JUSTICE AND SENTENCING

How to conceptualise and establish an equilibrium between the repressive, strongly formalised penal practice and the informal caring practice of restorative justice, in the light of the basic concepts and principles of a democratic legal system? According to this question we will analyse the place restorative justice principles can have in traditional (but evolving) sentencing practices and how a restorative outcome can be prioritised in sentencing decisions.

2.1. The Need for some Integration

Restorative justice is often seen as a practice and a justice model apart or different from the classic retributive criminal law model. There are, of course, good reasons for this division, because restorative justice brings in fundamentally different values and principles, such as meeting between the parties, communication between the parties, agreement by the parties, apology by the offender, restitution to the victim, change in the offender's behaviour, respect shown to all parties, assistance provided to any party that needs it and inclusion of the parties.[20] These principles should be ensured and protected when restorative justice is being implemented in the context of a punitively oriented criminal justice system and a dito-legal culture. However, this pertinent but often polarising concern has restrained us too long from seeing what is, or could be, in common between the restorative and the retributive model. Only in recent years, attempts have been made

19 J. BRAITHWAITE, *Restorative Justice and Responsive Regulation*, Oxford, Oxford University Press, 2001, 45-71; L. KURKI, "Evaluating Restorative Justice Practices", in A. VON HIRSCH, A.J. ROBERTS, A.E. BOTTOMS, K. ROACH and M. SCHIFF (eds) *Restorative Justice and Criminal Justice. Competing or reconcilable paradigms?*, Oxford, Hart Publishing, 2003, 293-314; J. LATIMER, C. DOWDEN and D. MUISE, *The effectiveness of Restorative Justice Practices: a Meta-analysis*, Ottawa, Department of Justice, Canada, Research and Statistic Division, 2001; P. MCCOLD, "A Survey of Assessment research on Mediation and Conferencing", in L. WALGRAVE (ed), *Repositioning Restorative Justice*, Cullompton, Willan Publishing, 2003, 67-120.

20 D.W. VAN NESS, "The Shape of Things to Come: A Framework for Thinking about a Restorative Justice System", in E.G.M. WEITEKAMP and H.J. KERNER (eds), *Restorative Justice. Theoretical Foundations*, Devon, Willan Publishing, 2002, 6.

to explore the common basis.[21] Brochu's paper rather confirms the earlier, diachronic view and describes the relation between the restorative and the retributive model more in terms of complementarity than in terms of integration. Our point is that we believe there are conceptual, practical and organisational ways to integrate restorative, rehabilitative and retributive elements into one system (without becoming dominantly punitive). We think, in particular, that at the level of sentencing this combination of "the best of three worlds" can be demonstrated and clarified (and, in the long run, realised). What is emerging is not just a complement to what already exists, but a re-thinking of the existing and a permanent modification of the new approach into the direction of a further, advanced model.

Let's become more concrete. Starting from the practice of victim-offender mediation,[22] Brochu is right when he refers to the dominant use of mediation for minor offences and its focus on juvenile law. We know, however, that mediation is also used for more serious crimes committed by adults[23]. Precisely this type of criminality lends itself to a more challenging and profound reflection on the relationship between restorative justice and the traditional, formal criminal justice. For these types of crimes, mediation cannot be reduced to an alternative or diversionary measure vis-à-vis the formal justice system, since it occurs parallel to prosecution in the perspective of dealing with the case by a sentencing judge. Here, we are obliged to think about the place and the meaning of the mutually negotiated solution between a victim and an offender in the framework of a criminal procedure.

What we have learned from practice and action-research, concerns the impossibility to reduce – for these more serious types of crime – the mediation process merely to an exchange and a communication between the two parties (the victim and the offender, possibly surrounded by supporting family members or others). For several reasons, what is happening at the horizontal level of inter-individual dynamics pre-supposes and requires a continuation, a translation and a support at the vertical level

---

21 K. DALY, "Revisiting the Relationship between Retributive and Restorative Justice", in H. STRANG and J. BRAITHWAITE (eds), *Restorative Justice: Philosophy to Practice*, Aldershot, Ashgate, 2000; A. VON HIRSCH, A.J. ROBERTS, A.E. BOTTOMS, K. ROACH and M. SCHIFF (eds) *Restorative Justice and Criminal Justice. Competing or reconcilable paradigms?*, Oxford, Hart Publishing, 2003.

22 We start from the example of mediation, just because we are most familiar with this particular method, which remains the most frequently used in Europe in the field of restorative justice. But the exercise could be done starting from the conferencing model as well.

23 I. AERTSEN, "Mediation bei schweren Straftaten – auf dem Weg zu einer neuen Rechtskultur?" in C. PELIKAN (ed), *Mediationsverfahren: Horizonte, Grenzen, Innensichten (Jahrbuch für Rechts-und Kriminalsoziologie)*, Baden-Baden, Nomos Verlaggesellschaft, 1999, 115-138.

of decision-making by the court. At least two arguments for this option should be mentioned:

1. Mediation practice reveals the psychological and social need of both parties to present to, and to see confirmed by, a public authority their mutual communication and – possibly – their solution. What they expect is that at least their personal and common efforts are being recognised and rewarded by the court. The victim often hopes for an official sign of denouncement of the offence, and, sometimes, for something additionally to be ordered to the offender.
2. Certainly for more serious types of crime, where the mediation outcome can influence the judicial decision-making, legal protection of both parties involved is necessary. Due process safeguards, general legal principles and other rights for victims and/or offenders should be respected. This is true, both regarding the mediation process and the mediation result (the agreement). This means concretely that a judge or a judicial authority should check whether important rights and principles were respected, for example: the right of legal or parental assistance, the impartiality of the mediator, power balances between the parties involved, the proportionality of the reparative action, etc. Some of these rights and principles should be controlled in each case (of a certain degree of seriousness), others require merely a control or general follow-up (where the judicial authority supervises some of these principles at the level of the mediation service). The sources for these rights and principles can be found – and should be elaborated further – in formal law and practice standards (laid down in supranational, national and local regulations and protocols).

What we have in mind is the creation of a forum, a place or a mechanism, where these two functions – public process and legal protection – can be put in operation. Two options are possible: either one locates both functions within the existing judicial structures, or one creates a new, intermediate level or structure (see e.g. the probation commissions in Belgium).

2.2. *Sentencing: Retributive and/or Restorative?*[24]

One could defend the idea that it is the role of the sentencing judge or a (new, possibly multidisciplinary) sentencing body to fulfil the two functions mentioned above. From a legal point of view, the fulfilment of the second

[24] Although we plead for a sentencing system that tries to integrate restorative, retributive and rehabilitative principles in an optimal way, for the sake of argument, we limit ourselves in this contribution to the retributive and restorative models.

function (legal protection) is not totally inconceivable. Moreover, this function could be enlarged with a facilitating one, i.e. a legal authority which provides and secures the equal access of all to (the right to) mediation. Maybe more challenging is the first perspective, namely finding a model where the horizontal communication between victim and offender could be transformed into a vertical dialogue with the sentencing authority. Yet, we believe this is the most innovative potential of restorative justice, which could throw a different light on the notion of retribution and punishment.

Imagine the following, hypothetical situation. What would happen if a victim and an offender, after having met each other one or several times with the help of a neutral third party, were invited (for the victim) or sued (for the offender) to have a meeting with the sentencing judge (one could imagine first a preliminary meeting with the judge, where the parties are still accompanied by a mediator, before meeting at the public session of the court)?[25] Both parties would explain to the judge what they have done so far: which topics they discussed, which types of experiences and meanings about the crime were exchanged,which emotions were expressed, and which solutions reached. And they would tell the judge about the hard and painful discussions they had, amongst others on what to expect from the court in their case, on what they believe to be the right "punishment". The judge would listen carefully, probably asking them more information or details, or arguing he could not agree with one of their agreements. He could ask the point of view of other stakeholders as well. And then, finally, he would decide.[26]

What would parties experience in this meeting with the sentencing judge? Normally, the judge would re-confirm explicitly the denouncement of the unlawful behaviour (already expressed by the public prosecutor when he referred the case to the mediation service). For both parties in the light of their former mediation experience (and for other people involved as well), this would have an important psychological and social significance. Simultaneously, the public character of the "wrong" would be underscored. But what about punishment? In some cases, the judge would find it inappropriate to impose an additional sanction on top of the reached

25 The North-American native practices of "sentencing circles" could be a source of inspiration: because of the physical presence of the prosecutor and/or the judge in the circle, there is a kind of integration at two levels: communication between the parties directly involved on the one hand, and decision-making by judicial authorities on the other hand.

26 We neglect the distinction between the judicial decision on guilt on the one hand, and the decision on the sanction on the other hand. It is clear that participation of both the victim and the offender – as presented here – refers to the second phase of the process.

mediation settlement, or he would conclude the case with a conditional sanction or a postponement. The latter we see in many files after mediation has been completed (at least in Belgian practice). In other cases, the judge could do more. First, he could legally confirm, by way of imposing an enforceable obligation, what the offender promised to do as an outcome of the mediation process (reparation to the victim or to others, participating in a training programme, etc.). Second, the judge could add something that did not result from the mediation process between the parties at all: an additional sanction or punishment. Maybe the judge is obliged to handle this way, because the law imposes a certain minimum sentence for a particular crime. But the judge in this case should explain to the parties (and to the others) why he is doing so, not in a general or stereotyped way, but if possible in a very concrete one, referring to the particular situation and earlier mediation work of both parties.

It is to be expected that this type of sanctioning will be experienced in a different way by both offenders and victims, compared to how they feel in their contacts with the judiciary at present. Without generalising, one can expect that many of them will feel more respected as a person, and that the sentence will be accepted more voluntarily. These expectations are supported by empirical evidence from research on victim-offender mediation[27] and by theory development, e.g. on the social-psychological concept of "procedural justice"[28]. This does not mean that the sanction – even when this is only a confirmation of what parties decided during the mediation process themselves – will not be experienced as a burden, or even as painful. But the *meaning* of this pain will be different, both for the sentencing judge and for offender and victim: the sanction will result from a constructive orientation on the notions of "responsibility" and "obligations", and thus will emerge less in a climate of "retribution" seen as pain infliction.

Although, according to Brochu and others, restorative justice is not aimed at providing "expiation" for the offender, here we see that this apparently retributive notion of expiation can achieve a particular content in a restorative-oriented sentencing practice, initiated by a public authority. "Expiation" refers, both in English and in French, to retribution and

---

27 M. UMBREIT, *The Handbook of Victim Offender Mediation. An Essential Guide to Practice and Research*, San Francisco, Jossey-Bass, 2001, 161-252.

28 E.A. LIND & T.R. TYLER, *The Social Psychology of Procedural Justice*, New York, Plenum Press, 1988; H. STRANG, *Repair or Revenge. Victims and Restorative Justice*, Oxford, Oxford University Press, 2002.

penance or atonement, but also to compensation, satisfaction and conciliation (*"Fête des expiations"*: Great Conciliation Day).

In conclusion, what should be preserved from the retributive sentencing model is ensuring legal protection and communicating public censure, done in a concrete way and not merely at an abstract level. In particular, the court has a role of guardian of the public interest: "Since the crime is a public wrong, the victim must not just speak for herself, but for the community as a whole; and the offender must not speak just to her, but through her to the whole community".[29] This means that the dialogue between victim, offender and judge at the level of sentencing has to be broadened to representatives of the larger community. But the aspect of additional infliction of pain, taken for granted and handled as a self-evident and normal reflex (the standard in the retributive approach), in a restorative sentencing approach would be reduced considerably. The judge would sentence as much as possible on the basis of the personal involvement and commitments of the parties.[30]

2.3. Types of Morality

According to Brochu, "The sought objective [in restorative justice] is no longer a moral rebalance [...]". "Crime is viewed primarily as a conflict between individuals that results in injuries and secondly, as a violation against the Law" (see p. 81 in this volume). Brochu recognises in restorative justice processes three key actors: offender, victim and society. "Thus, these key actors must take an active participation in dialogue and negotiation to settle the conflict situation" (p. 82). "This process entails levels of a psychological, social and/or symbolic nature for the implied actors. Each party must assume its responsibilities in order to succeed" (p. 82). "[...] the community must provide the support as well as the incentives necessary to proceed in an optimal way and without losers" (p. 82).

In short, for Brochu restorative justice is centred on the victim-offender relation in the context of the community. This approach is, without any doubt, the dominant one among restorative justice practitioners and advocates. On the other hand, restorative justice practices are criticised because of their individualising character, and attempts are made to situate

---

29 R.A. DUFF, "Restoration and Retribution", in A. VON HIRSCH, A.J. ROBERTS, A.E. BOTTOMS, K. ROACH and M. SCHIFF (eds) *Restorative Justice and Criminal Justice. Competing or Reconcilable Paradigms?*, Oxford, Hart Publishing, 2003, 56-58.

30 See also J. BRAITHWAITE, "In Search of Restorative Jurisprudence" in L. WALGRAVE (ed), *Restorative Justice and the Law*, Cullompton, Willan Publishing, 2002, 150-167.

the conflict – at least in a conceptual way – not only at the level of the community, but also at the level of the law and the state. And here, from a restorative justice perspective, new room emerges for a moral approach, which involves different types of morality, and not just one type (namely the morality of the law). How different types of morality can be involved and integrated in restorative justice practices, and how this concretely can be conceived in the direction of a "moral rebalance", has been elaborated by Sweigert.[31]

Sweigert in his restorative justice thinking employs a dual notion of criminality: the criminal offence as violation of concrete relations, but also as violation of universal, rationally established norms. From this it follows that the offender also has a moral obligation to the state. For Sweigert, this approach refers to processes of moral concern with, and moral education in, "the common good", as this is considered in the American intellectual traditions of both the "civic virtue" and the "civil society" approaches. A community-based restorative justice reveals, according to Sweigert, three characteristics and guiding principles that refer to a maximum potential for moral education in the common good:

- Restorative justice brings together two types of moral authority into a mutually nourishing relationship: the morality of personal communal-based traditions and the morality of impersonal and universal norms. From this follows the pedagogical principle of the complementarity of communal and universal norms.
- Restorative justice directs its efforts and processes to "the space between places" in social relations, and not so much to individuals, families or institutions. The action thus takes place in "the space where these important social bodies intersect". Hence the second pedagogical principle: the locus of moral education lies in the overlapping of manifold social experience.
- Restorative justice employs all community resources in order to take the initiative and initiate change regarding criminality-based problems. This path is preferable to a one-sided focus on the offender. The third pedagogical principle then says that the optimum model for moral development is one of community development.

Concerning the first characteristic, the moral authority of universal norms – usually the most difficult to recognise in mediation or restorative justice – is present in two ways: (1) in accepting the principle of voluntary and equal participation, and (2) through the moral duty to comply with

31 F. SWEIGERT, *Learning the Common Good: Principles of Community-Based Moral Education in Restorative Justice*, Unpublished paper, University of Minnesota, 1997.

obligations entered into voluntarily and consensually. The moral authority of the state will make it possible that the moral authority of the community – which we recognise in the concrete functioning of restorative justice models – "does its work effectively". The state creates a general framework and takes up its responsibility, more specifically in locating the offender, leading the investigation, establishing the seriousness of the offence and protecting the fundamental legal rights of the persons involved.

In respect to the second principle, the necessarily intermediate character of a mediation service becomes clear. Offenders, victims, supporting persons, social workers, government officials, the public prosecutor and judges come together in a (not yet existing) neutral space, without this space becoming the domain of one of them or belonging exclusively to one of them. It is due to the neutrality of this place that the participants are open to others and are able to contribute morally as equals, not determined by the rationality of one given actor. In this collective, emancipatory and mutual process of moral learning lays the deeper significance of restorative justice. This implies that it is "learning" rather than "teaching" that leads to the development of morality in society.

In other words, what we find here is an intermediate forum where the interaction can take place between the horizontal and the vertical approach as we mentioned above. This forum creates possibilities for rebalancing the morality after a crime is committed, but also for redefining and rebalancing moral values as they evolve in society in general. This type of "intermediate institution of jurisprudence" based on restorative justice principles is, to a large degree, hypothetical. Nevertheless, specific methods could be conceptualised and developed in practice, extending existing models of mediation, conferencing or sentencing circles.

3. A BELGIAN PROPOSAL FOR SENTENCING REFORM

We conclude with a brief outline of a Belgian attempt to introduce restorative justice principles in sentencing. A former Minister of Justice, M. Verwilghen, promoted restorative justice as the leading idea of a new penal law. In March 2000 a Commission was set up to advise the Minister on reforming the sentencing system towards a more restorative oriented approach.[32]

[32] In March 2003, the final report has been handed over to the Minister: Commission "Tribunaux de l'application des peines, statut juridique externe des détenus et fixation de la peine", Rapport Final, Deuxième partie, Fixation de la peine.

3.1. General Framework

The commission's main aim was to look for a new sentencing framework. However, a complete reform of the existing penal law has never been considered. Proposals have been formulated to achieve more legal security. Consistency in sentencing with a strict reductionist option was at the forefront. We mention the following principles proposed to be enacted into the law:[33]

1. The enactment of general principles for a fair criminal justice system;
2. The enactment of principles for just sentencing;
3. The enactment of purposes of sentencing;
4. The enactment of principles for a communicative and participatory criminal justice system;
5. The introduction of a new framework and hierarchy of sentencing options;
6. The division of the criminal process into the decision on guilt and the decision-making process on the sentence.

The main philosophy behind the proposals is the subsidiarity of penal intervention and the strive for a reductionist (imprisonment should be the real *ultimum remedium*) and problem-solving system that prioritises restorative outcomes. Restorative and problem-solving options should not be complementary to retributive justice, but should receive priority. To prevent that "restorative justice would complement the penal panoply" as Brochu rightly remarks (see p. 86 in this volume), only four purposes of sentencing are proposed to be enacted in the law, viz.:

1. To express disapproval of the unlawful behaviour (censure);
2. To support problem-solving and restoration of the damage caused by the crime;
3. To encourage social integration (social integration and restoration are linked);
4. To protect society via the incapacitation of the offender.

These four sentencing aims represent the three dominant punishment models, viz. the retributive, the restorative and the rehabilitative. A strict hierarchy amongst these goals has not been promoted, but the general principle of parsimony in punishment is proposed as the guiding line for the sentencing judge.

---

33 This is not a complete list of the proposals of the commission.

3.2. Principles for a Communicative and Participative Sentencing / Criminal Justice System

With the principles for a communicative and participative sentencing / criminal justice system, the commission seeks to establish a new partnership amongst the different relevant actors involved. A major principle to be introduced is "Enabling the active participation of the different parties involved". In general the judge should encourage offenders and victims to express their point of view. The different parties should get the right to speak up and communicate more freely in court. This goes further than the current position "civil parties" have nowadays. Also other actors should be able to speak up during the trial, such as people who have a close relationship with the victim or the offender. The initiative to communicate can be taken by the judge or by the parties involved. These parties will not have the duty to take an oath. As a consequence, the information given will not have the status of a testimony and will be less formal. These proposals mainly seek to make communication in the court less official, less rule-oriented and hopefully also more humane. The overly ritualised, strict hierarchical, offender oriented and formal context at the court however does not encourage or facilitate dialogue on equal terms between conflicting parties. Consequently, the expectations of victims and offender may not be too high. Therefore, we should be aware of the danger of secondary victimisation and of further stigmatising the offender through these streams of information. However, if we want to be consistent with the purpose of a sentencing system that aims for restoration, conditions for better and more direct communication at court are indispensable.

The general recommendation is thus to create more openness for interaction and communication between parties before and during the trial at the court. It is clear that the communication between parties should be initiated long before the case appears before the judge. In some jurisdictions in Belgium it can take one or two years before a case is handled at the court. Then it can be too late or no longer appropriate to start a negotiation. The commission therefore proposes that mediation between victim and offender should be made available in each phase of the criminal justice process.

3.3. A Place for Narratives in Court?

Pleading for more communication at the court is, however, not unproblematic. Possible side effects or even perverse effects of bringing more lay voices to the sentencing process should be mentioned. An important argument against close involvement of victims or other relevant actors in the sentencing process concerns the risk of introducing or strengthening an extremely emotional – and often retributive and punitive – tone, in a decision-making process that should be guided by rational principles of proportionality and fairness. The question is whether the judge, who has to decide in such a complex and sensitive context, is able to manage and control a possible punitive bias in his decision making. In other words, we should be very cautious not to move backwards in the important function of the criminal justice system of channelling raw emotions with regard to crime and punishment.

Typically for a restorative justice approach is that participants in a mediation process will not just discuss the offence alone. Also circumstances related to the offence, previous incidents, previous interaction between offenders and victims and matters which have occurred since the offence, will be brought into the negotiation process. Involving narratives of other actors, who are in a direct or indirect relationship with one of the parties, can however be slippery. Shapland points out that including material not related to the instant offence can carry dangers to offender and victim. "Apology [...] is in fact a very complex account, embodying stories which redefine the presentation of the offence and the character of the offender, and which are directed at all the participants present. Legal representatives undertake this task as a proxy, sifting out material which is irrelevant, in the court's culture and perception, to sentence. They thus sift out material about other interactions between victim and offender, but leave in material about previous wrongdoing leading to convictions."[34] Allowing information in the court that goes beyond the instance offence[35] and thus encouraging individualisation in sentencing, can have a positive result if it resolves not just the current offence, both also deals with underlying patterns of behaviour. On the other hand, this approach also can have other, less desirable consequences. The outcome may be a judgement, not just on that particular offence, but also on all presumed undesirable conduct of the offender. And who should decide which information is relevant for the case and which information is not? At present it is still the judge who has the power to decide on who has the right to speak and about what should be communicated in court. As a result, context information on the offence and the behaviour of the offender can be used and abused to justify harsh(er) punishment.

We thus agree with Brochu that giving the victim a too central role in the negotiation procedures *can* add an additional punitive element in the penal

---

34 J. SHAPLAND, "Restorative Justice and Criminal Justice: Just Responses to Crime?" in A. VON HIRSCH, A.E. BOTTOMS, K. ROACH and M. SCHIFF (eds) *Restorative Justice and Criminal Justice. Competing or reconcilable paradigms?*, Oxford, Hart Publishing, 2003, 205

35 This is also encouraged in a rehabilitative sentencing model.

process. Their account in court should be limited to their own experiences and as in the Belgian Assisen procedure, victims should not be allowed to unilaterally express themselves or advise the judge on the punishment.

3.4. Some Conditions for a Successful Restorative, thus Communicative and Participative Sentencing Process

The importance of introducing a culture of mutual respect in criminal justice matters has to be underlined. It is clear that fair and open communication in court is impossible in the current ritualised court context, which is characterised by unequal power relations between the different parties. A better and more adequate training of judges to prepare them for their difficult task to enhance communication between different parties on an equal basis is indispensable. To change a system we cannot limit ourselves to enacting some beautiful principles in law. Changing the cultural context is even more important. With regard to the latter there is still a long way to go. It will take years, not to say generations to sensitise the mainly classical, purely retributively thinking judges towards a criminal justice system primarily driven by restorative and rehabilitative principles. The availability of a proper infrastructure, regulation and personnel to support and orientate persons involved and to inform prosecutors and judges is another important condition for progress. Besides, the introduction of an intermediate actor (e.g. a mediator) or an intermediate phase into the sentencing process can be defended. It should be recommended that the core restorative business takes place outside the court and before the sentencing process starts. During this phase of mediation, raw emotions could be uttered by the parties involved and channelled by the professional mediator. The meeting at the court could thus better be prepared. And last but not least, the responsibility of society and penal policy makers is of vital importance. Not only the actors involved in criminal justice have to be sensitised towards the ideas of a more communicative, participative and restorative oriented punishment, but also the general public has to become familiarised with these ideas and aims. It concerns an approach that implies a responsabilisation of all parties involved, including the victim.

To end, we point at the modest potential of the proposals of the Belgian sentencing commission in the short term. Trials in court in the presence of both offenders and victims are still a minority. Although restorative justice also contains perspectives at a structural societal level, the problem of the penal crisis we nowadays experience will not be solved rapidly.[36]

[36] I. Aertsen, *Slachtoffer-daderbemiddeling: een onderzoek naar de ontwikkeling van een herstelgerichte strafrechtsbedeling*, Leuven, Leuven University Press, 2004.

PART THREE.
PUNISHMENT AND THE MORALITY OF LAW

7. PUNISHMENT AND THE MORALITY OF LAW

ANTONY DUFF[1]

The themes of this paper connect rather closely with those of the other two plenary papers in this volume, by Erik Claes and Serge Brochu, since it concerns both the role of punishment in what purport to be democratic, liberal legal systems, and the relationship between "punitive" and "restorative" justice.

I will begin, in section 1, by making my topic a little more precise, to focus not on the meaning, justification or character of criminal punishment in the abstract, but on what proper role it can play in a liberal democracy: as we will see, this gives the problem of punishment a particular, and particularly troubling, significance. In section 2 I will sketch a conception of punishment that, I will argue, shows how it could be appropriate in a liberal democracy; and in section 3 I will argue that such an account of punishment should satisfy at least some of the legitimate concerns of advocates of "restorative justice", whilst rejecting the sharp distinction that both they and their critics so often draw between restorative and punitive measures.

Before embarking on this discussion, I should emphasise one point that must apply to any normative theory of punishment (that is, any theory that aims to show what punishment *ought* to be), but that is too often ignored by critics. The point is, simply, that a normative theory of punishment does not aim to describe, or justify, our existing penal practices; such theories are therefore not refuted simply by showing that they do not match existing penal realities. Given the manifest deficiencies in our existing practices, a theory that seemed to justify them would indeed, by that very fact, cast doubt on its normative credentials: we would expect a plausible normative theory to provide not a comforting justification of the penal status quo, but rather a normative ideal of punishment, towards which we can strive and against which we can judge and criticise our existing practices. If the ideal is far distant from the actual (and mine will be far distant), if we can see no rapid route from where we are now to where we ought to be (and my account admittedly offers us no such route), we face a serious problem,

---

1 This paper was written during my tenure of a Leverhulme Research Fellowship; I am very grateful to the Leverhulme Trust for this support. I am also grateful to the organizers of the 10th Aquinas Conference for their invitation to give a paper at the Conference; to my respondents, Lode Walgrave and Arnold Burms, and to the participants in the Conference, for their helpful comments.

and might have to question the practicability of the ideal, or compromise our attachment to it: but it is important that we begin by trying to articulate a normative ideal that is plausible as an ideal – if only to induce a suitable humility and caution in our attitude towards our existing practices.

1. HOW CAN CITIZENS PUNISH EACH OTHER?

Criminal punishment, involving as it does the official imposition on individuals of measures that are intended to be burdensome or painful,[2] is morally problematic on any tolerable view of the state: but it is distinctively problematic in states that purport to be liberal democracies. We need to ask what criminal punishment could be, what it could mean, and how (if at all) it could be justified, in a liberal democracy; and we will soon find that, if we take seriously the values that are central to the ideal of liberal democracy (such values as autonomy, freedom, and a mutual recognition of and respect for each other as fellow citizens), the answer is far from clear.

We might begin by asking how a liberal democratic state can punish its citizens, meaning by that both how a system of criminal punishment could be justified in such a state, and what shape it could justifiably take. But to ask thus abstractly about what "the state" can justifiably do is to evade part of the force of the problematic of punishment in liberal democracies. For a liberal democracy claims to act in the name of, as the authorised agent of, its citizens: that is, of all of us. Our question must therefore instead be "How can we punish our fellow citizens?"; or even, in recognition of our commonality as citizens, "How can we punish our neighbours?" or "How can we punish ourselves?".

To ask these questions is to ask in part about the state's right, and thus about our right, to impose punishments on its citizens. But it is to ask too whether and how criminal punishment can treat those who are punished (and those threatened with punishment) as citizens: is this a kind of treatment that is compatible with a full recognition of or respect for their citizenship? We can put this question in Kantian terms: can criminal punishment treat those on whom it is imposed "as ends in themselves", or as responsible moral agents who deserve respect for their rational humanity? Or we could put it in more communitarian terms: can criminal

---

2 Although there are plenty of (in the end tedious and unproductive) controversies about the precise meaning of "punishment" – on which see recently D. SCHEID, "Note on Defining "Punishment'", (1980) 10 *Canadian Journal of Philosophy* 453 – it is not controversial that punishment, unlike other kinds of officially imposed measure that might in fact be and be known to be burdensome, is intended to be burdensome: if what is imposed on an offender is not burdensome to him, it has failed as a punishment.

punishment show those who are punished the respect and concern we owe them as our fellow citizens? In either case (I will say a bit more below about these different ways of posing the question), the issue concerns the compatibility of criminal punishment with a recognition of citizenship.[3]

Now on some penal theories, this is not a question that need concern us. I have talked as if those who commit crimes retain the full rights and moral standing of citizens, so that if we are to justify punishing them we must show how punishment is consistent with a due respect for them as citizens: but some theorists argue that by committing a crime the offender forfeits his rights, his moral standing, as a citizen.[4] The *innocent* have a right to be protected against mistaken convictions and unjust punishments (as well as against crime), and we must ensure that our criminal justice system gives them such protection: but the *guilty*, who have by their own voluntary wrongdoing forfeited their civic standing, can retain no such claims of justice or respect on us. We should of course treat them as humanely as we can (they are still human beings); we should make it possible for them to regain their civic rights, even help them to do so: but we need not try to show that the punishments to which they are subjected still respect their rights or standing as citizens, since to be liable to punishment is to have lost those rights and that standing.

Some such view of criminals as this is depressingly often implicit, or sometimes explicit, in contemporary penal rhetoric and practice. Politicians talk of a "war on crime", a war which too easily becomes a war on criminals; criminals are portrayed, and feared, as enemies (of the state, of the community), as a "them" against whom "we", the law-abiding and innocent, must be protected – which is to fail to see them as our fellow citizens. (More precisely, this is how some criminals are seen; it is not typically how those who commit crimes that "people like us" commit – tax evaders, drunken or reckless drivers, white collar criminals – are portrayed.)

There is, I think, a real question about whether there are some crimes, or some careers of persistent crime, which are so serious, so dangerous, and manifesting such complete rejection of the polity's essential values,

---

3 My focus in this paper is on domestic systems of criminal law, dealing primarily with crimes committed by and against citizens of the states whose systems they are. The account would need to be modestly extended to deal with crimes committed by or against visitors to a state. More significantly, I cannot discuss here the important issues raised by recent developments in international criminal law, including the creation of the International Criminal Court; we could say, though, that they embody a claim that for some crimes the perpetrator is answerable not just to his fellow citizens in their domestic arena, but to all his fellow human beings in virtue of their shared humanity.

4 See e.g. A.H. GOLDMAN, "Toward a New Theory of Punishment", (1982) 1 *Law and Philosophy* 57; C. W. MORRIS, *"Punishment and Loss of Moral Standing"*, (1991) 21 *Canadian Journal of Philosophy* 53; for criticism, see R.A. DUFF, *Punishment, Communication, and Community*, New York, Oxford University Press, 2001, 14-16.

that they should cast doubt on the offender's continuing status as a citizen: can we ever properly say that an offender has excluded himself from citizenship by his crimes?[5] There are also serious questions, which we cannot pursue here, about how we should respond to terrorist crimes committed by those who deny fellow citizenship with those whom they attack. I think, however, that only a very shallow kind of liberalism could make it that easy to lose one's standing as a citizen: for the great majority of offences and offenders, we must surely see them, not as outlaws who have put themselves beyond the civic pale, but as fellow citizens who, although they have done wrong, have not thereby lost their claim on our respect and our concern. I do not have space to justify that belief here, and I do not claim that it is expressed in the ways in which offenders are actually treated by our existing systems of criminal justice (I will comment on this point shortly): but it seems to me to be an essential starting point for any civilised penal theory.

Such a claim about the moral standing, the moral claims, of offenders was also central to the retributivist revival that was such a striking feature of the late 20th century penal debates. There had always, of course, been concerns about the rights of the innocent – concerns which led, given the well-founded objection that purely consequentialist theories could not provide the innocent with adequate protection against penal victimisation, to familiar side-constrained versions of consequentialism: we should use punishment as a technique for preventing crime, subject to the side-constraint that we should not punish the innocent even if that would be an effective means of preventing crime.[6] The new retributivists, however, argued that even side-constrained versions of consequentialism failed to do justice to the guilty: to use punishment simply as a method of deterrence, incapacitation or compulsory "reform" was to fail to respect the moral standing, the moral agency, of those subjected to it.[7]

---

5 See R.A. DUFF, *op.cit.* note 4 above, 164-74.

6 See most famously H.L.A. HART, *Punishment and Responsibility*, Oxford, Oxford University Press, 1968, and the refinement of a Hartian account developed in D. SCHEID, "Constructing a Theory of Punishment, Desert and the Distribution of Punishments" (1997) 10 *Canadian Journal of Law and Jurisprudence* 441; see also N. WALKER, *Why Punish?*, Oxford, Oxford University Press, 1991, ch. 11. Some consequentialists do of course argue that they can provide the innocent with the protection due to them within a purely consequentialist theory: see e.g. J. BRAITHWAITE and P. PETTIT, *Not Just Deserts*, Oxford, Oxford University Press, 1990.

7 For different versions of this argument see C.S. LEWIS, "The Humanitarian Theory of Punishment" (1953) 6 *Res Judicatae*, reprinted in W. SELLARS and J. HOSPERS (eds); *Readings in Ethical Theory* (2nd ed), New York, Appleton-Century-Crofts, 1970; H. MORRIS, "Persons and Punishment" (1968) 52 *The Monist* 475; J.G. MURPHY, "Marxism and Retribution" (1973) 2 *Philosophy and Public Affairs*, 217. R.A. DUFF, *Trials and Punishments*, Cambridge, Cambridge University Press, 1986, 170-86.

I want to give these claims about the moral standing of the guilty a slightly more precise focus by representing them as claims about liberal citizenship: to justify criminal punishment in a liberal democracy, we must be able to show that it can treat and respect those who suffer punishment as citizens. But what is it to treat, or to fail to treat, someone as a citizen?

There are of course different species of liberalism, offering different conceptions of what it is to be a citizen of a liberal polity. In particular, we must distinguish individualist versions of liberalism which often appeal to contractualist theories to explain how separate individuals could have reason to commit themselves to a political association, from more communitarian versions of liberalism that locate such liberal values as autonomy, freedom and pluralism in a political community that is defined and validated not by the contractual choices of individuals to join it or to stay within it, but by the mutual recognition of its members as sharing this way of life.[8] We can, however, identify some central elements of any plausible liberal conception of citizenship. (I will describe these elements in the language of a communitarian liberalism; but those descriptions could be translated into more individualist terms.)

We can begin by contrasting citizens with subjects. Subjects are bound by a sovereign's laws, laws which are addressed to them as commands. "Do this, or else!" is the paradigmatic form of a sovereign's law – an order backed by a threatened sanction. This is how traditional legal positivism portrayed law as such; but what it portrayed was a law fit for subjects, not for citizens. Citizens are of course bound by the law, and by the normative demands of the polity: but they are not bound in the way that subjects are bound. Subjects are bound by a law that is not theirs, but the sovereign's: they must obey another's will. Citizens, by contrast, are bound by a law that is their law, as the law of the polity to which they belong and which they help to define: their law is a common law that speaks to them in the voice, not of an alien sovereign, but of their own supposedly shared political values.[9] The demands of the law are thus not the commands of a sovereign who threatens sanctions against the disobedient, but the normative claims of values to which they should already be committed as citizens of the polity.

---

8 See further R.A. DUFF, *op.cit.* note 4 above, 35-79.

9 On the idea of common law, see G. POSTEMA, *Bentham and the Common Law Tradition*, Oxford University Press, Oxford, 1986, chs. 1-2; also R. COTTERELL, *Law's Community*, Oxford, Oxford University Press, 1995, ch. 11. My concern is with the meaning embodied in the rhetoric of the common law tradition, rather than with the political reality of the common law as it actually developed in England: whilst Bentham's scathing critique of that reality was well-founded, the rhetoric of the common law appealed to values that we should take seriously.

This distinction should sharpen our problematic question about punishment. It is easy to see how a sovereign could use punishment on her subjects. It could serve, most obviously, as a coercive threat to secure obedience from the recalcitrant, although it could also no doubt be used to incapacitate the dangerous, or to inflict retribution on the disobedient: but if we have accepted the idea of a sovereign, it is hard to deny her the right to use punishment to enforce her power. What is (rightly) more problematic is the question of how citizens living under the common law of a liberal polity could have a legitimate use for punishment: for, we might ask, is not punishment inevitably an attempt to subject people to the superior, sovereign power of those who impose it – to treat them, that is, as subjects?

A second contrast, between civic inclusion and civic exclusion, will sharpen this question yet further.[10]

Civic inclusion is a matter of being recognised, and treated, as a member of the political community. It requires political inclusion: being able and encouraged (or even required, in a demanding polity) to participate in the political process by which the polity governs itself. It requires material inclusion: sharing in the material benefits and opportunities available in the polity, especially those that bear on our welfare interests. And it requires normative inclusion: being treated by one's fellow citizens, and by the law and the state, as one who shares in the polity's defining and essential values – as someone who is both protected and bound by them. Civic exclusion, by contrast involves the failure of one or more of these types of inclusion: a person is excluded, and so suffers civic injustice (whether or not that exclusion is deliberate) insofar as she is precluded from the kinds of political participation that are essential to liberal citizenship, or from fair access to those benefits and opportunities that are available to other members of the polity; or insofar as she is not taken to share in either the rights or the duties, the protections or the demands, that flow from the polity's values. We treat others as citizens insofar as we treat them inclusively in these ways; we fail to treat them as our fellow citizens insofar as we exclude them or are complicit in their exclusion in any of these ways.

Now it is clear that criminal punishment can be, and all too often is, a powerful means of exclusion (it is also clear that it is all too often inflicted on people who have already suffered other and continuing serious kinds of civic exclusion). This is most dramatically visible in the case of imprison-

---

10 Talk of "inclusion" as an essential social good has become prominent in political rhetoric in the UK during the last decade. It might be tempting to dismiss it as mere rhetoric, but I think it is worth taking seriously, since by doing so we can expose the hollowness of some of the rhetoric of inclusion by showing what is involved in taking inclusion seriously.

ment, which physically excludes the prisoner from the community's ordinary life, and whose message is so often that he has no place in the polity (think of the meaning of "Three strikes and you're out"); it is made even more obvious when imprisonment brings with it the kind of "civic death",[11] involving formal exclusion from political participation and other civic amenities after as well as during incarceration, that sometimes attaches to imprisonment for a felony. It is also a feature, or an obvious side-effect, of other kinds of punishment which stigmatise the offender as an outsider, and leave him no effective way back into participation in the rights and benefits of community.

Some familiar normative accounts of the proper aims of punishment also portray it as an exclusionary mechanism. If punishment is justified as a means of incapacitating criminals, for instance, it is justified as a means of excluding them from the community, portraying them as dangerous beasts to be caged, not as fellow citizens with whom we can live and reason.[12] If it is justified simply as a deterrent it is portrayed as a technique of control which addresses both offenders and potential offenders not in the language of the values of their polity that they are supposed to share, but in a brutal language of threats and self-preservation: but that is to treat them as normative outsiders, rather than as members of the normative political community – as, as Hegel famously put it, "dog[s] instead of with the freedom and respect due to" them as moral agents.[13]

Punishment is often in fact exclusionary, in both its meaning and its effects. Insofar as it is exclusionary, it is incompatible with a recognition of offenders as our fellow citizens: if we exclude someone from our political community, we deny, instead of recognising, her fellow citizenship. The crucial question is whether punishment *must* be exclusionary. If it cannot but exclude those who are punished, it could be justified only by arguing that those who commit crimes thereby forfeit their standing as citizens, but I have suggested that we must resist that view. If we are to resist it, however,

---

11 See L WACQUANT, "Deadly Symbiosis" (2001) 3 *Punishment and Society* 95, 119-20; the "After Prison Initiative", http://www.soros.org/annual/2001_us/us_2001_cji.pdf.

12 See e.g. P.W. GREENWOOD and A. ABRAHAMSE, *Selective Incapacitation*, Santa Monica, California, Rand Corporation, 1982; J.Q. WILSON, Thinking about Crime (rev ed), Basic Books, New York, 1983, ch. VIII: as against N. LACEY, "Dangerousness and Criminal Justice", (1983) 36 *Current Legal Problems* 31; A. VON HIRSCH and A. ASHWORTH (eds), *Principled Sentencing*, Oxford, Hart Publishing, 1998, 121-38, on selective incapacitation; M. FEELY and J. SIMON, "The New Penology: Notes of the Emerging Strategy for Corrections and its Implications" (1992) 30 *Criminology* 49, on actuarial justice.

13 See G.W.F. HEGEL, *The Philosophy of Right* (trans. T.M. Knox, 1942), Oxford, Oxford University Press, 1821, 246; A. VON HIRSCH *Censure and Sanctions*, Oxford, Oxford University Press, 1993, 11. I think this is the most plausible way of explaining the familiar Kantian charge that deterrent punishment treats those punished "merely as means"; see J.G. MURPHY, *op.cit.* note 7 above.

while still justifying criminal punishment, we must show that punishment could be inclusionary, rather than exclusionary: that it could genuinely treat those who are punished as fellow citizens. The challenge for liberal penal theorists is to show how this is possible.

A third idea that must be central to any notion of liberal democracy is that of responsible agency – which is obviously bound up with idea(l)s of autonomy and freedom: to be a citizen of a liberal polity is to be, and to be treated as, a responsible moral agent. (Of course, not all members of a polity will be responsible agents: some are children, who have not yet attained responsible maturity, and others are victims of mental disorders or disabilities that undermine their capacity for responsible agency. Their membership of the community is not undermined by such disabilities: they have a strong claim on our concern and protection, and they share in whatever of the polity's goods they are able to enjoy. But their citizenship is qualified by their inability to participate rationally in the governance either of their own lives or of the community.) I have space here only to indicate a few significant features of responsible agency, of what it is to be a responsible agent and of the kinds of treatment by others that this status makes appropriate or inappropriate, that bear on our present concerns.

A responsible moral agent is a practically rational being: someone who is capable both of engaging in practical reasoning about the good and of actualising the results of that reasoning in her actions. She can recognise reasons for action, including those provided by morality and the law, and be moved by them; she can decide what to do, and guide her actions by her grasp of reasons for action; she can play her part in the political and moral discussions that occupy her community.[14] To treat her as a responsible moral agent is to treat her in ways that respect and respond to these capacities for rational thought and action, and for recognising and being motivated by appropriate values: this is also, in Kantian terms, part of what it is to respect her "as an end in herself", and in liberal communitarian terms to treat her as someone who shares in the values of the polity – as someone who is both bound and protected by those values.

I will simply note here three important aspects of such treatment. First, we must not seek merely to bully, to manipulate (for instance by deception) or to coerce our fellow citizens into behaving as we wish them to behave: such methods clearly fail to treat or to respect them as responsible agents. Second, we may properly try to influence or guide their conduct, to bring them to do what they would not otherwise have done: respect for the

---

[14] Which is to say that she is an autonomous agent, but we cannot explore the various meanings of that notion here: for useful discussions, see J. RAZ, *The Morality of Freedom*, Oxford University Press, Oxford, 1986, 369-429; G. SHER, *Beyond Neutrality*, Cambridge, Cambridge University Press, 1997, chs. 2-3.

other's rational agency does not preclude me from attempting to persuade her to act differently. What it does require, however, is that I try to influence her conduct only by offering her reasons to act differently: reasons which I take to be good reasons, but which it is in the end up to her to accept or not to accept.[15] Third, respect for another as a responsible agent is fully consistent with criticising or blaming her for wrongs that she commits: indeed, if I take seriously the values to which both of us are supposedly committed I must be ready to criticise her for violating those values (and to accept her criticism of my violations); to ignore her wrongdoing would be to betray those values, and to fail to take her seriously as a moral agent. This is not to suggest that we should be moral busybodies constantly seeking for wrongs to condemn: quite apart from the fact that we ought to pay more attention to the beams in our own eyes than to the motes in the eyes of others,[16] we must distinguish the private realms of others' lives that are not our business from the public realm in which we have a proper interest.[17] But if we are to take our fellow citizens seriously as responsible moral agents, we must be prepared to call them to account for, and to blame them for, wrongs that they commit when those wrongs are properly our business.

A system of criminal law can in various ways claim to address the citizens as responsible moral agents, and to treat them as members of the normative community. It can address them not in the peremptory tones of a sovereign's commands, but in appropriately normative tones that speak of the polity's values: we can understand the criminal law's definitions of offences not as a series of brute orders, "Do not do this, or else!", but rather as specifications of a range of public wrongs – of kinds of conduct that violate the polity's central values, from which the citizens therefore have good reason to refrain. When the criminal law defines theft, and rape, and tax evasion, as crimes, it declares them to be public wrongs, and appeals to the citizens to recognise and to be moved by the good reasons that they have to refrain from such conduct.[18] Furthermore, we can see the criminal trial

---

15 This is not to say that *every* use of force or violence against another person involves a failure to respect his autonomy, or his responsible moral agency: we can on this account legitimately use violence as a defensive response to another's wrongful attack. For a useful general discussion of self-defence and its justification, see S. UNIACKE, *Permissible Killing*, Cambridge, Cambridge University Press, 1994.

16 St Matthew's Gospel, vii.3.

17 The distinction between the "public" and the "private" is of course also crucial to liberalism. It requires very careful analysis: we should note in particular that it is not given in advance of, as a basis for, an account of the kinds of matter that do, or do not, properly concern the whole polity; it rather expresses the conclusion of such an account. See further R.A. DUFF, *op.cit.* note 4 above, 45-47, 125-29.

18 For reasons of space, I must pass over here the crucial but controversial distinction between *mala in se* and *mala prohibita* – between crimes which are wrong independently of the criminal law, whose wrongfulness is declared rather than created by the law; and crimes which are wrong only because they are so defined by the law.

(in ideal theory, although rarely in actual practice) as a process through which citizens are called to answer a charge that they have committed a wrong – as a process that calls them to account for their wrongdoing, and condemns them for it through a formal conviction if that charge is proved: we can thus see it as a process which addresses the citizens as responsible moral agents, and as members of the normative political community, by holding them responsible for the wrongs that they commit.[19]

But what of criminal punishment? Even if the criminal law and the criminal trial address the citizens as responsible moral agents who are bound and protected by the polity's values, is not the punishment that follows a conviction simply a coercive imposition on the offender, which treats him simply as a patient or object? How could punishment treat those on whom it is imposed not merely as its passive recipients, but as responsible agents?

Some would argue that it cannot, and that what this shows is not that we must look more carefully for an adequate justification of criminal punishment in liberal democracies, but that we should recognise that it simply cannot be justified, and should therefore be abolished. This is the abolitionists' challenge.[20] Punishment, they argue, is an oppressive, destructive practice that serves neither justice nor any real human good: rather than trying to reform it, we should try to do without it. This is not to say that we should do nothing about "crime", although some would say that we should think of "conflicts", or "troubles", that need to be resolved by those involved in them, rather than of crimes that require punishment. But we should, many would suggest, look for "restorative" rather than for "retributive" justice: for procedures, including various types of mediation process, which will help those involved in the conflicts to repair the harm that was done, to restore peace, and to reconcile themselves with each other.[21]

---

19 See further R.A. DUFF, *op.cit.* note 7 above, ch. 4.

20 For some central examples of the various and diverse strands of abolitionism see T. MATHIESEN, *The Politics of Abolition*, London, Martin Robertson, 1974; N. CHRISTIE *Limits to Pain*, Martin Robertson, London 1981; L. HULSMAN, "Critical Criminology and the Concept of Crime", (1986) 10 *Contemporary Crises* 63; W. DE HAAN, *The Politics of Redress*, London, Unwin Hyman, 1990; H. BIANCHI, *Justice as Sanctuary*, Bloomington, Indiana University Press, 1994.

21 The literature on restorative justice is also vast. For useful introductions, see J. BRAITHWAITE, *"Restorative Justice: Assessing Optimistic and Pessimistic Accounts"*, (1999) 23 *Crime and Justice: a Review of Research* (ed. M. Tonry; Chicago, University of Chicago Press) 1; L. WALGRAVE, "Beyond Rehabilitation: In Search of a Constructive Alternative in the Judicial Response to Juvenile Crime", (1994) 2 *European Journal on Criminal Policy and Research* 57; G. JOHNSTONE, *Restorative Justice: Ideas, Values, Debates*, Cullompton, Willan Publishing, 2002. For critical debate, see A. VON HIRSCH et al (eds), *Restorative Justice and Criminal Justice: Competing or Reconcilable Paradigms?*, Oxford, Hart Publishing, 2003.

Can penal theory meet the abolitionist challenge: can it show that punishment does have a legitimate place in a liberal democratic political community? Restorative justice movements can claim to take community, inclusion and responsibility seriously: they understand crime as a disturbance of relationships within a community, between its members; the essential aim is to restore those relationships, by processes that involve, and thus include, all the parties to the disturbance; and those processes depend on a view of the participants as responsible agents – as being responsible to each other for resolving their problems. Many advocates of restorative justice think that the pursuit of such reconciliatory aims as these is quite inconsistent with the infliction of punishment – and many critics of restorative justice agree, arguing that we must retain the "punishment paradigm", rather than replacing it by the "restorative paradigm".[22] In the next two sections, however, I will sketch a theory of punishment that shows punishment to be consistent with, indeed expressive of, a regard for offenders as our fellow citizens, and that also embodies some of the reconciliatory aims of restorative justice.

2. PUNISHMENT AND COMMUNICATION

One increasingly prominent theme in recent penal theorising has been that of punishment as expression or communication: we are to attend not merely to punishment's effects, to what it brings about, but to its meaning, to what it says (and to whom it says it). This is obviously an important topic for penal sociology and psychology – for any attempt to understand the roles that punishment actually plays in our societies: but it might also be significant for normative penal theory – for the attempt to determine whether and how punishment could be justified; perhaps we can justify it in expressive or communicative terms.[23]

Punishment can of course communicate many different messages, whilst different modes of punishment can communicate distinctive messages of their own. Penal theorists should pay more attention to the particular meanings of particular modes of punishment than they usually pay, but for the moment we can attend to the kind of meaning that it might be appropriate for punishment to communicate simply qua punishment.

---

22 On the "punishment" and "restorative" paradigms, see A.J. ASHWORTH, "Some Doubts about Restorative Justice", (1993) 4 *Criminal Law Forum* 277.

23 Joel Feinberg deserves the credit for bringing the expressive dimension of punishment back into the normative debate: J. FEINBERG, "The Expressive Function of Punishment" in his *Doing and Deserving*, Princeton, Princeton University Press, 1970; see generally A.J. SKILLEN, "How to Say Things with Walls", (1980) 55 *Philosophy*, 509; I. PRIMORATZ, "Punishment as Language", (1989) 64 *Philosophy* 187.

Central to that meaning is censure, or condemnation: by punishing a person, we censure or condemn her for the criminal wrongdoing for which the punishment is imposed. That is the defining difference between a fine as punishment and a tax;[24] between a prison term imposed as a punishment, and detention imposed as quarantine; between a Community Service Order imposed as a punishment, and a requirement to undertake unpaid work for the community as a matter of civic duty: in each case the punishment communicates a censure or condemnation that the latter does not. That censure is communicated to the offender: punishment conveys the same message to her as was conveyed by her conviction at her trial, that she committed a criminal wrong which merits such forceful censure. But in communicating to her, punishment also communicates to others – to the victim (when there was one), and to the wider political community: it shows that we, as a polity, take the victim's wrong seriously, and displays our public commitment to the values that the crime violated.

Now this dimension of punishment can play a role in different types of normative penal theory. Consequentialists, who justify punishment as an efficient means of preventing crime, can argue that censure is a useful technique: if we want to dissuade people from certain kinds of harmful conduct, we may do better to threaten them with forceful censure than merely with prudential deterrents – to appeal to their shame, not only to their cruder self-interest.[25] But if we see censure simply as one among other possible techniques that we might use to dissuade people from crime, we have come no closer to showing how punishment could respect those who are punished as responsible moral agents, or as fellow members of a normative political community: we still portray them as beings whom we must manipulate to achieve our social goals; we will use shame, rather than a cruder system of deterrence, only if it promises to be a more efficient means to those goals. What we rather need to show is how penal censure is an intrinsically appropriate response to the wrongdoings of citizens as responsible moral agents, not merely an efficient technique for modifying their conduct; and we can do that by offering a retributivist rather than a consequentialist account of punishment as censure.[26]

---

[24] Even if taxation is used to discourage an activity, its message is that the activity is legitimate so long as the tax is paid. Some people might treat the fine simply as a tax, but that is to ignore its intended meaning.

[25] See J. BRAITHWAITE, *Crime, Shame and Reintegration*, Cambridge, Cambridge University Press, 1989; J. BRAITHWAITE and P. PETTIT, *op.cit.* note 6 above, esp. 87-92.

[26] I have only gestured here at the objections to a consequentialist account of censure: see further R.A. DUFF, *op.cit.* note 7 above, ch. 2; on Braithwaite and Pettit, see A. VON HIRSCH and A. ASHWORTH, "Not Not Just Deserts: A Response to Braithwaite and Pettit", (1992) 12 *Oxford Journal of Legal Studies* 83.

A conception of punishment as the communication of censure seems well suited to make plausible moral sense of the retributivist slogan that "the guilty deserve to suffer" – and that it is the state's responsibility to ensure that they suffer as they deserve. A crucial challenge for retributivists is to explain what that slogan means. What do the guilty deserve to suffer? Why do they deserve to suffer it – why is suffering an appropriate response to crime? Why should it be the state's task to inflict that suffering? An account of punishment as the communication of censure can offer plausible answers to these questions.

If I have done wrong, I deserve to be censured and criticised by those whom I wronged, and by other members of the community whose values that wrong violated: such censure is, typically and intentionally, painful – it hurts to be criticised and condemned by my fellows. Censure from others is also apt, in a receptive wrongdoer, to induce self-censure or remorse: I come to recognise and condemn my own crime as a wrong – and remorse is also intrinsically painful. These then are two related kinds of suffering that wrongdoers deserve – the pain of being criticised and the pain of remorse; and punishment, as censure, is meant to induce such suffering.

It might be said that the previous paragraph showed at most that it is *good* if wrongdoers suffer the pains of censure and remorse: but that this does not show that anyone has either the right or the duty to seek to inflict such suffering, let alone that it should be the state's duty.[27] That further step is, however, easy to justify. In a legitimate system of criminal law, crimes are public wrongs – wrongs that violate the political community's essential values, and that therefore properly concern the whole polity.[28] They therefore require a public response – an authoritative public condemnation of the wrong and censure of the wrongdoer. We owe this, we can say, to the victim of the wrong, since to fail to condemn the wrong is to fail to take it, and her, seriously; we owe it to her as our fellow citizen to offer her this moral support, this vindication of her moral standing. We owe it to the values that were violated and to the polity whose values they are: for to be committed to those values and to that polity is to be prepared to respond critically to such attacks on them. We also owe it to the wrongdoer himself, since to take him seriously as a moral agent is to be prepared, *inter alia*, to respond critically to his wrongdoings. The criminal law, as a system of norms which define a range of public wrongs, and the criminal trial, as a

---

27 This distinction between showing that punishment is a good, and showing that the state has the right or the duty to inflict punishment, is usefully emphasized by J.G. MURPHY, *op.cit.* note 7 above; see also D. HUSAK, "Why Punish the Deserving?", (1992) 26 *Nous* 447.

28 On the meaning of "public wrong" here, see further S.E. MARSHALL and R.A. DUFF, "Criminalisation and Sharing Wrongs", (1998) 11 *Canadian Journal of Law & Jurisprudence* 7.

process through which citizens are called to answer for the wrongs they have committed, give appropriate institutional form to the polity's concern for the values on which it depends. Criminal punishment, as a method of forcefully communicating censure to wrongdoers, can now be seen to fit neatly into that institutional structure: it gives a further, more forceful expression to the censure that the criminal conviction initially conveys.

If we can portray and justify punishment as a method of communicating the censure that offenders deserve, we can also show it to be consistent with, indeed expressive of, the ideals of liberal political community. Punishment as censure, like the criminal law itself, speaks to offenders not as subjects, but as citizens, as members of the political community. It addresses them not in the language of merely coercive power, but in the language of values which they should recognise and accept as members of that polity; it presents their wrongdoings to them not as disobedience which invites retaliation, but as wrongs against their fellow citizens, for whom they should care, and against values that they should recognise as their own. Far from excluding them from the normative political community, punishment as thus conceived treats them as members of that community who are bound as well as protected by its values: for to censure someone is to treat them as a participant in our shared normative life.

Furthermore, punishment as censure treats those who are punished as responsible moral agents. It constitutes an appropriate response to their wrongdoings, since censure recognises and takes seriously the wrongdoer's status as a responsible agent; we cannot properly censure those whom we do not regard as responsible.[29] It also constitutes an appropriate way of trying to modify their future behaviour. Of course we hope that those who are punished will thereby be persuaded to refrain from crime in future, but we seek to secure that result only by offering them good and relevant reasons for thus refraining. Punishment as censure is not intended to coerce or manipulate offenders into refraining from crime: it speaks to them in the normative language in which the criminal law speaks; it speaks of the wrongs that they committed, and of the values that they violated; it asks them, as censure always asks those who are censured, to recognise that they did wrong and to refrain from future wrongdoing because they see it to be wrong.

---

29 It is worth distinguishing several facets to responsibility in this context. In censuring someone we assume that he *was* responsible for his wrongdoing, in that he was a rationally competent agent who had no excuse for what he did; we assume that he *is now* a responsible agent, in that he is capable of understanding and of responding appropriately to our censure; and we assume that he is responsible *to us* for his wrongdoing, in that we have the standing to call him to account for it.

Finally, we may note that punishment as the communication of censure treats offenders as agents, not merely as its passive recipients. The point here is not merely that punishment is imposed on them for their previous wrongful conduct as agents, but rather that as an exercise in communication it seeks a rational response from them: for it seeks their acceptance of the censure as justified; it seeks their recognition of the wrong they committed as a wrong which they should now repent; and it seeks thus to persuade them to refrain from future crimes.

There is, however, an obvious and major question to be asked about any such attempt to justify criminal punishment, in anything like the forms with which we are now familiar, as a process of communicating censure: why choose *this* medium of communication?

Suppose we agree that we should have an institution whose main task is to communicate to criminal offenders, formally and authoritatively, the censure they deserve for their crimes. There are various ways in which censure could be communicated with appropriate formality and authority. It could be done verbally – through a suitable speech from the judge after the offender's conviction (as well as by the conviction itself), through a formal meeting at which others have the chance to add their censure to that of the court, through other kinds of public denunciation. Or it could be done through a system of purely symbolic penalties, which will be painful only insofar as the offender recognises and is moved by their censorious meaning; imagine, for instance, a system under which thieves had to keep (for a suitable time) a notice stuck to their bathroom mirror saying "I am a thief", or those guilty of physical assaults were required to keep pictures of their victims somewhere where they could not but see them. Our own systems of criminal law, however, go well beyond such verbal condemnations or purely symbolic punishments: they impose "hard treatment" punishments, which are burdensome or painful independently of their censorious meaning.[30] We deprive offenders of their liberty by imprisoning them, of their money by fining them or requiring them to pay compensation, of their time by requiring them to undertake community service: all of these penalties constitute penal hard treatment, since offenders who are deaf to or wholly unmoved by their censorious message will still find them, and are still meant to find them, burdensome.

[30] On penal "hard treatment" and the problem of justifying it from within an expressive account, see J. FEINBERG, *op.cit.* note 23 above. But the label might be misleading, since it could suggest something seriously oppressive or coercive, like imprisonment; it should rather be understood as covering *every* kind of punishment that is burdensome independently of its censorious meaning.

Let us accept that such hard treatment punishments *can* communicate the censure that the offender deserves. But the question is: why *should* we choose this medium of communication rather than one that involves no such hard treatment? If our aim is simply to communicate the appropriate kind of censure, why should we not rest content with purely verbal denunciations, or with purely symbolic punishments?

There are, at first glance, two ways to answer this question. One accepts that the need to communicate censure, to try to engage the offender in this kind of normative dialogue, cannot itself justify using penal hard treatment as the medium of communication: to justify that, we must look beyond a retributivist concern with deserved censure, to a consequentialist concern for effective crime prevention. We accept that the criminal law must initially address citizens in the normative language of the values on which it, and the polity, depend: that it must speak to them as members of that normative community, of the wrongfulness of the conduct that it condemns. We also recognise, however, that some (too many) will be unpersuaded by such a normative appeal: neither the moral authority of the criminal law, nor the prospect or fact of a criminal conviction and the formal censure that it expresses, will dissuade them from crime. If we do nothing more to dissuade such people from crime, the results will be damaging both to the victims of the crimes they go on to commit and to the community at large. For the sake of those victims and of the peace and security of the polity, we should therefore communicate the censure that wrongdoers deserve through a medium, penal hard treatment, which will also provide a purely prudential deterrent for those who are not moved by the law's moral appeal; the law must speak to those who are deaf to its moral voice in a language of self-interest and of threats that they will understand and by which – we can hope – they might be persuaded.[31]

On this view punishment is justified partly as the communication of the censure that the offender deserves, but partly (as to the choice of hard treatment as the medium) as a deterrent. This might seem to be both realistic and morally plausible. The criminal law does address its citizens as responsible moral agents, as members of the normative polity: it speaks

[31] See e.g. J. FEINBERG J., *op.cit.* note 23 above; B.M. BAKER, "Consequentialism, Punishment and Autonomy" in W. CRAGG (ed), *Retributivism and Its Critics*, Stuttgart, Franz Steiner, 1992, 149. A. Von Hirsch offers a more subtle account, which I cannot discuss here (A. VON HIRSCH, Censure and Sanctions, Oxford, Oxford University Press, 1993, ch. 2; see also U. NARAYAN, "Appropriate Reponses and Preventive Benefit: Justifying Censure and Hart Treatment in Legal Punishment", (1993) 13 *Oxford Journal of Legal Studies* 166); for critical discussion see A.E. BOTTOMS, "Five Puzzles in von Hirsch's Theory of Punishment", in A.J. ASHWORTH & M. WASIK (eds), *Fundamentals of Sentencing Theory*, Oxford, Oxford University Press, 1998, 53; R.A. DUFF, *op.cit.* note 4 above, 86-88.

to them of wrongs that they should not commit, and censures them if they commit such wrongs. It also, however, recognises the limits of normative community – the extent to which some citizens are not committed to the polity's values or susceptible to persuasion by the law's moral voice. In seeking to deter such people, it still addresses them as rational agents: it seeks to dissuade them from crime by offering them what they will see as good reasons to desist from crime. It might no longer address them as responsible *moral* agents, since the reasons it offers them are prudential rather than moral: but that simply marks a recognition of the limits of moral reason in motivating human conduct. The law must deal with us as we are, not as we should ideally be; and we (too many of us) are beings who will not be sufficiently persuaded by purely moral appeals to conform our conduct to the basic moral requirements of human life.

Now in some moods, I confess, some such view as this seems to me to be right: if we are to justify a system of criminal punishment that uses penal hard treatment, in a world at all like our own, we must do so along such lines. I also think, however, that such a justification falls far short of being wholly satisfactory: for what we are in effect saying to those against whom penal hard treatment is used as a deterrent is "We can no longer address you as fellow citizens of a normative community; we will instead address you as amoral beings who can understand only the language of threats and self-interest". If this is the best we can do, we might still be able to think that such a system of punishment is justified, as a means to securing the kind of social peace and security upon which a liberal democracy must depend: but we cannot think that the penal system itself fully expresses the ideals of such a democracy, or treats those on whom it inflicts hard treatment punishments as full members of such a polity.

The second way of answering the question about penal hard treatment argues that we can justify that medium of communication in terms of the aims intrinsic to the idea of punishment as a communicative enterprise: we should communicate censure by appropriate kinds of hard treatment, rather than by purely verbal or symbolic means, because that will serve the aims of the communicative enterprise more adequately. Such an answer depends on a richer account of the aims of the communicative process than simply communicating censure: an account of punishment as a *two-way* process of communication between community and offender (and victim). Hard treatment is crucial to both aspects of this mutually communicative enterprise.[32]

---

32 For a detailed development and defence of this kind of account, see R.A. DUFF, *op.cit.* note 4 above, especially chs. 3-5.

First, in communicating censure from the community to the offender, the aim should not be merely to ensure that he hears the censure, but to persuade him to attend to it, in the hope that he will be persuaded by it to repent his crime (and thus also to see the need to reform his future conduct). But merely verbal or symbolic punishments are likely to be inadequate, since they are all too easily ignored or forgotten: it is a depressingly familiar human characteristic, one which most of us can recognise all too well in ourselves, that we find it hard to give our wrongdoings the serious attention that they need, and all too easy to distract ourselves from thinking about them. One function of hard treatment punishment, then, is to make it harder for the offender to ignore the message that punishment aims to communicate: it is a way of helping to keep his attention focused on his wrongdoing and its implications, with a view to inducing and strengthening a properly repentant understanding of what he has done.[33]

Second, something also needs to be communicated from the offender to the community and to the victim (when there is a victim). He has committed a wrong against the victim, and against the whole community, and he must "make up" for that wrong, by making reparation to them. In the context of the criminal law, what matters is not reparation for whatever harm he caused (that is a matter of civil rather than criminal law), but moral reparation for the wrong that he has done. Central to such a moral reparation is apology. If I recognise that I wronged you, I must also recognise that I owe you an apology: that is how I can attempt to repair the wrong. Apology expresses, or purports to express, my repentant recognition of that wrong: it owns the wrong as mine, whilst disowning it as something that I now repudiate; it implies, as repentance always implies, a commitment to avoid doing such wrongs in future; it expresses my desire to seek forgiveness from and reconciliation with the person I wronged.

Now in many cases of moral wrongdoing, a verbal apology is sufficient: nothing more is or should be expected. Sometimes, however, when the wrong is more serious, or when victim and wrongdoer do not stand in the kind of relationship in which mere words can carry enough moral weight, words are not enough, since words can be too cheap and easy: if the apology is to address the seriousness of the wrong and show the victim that the wrong is taken seriously, if it is to focus the wrongdoer's attention on the wrong as it should be focused, it must take a more than merely verbal form. That "more than merely verbal form" will involve something

[33] I cannot pursue here the question of what modes of punishment will be appropriate to this communicative purpose: but we should think less about such familiar punishments as fines and imprisonment, and more about such punishments as probation and Community Service Orders.

burdensome that the wrongdoer undertakes – some task that he undertakes for the benefit of the victim or the community, some penitential suffering that he undergoes, or perhaps some burdensome programme aimed at dealing with the roots of his wrongdoing. The key point is that it must be burdensome to him if it is to serve its apologetic purpose: something that was not burdensome, something that cost no more than mere words, would be no more adequate an apology than mere words; and if I am to give material form to my repentant recognition of the burden of guilt that I now carry, that form must itself be something burdensome.[34]

The second communicative aspect of punishment, then, is the communication of apology from the offender to those whom she wronged – the direct victim, and the wider community: the penal hard treatment gives material form, and thus greater moral force, to that apology. Of course, we know that many – probably most – offenders who undergo punishment are not, at least initially, genuinely apologetic; in undergoing their punishment they are not expressing a genuinely repentant recognition of the wrong they have done. Criminal punishment is thus on this account a species of forced or required apology: the offender is required to apologise, i.e. to go through the motions of apology, even if she does not mean it.

It might now be objected that such required apologies lack real value – that only sincere apologies have any value; and that to require or force people to apologise is inconsistent with the respect for autonomy and for privacy of conscience that a liberal polity should display. As to the first of these objections, there is still value even in required apologies whose sincerity is doubtful: for they make clear to the offender what he ought to do (i.e. apologise sincerely), and to the victim that the community takes seriously the wrong she suffered. As to the second objection, we must recognise that what punishment requires of the offender is not his actual repentance (*that* cannot be forced), but that he undergoes these rituals of apology and moral reparation: this respects his autonomy and privacy, since it is still up to him to make or refuse to make the apology genuine. It is still an exercise in rational communication, rather than in mere manipulation or coercion, in that it constitutes at attempt to persuade him to recognise and repent what he has done – an attempt which must leave him free to remain unpersuaded. By requiring him to undergo some burdensome hard treatment that would constitute suitable reparation for

---

[34] The case of apology is just one of many contexts in which we might need to express ourselves in material rather than merely verbal form: consider, for instance, the way in which we might express gratitude for a great benefit done to us not just by words of thanks, but by offering a gift or reward to our benefactor; or the ways in which we give material form to grief through the rituals and ceremonies of mourning.

the wrong that he did, we hope he will come to recognise the appropriateness of and the need for that reparation himself – that he will come to make it his own: but we still leave it to him, as a responsible moral agent, to be persuaded or to remain unpersuaded.

Criminal punishment, on this account, is a species of secular penance: it is a burden that the wrongdoer is required to accept, in order both to induce and deepen her own repentant recognition of the wrong she has done, and to communicate to her victim and to her fellow citizens her repentantly desire to make reparation to them and reconcile herself with them.[35]

3. RETRIBUTION AND RESTORATION

There is, of course, much more that needs to be said by way of explanation and defence of the account of punishment I have sketched. To mention just three further issues, more needs to be said about how such a theory could be put into practice – what kinds of procedure, what kinds of sentence it would sanction; about the kind of normative political community that it seems to presuppose, and whether we live in such communities; and about its consistency with such liberal values as respect for individual freedom and autonomy, since some liberals will argue that any such attempt to persuade offenders to repent constitutes an illegitimate intrusion into the private realm of conscience. I cannot pursue these issues here, but want instead to end by suggesting that this account of punishment can do justice to some of the main concerns that motivate the restorative justice movement, whilst showing how the kind of "restoration" that crime makes necessary can and should be pursued not by looking for "restorative" alternatives to punishment, but through a system of appropriate, penitential punishments – how, that is, "restoration" can be achieved and should be sought through "retribution".

Advocates of restorative justice seek some process that will "repair" the damage that has been done, or "restore" the relationships that have been injured or fractured; some process that will reconcile the parties affected by the crime. Now reparation, restoration and reconciliation are, on my account, central functions of punishment: by making the kind of moral

---

35 My account has something in common with "moral education" theories of punishment (e.g. H. MORRIS, "A Paternalistic Theory of Punishment", (1981) 18 *American Philosophical Quarterly* 263; J. HAMPTON, "The Moral Education Theory of Punishment", (1984) 13 *Philosophy and Public Affairs* 208. But, first, to talk of education suggests a patronizing view of offenders as less than mature agents, and thus as less than full citizens. Second, it is not clear that what most offenders need is *education* about what is wrong, as distinct from being persuaded to attend to the wrongness of their conduct. Third, if they need education, it is not clear why we should choose penal hard treatment as our educational method.

reparation that punishment essentially involves, the wrongdoer repairs his civic relationships, both with his victim and with the wider polity whose values he flouted, and thus reconciles himself with his fellow citizens; by accepting that reparation, by accepting that in undergoing punishment he has "paid his debt", his fellow citizens reconcile themselves with him. (We must again bear in mind that this is a normative theory, which speaks of how we *ought* to treat offenders; I do not claim that offenders' fellow citizens do in fact typically reconcile themselves in this way.) The essential difference between my account and theories of restorative justice is that I argue that the reparation that crime requires must involve punishment, whereas they do not. It might seem that the onus is then on me to show why reparation, restoration and reconciliation must involve punishment, the deliberate infliction of suffering: of course making reparation might in fact be burdensome for the offender, if it requires resources that he cannot easily spare, but why should we *aim* to make it burdensome, or to "deliver pain" to the offender?[36]

The answer to this question has to do with the significance of wrongdoing. If what needs to be repaired is simply some harm, reparation need not be burdensome or painful: thus when a civil court determines the damages to be paid by a defendant who has been found liable for some loss or harm, it focuses on what level of damages will be sufficient to pay for that loss or harm, not on what will hurt the defendant.[37] But it is a defining feature of the criminal as distinct from the civil law that it focuses on wrongs, not harms: even if most crimes cause or threaten harm, what justifies making them crimes, rather than matters for the civil law, is the wrongful character of the harm that they cause or threaten. We have a criminal law because we take wrongdoing, as something distinct from mere harm-causing, seriously; and we must therefore ask what could count as "repairing" the

---

36 On "pain delivery", see N. CHRISTIE, *op.cit.* note 20 above; on the significance of the point that, for restorative justice theorists, making reparation might in fact be burdensome, but is not designedly so, see L. WALGRAVE, *op.cit.* note 21 above. Walgrave is prepared, as restorative justice theorists should be, to impose "coerced restorative sanctions" (L. WALGRAVE, "Not Punishing Children but Committing them to Restore", in I. WEIJERS and R.A. DUFF (eds), *Punishing Juveniles: Principle and Critique*, Oxford, Hart Publishing, 2002), but they should not be *intended* to be painful or burdensome.

37 There are of course exceptions to this: not only when a court explicitly awards "punitive damages", but also when it is obvious that the level of damages is being fixed so as to make sure that it hurts the defendant, as sometimes happens in libel cases. I cannot discuss such cases here, but suggest that they are cases in which attention is focused on the *wrong* done by the defendant and on what can "repair" it: the jury wants to make sure that the price to be paid is sufficient (relative to the defendant's means) to do justice to the wrong done. If I am right about this, such cases actually support my argument here.

offender's wrong, or "restoring" the victim, or reconciling the offender with her fellow citizens in a way that does justice to that wrong.

The previous section sketched my answer to this question.[38] What repairs or restores the victim is his fellow citizens' recognition of the wrong done to him, a recognition expressed in their condemnation of the offender as well as in their sympathetic responses to him; and more crucially the apology and moral reparation provided, through punishment, by the offender. So too what will suffice (what will morally suffice) to restore the civic relationships damaged by the crime – the relationships between offender, victim and their fellow citizens as members of the polity – is a process that addresses the wrong done by the offender, since it was the wrong done that damaged those relationships, by flouting the values by which those relationships are defined. But such a process, if it is to address the wrong seriously, must involve an attempt to bring the offender to recognise the wrong and its implications – a recognition that, if genuine, will lead the offender to a repentant desire to make reparative apology to those whom she has wronged. Punishment as I have sketched it, as a process of penitential communication, is just such a process; and I have tried to explain why it is essential to that process that the offender undergoes or undertakes something burdensome or painful, since something that was not thus burdensome or painful could not serve the two-way communicative aims of the process.

Although some restorative theorists are uneasy with the focus on wrongdoing that I have claimed is essential to criminal law,[39] others do take wrongdoing seriously; many recognise, indeed emphasise, the importance of apology.[40] What I am suggesting to them is that, if we do take wrongdoing and the need to repair it seriously, we should recognise that the kind of "repair" it requires must involve the offender's punishment – punishment understood, not as the mere infliction of pain for its own sake (as "retribution" has too often been understood), but as the kind of secular penance I have described.

---

38 See further R.A. DUFF, "Restorative Punishment and Punitive Restoration", in L. WALGRAVE (ed) *Restorative Justice and the Law*, Cullompton, Willan Publishing, 2002; "Restoration and Retribution", in A. VON HIRSCH et al. (eds), *Restorative Justice and Criminal Justice: Competing or Reconcilable Paradigms?*, Oxford, Hart Publishing, 2003.

39 Which is why Christie prefers to talk of "conflicts", and Hulsman of "troubles", rather than of "crimes": see N. CHRISTIE "Conflicts as Property" (1977) 17 *British Journal of Criminology* 1; L. HULSMAN, *op.cit.* note 20 above – on which see R.A. DUFF, *op.cit.* note 4 above, 60-64.

40 Some even talk in terms that come close to mine: see, e.g., D.W. VAN NESS, "New Wine and Old Wineskins: Four Challenges of Restorative Justice" (1993) 4 *Criminal Law Reform* 255, quoting J. O. HALEY on the importance of "confession, repentance and absolution"; see also N. CHRISTIE, *op.cit.* note 39 above.

I have tried to show that the question of whether, and how, criminal punishment can be consistent with the values of a liberal democratic polity is both important and difficult, and I have argued that the best way to render it thus consistent is to portray it in retributivist terms as a communicative enterprise between the polity and its citizens. The further question then is whether we can justify the choice of penal hard treatment as the medium of communication in similar terms, as being necessary to secure the suffering that offenders deserve to undergo; or whether we can justify it only by adding some kind of consequentialist, deterrent rationale to the initial retributivist rationale of communicating deserved censure. I have tried to make sense of the former approach: what justice requires (what the offender deserves) is not merely that the offender be censured, but that the censure be given a burdensome material form that will be adequate to the seriousness of the wrong – adequate both as a vehicle for repentance, and as moral reparation for that wrong. That account is not *purely* retributivist, since it gives punishment a forward-looking as well as a backward-looking rationale: punishment aims to secure repentance, self-reform (the offender's commitment to correct her future behaviour), and reconciliation. But it is essentially retributivist, in that punishment's primary justification is found in its relationship to the past crime, as a legitimate response to that crime; and I have argued that this type of retributivism, far from expressing the kind of primitive and vindictive desire to inflict pain of which critics of "retributive justice" often accuse it, is actually focused on aims that are closely related to those emphasised by advocates of restorative justice. If we take seriously the idea that what must be repaired is an offender's wrongdoing, and its impact on and implications for the offender's relationships with his fellow citizens, we can recognise that that repair must be punitive.

8. RETRIBUTIVISM AND THE QUALITY OF SOCIAL LIFE: A REPLY TO DUFF

LODE WALGRAVE

Antony Duff's approach is normative. As he rightly recalls, a normative theory on criminal justice does not describe how the justice system is currently functioning, but how it *should* function, according to normative principles and their derivatives. Critics on such theory should therefore mainly be based on normative reflections. However, normative theories are not purely abstract. They cannot deny empirical findings, nor can they be too distant from real feasibility considerations.[1] To be clear from the beginning: I do share Duff's criticism on the current punishment practice. I do notagree, however, with his principled option for punishment as the mainstream response to crime, for socio-ethical and instrumental reasons.

1. RETRIBUTIVISM AND INSTRUMENTALISM

Duff positions himself as a retributivist (or "deontologist"), as opposed to instrumentalists (or consequentionalists).[2]

Several versions of retributivism exist, but they all basically go back to the Kantian principle that punishing the wrongdoing is a categorical imperative. It is inherent in morality that wrongdoing must be responded to by imposing hard treatment on the wrongdoer. The offender intrinsically deserves to be punished. It is even stated that the offender has the right to be punished, because this would position him as a morally responsible person. Contrary to consequentionalism, retributivism (or deontologism) does not primarily ask questions about possible targets or effects of punishment. The reasons for the pain infliction are sought in a conception of equality (by rectifying the illegitimate advantage, obtained by the crime), or in the expression of blame. Retributivists look for principles in order to implement the categorical imperative in an as just as possible way. They

1 J. BRAITHWAITE and P. PETTIT, "Republicanism and Restorative Justice: an Explanatory and Normative Connection", in H. STRANG and J. BRAITHWAITE (eds), *Restorative Justice. Philosophy to Practice,* Aldershot, Ashgate, 2000, 145-163.

2 A. VON HIRSCH, "Penal Theories" in M. TONRY (ed), *The Handbook of Crime and Punishment,* New York/ Oxford, Oxford University Press, 1998.

therefore subject penal law to a series of prescriptions, such as the legality principle, the due process principle, and the proportionality principle. So, for example, the amount of pain to be inflicted depends on the amount of illegitimate advantage or the degree of blameworthiness of the crime.[3] By referring uniquely to the crime already committed, retributivists base sentencing on retrospective considerations, and find therein the stakes for assuring proportionality.

However, the retributivist/instrumentalist opposition may be overrated. In its extreme form, retributivism would loose contact with real life. A purely principled approach would drift the system away from changes in social ethics and beliefs, and would leave no space for human relations which include mutual understanding, apologies and forgiveness.[4] A purely deontological theory also seems not achievable. It always hides at least some consequentionalist aims. Von Hirsch, for example, stresses the need for punishment because of the need for censure, and censure is needed to keep morality.[5] It is "simply a part of morality that holds people accountable for their conduct", von Hirsch approvingly quotes Strawson.[6] But why should we keep morality? Morality is not given by nature, it is not an absolutist system, but it is a pragmatist social construction, based on civilisation, to keep life in community liveable.[7] Morality itself thus serves a target, and preserving morality through censure indirectly serves the same target.

Consequentionalist theories, on the contrary, do reflect on the purpose of the criminal justice system, and derive constraints from these purposes. Adherents of such a theoretical approach accept the evil of punishment, because they believe that it helps to achieve greater social goods, such as social order and peace, by deterring potential offenders, converting offenders, or assuring the public of the law enforcement.

But, again, a pure consequentionalist theory is not tenable. It would mean that the end always justifies the means. The aim of rehabilitation, for example, as put forward for juvenile justice, cannot justify endless intervention. Juveniles, their families and victims have rights to be respected, regardless of the rehabilitative purpose. Here, principled (often

---

3 A. VON HIRSCH, *Censure and Sanctions*, Oxford, Clarendon Press, 1993.

4 M. NUSSBAUM, "Equity and Mercy", (1993) 22 *Philosophy and Public Affairs* 2.

5 A. VON HIRSCH *Censure and Sanctions*, Oxford Clarendon Press, 1993.

6 A. VON HIRSCH *Censure and Sanctions*, Oxford Clarendon Press, 1993, 9.

7 Since Freud and Durkheim, norms and values have increasingly been seen as pragmatic constructions, made in order to keep life in community and society liveable. If the norm itself is a utilitarian based concept, the norm-enforcement should primarily also be utilitarian in nature. The norms and values are the norms and values of the community (and not of nature, nor of a superior power), and community should be given something back through its norm-enforcing. That is a consequentionalist reasoning.

deontological) reasons do limit the rehabilitative purpose. Extreme instrumentalism can lead to punishing the innocent or to draconian punishments. Therefore, the instrumentalist justifications of punishment always are limited by some (possibly hidden) deontological principles.

It is difficult to begin theorising on criminal punishment without reflecting first on targets. If we did not indicate an objective for the criminal justice system, why would we keep it? If we do not expect any positive effect from that system, what should we fear from abolishing this very expensive and grievous system? Basically, criminal justice must deserve its right to exist through the targets it promotes.

There is a deep tension between the fundamentals of our democratic constitutional states, i.e. the protection and promotion of the citizens' rights and freedoms, on the one hand, and the essentials of the coercive judicial system, being the reduction of citizens' freedoms, on the other. That is why the criminal justice system must be used parsimoniously and only in clearly defined exceptional situations. Coercion and reduction of freedom can apply in a situation of emergency only. These situations must clearly be defined, referring to commonly acceptable goals. Only then should we reflect on the means to achieve the goals. Punishment is a means, and not a value on its own. We shall discuss whether or not punishment is an appropriate means.

2. WHAT IS A WRONG?

For Antony Duff, and in line with retributivism, punishment is needed to mark the wrong. This argument is basically grounded on ethical foundations. But what is a wrong? Surprisingly, retributivists seldom question the ethical value of the norm system itself, which the punishment is supposed to enforce.[8] With some exceptions,[9] retributivists seem to equate legal order with moral order. But that is far from evident.

Criminal punishment is used to enforce any legal system. It is used in our democratic regimes and in the most dictatorial regimes as well. It is an act of power to express disapproval, possibly to enforce compliance, but it is neutral about the value system it enforces. Ethical questions about legal order should always be asked, including about the legal order in our Western democracies. Why, for example, is penal law predominantly geared to public order, individual physical integrity and property, and not, for example, to social peace, solidarity, and social and economic equity? Retributive punishments are used to enforce any legal rule, including the

---

8 A. FATIC, *Punishment and Restorative Crime-Handling*, Aldershot, Avebury, 1995.

9 For example M. MOORE, "The moral Worth of Retribution" in J. MURPHY (ed), *Punishment and Rehabilitation*, Belmont CA, Wadsworth Publishing, 1995.

most immoral ones. Leaving enforcement through pain infliction open to all these possibilities is a very dangerous game, as daily practice overwhelmingly demonstrates.

Is there an intrinsic wrong, linked to human nature? Do *mala in se* exist, and how are they defined? There may be good arguments to conclude that such wrongs exist. However, they appear not to be clearly respected in our political communities. The death penalty, killing in war, using power for self interest, causing harsh living conditions for populations, all are actions which could be called "intrinsically immoral", but which are committed in and by self declared "model democracies". In political and in professional life, lying and cheating is common. In sports, committing so called "professional faults" is the rule. Rejecting a "wrong" is probably less inspired by a general human attachment to "the right", than by a pragmatic aversion of what we experience as a threat for our personal and social lives and our comfort.[10] Deep down, ethical categories, distinguishing right from wrong, seem to rest upon (well conceived?) self interest. We can only hope that self interest is understood in terms of being a participant in harmoniously living collectivities, leading to mutual respect, solidarity and taking active responsibility.

Even if we were able to define moral wrongs, should they all be subjected to possible public intervention? I would not say so. It would lead to ethical absolutism. We might fear then a kind of "Talibanisation" of society. Public order and norm enforcement must be limited to what is needed for the quality of public life. Why, for example is it debated whether criminal justice should intervene in some types of sexual behaviour among consenting adults, or in the use of drugs? Because, for some, such behaviour is not harmful to other people nor to social life in general. Here is probably the criterion to define a "public wrong", as the reason for public intervention: the harm it causes to fellow citizens and to social life in general.

In an article with Jareborg, von Hirsch distinguishes four types of "damages to standards of living" (physical integrity, material support, freedom from humiliation and privacy/autonomy).[11] Boutellier advances "victimalisation" as the "moral minimum" to underpin a commonly acceptable criminal justice system.[12] John Braithwaite and P. Pettit speak

---

10 "Le crime ne blesse les sentiments que d'une façon secondaire et dérivée. Primitivement, ce sont les intérêts qu'il lèse" (MAXWELL 1914, cit. in C. DEBUYST, "Pour introduire une histoire de la criminologie. Les problématiques du départ", (1990) 14 *Déviance et Société* 347-376. See also Durkheim and Freud, as mentioned in footnote 7.

11 A. VON HIRSCH and N. JAREBORG, "Gauging Criminal Harm: a Living -Standard Analysis" (1991) 11 *Oxford Journal of Legal Studies* 1-38.

12 H. BOUTELLIER, "Beyond the Criminal Justice Paradox. Alternatives between Law and Morality" (1995) 4 *European Journal on Criminal Policy and Research* 7-20.

in terms of "intrusion into dominion"[13]. They all consider the harm or damage to others and/or to collective life as the reason to criminalise certain behaviour.

That brings us to two questions:

- Can one keep a moral category "wrongfulness", distinguished from "harmfulness", to gear public intervention against certain behaviour, as Antony Duff does?
- If harmfulness is the basic reason to justify criminalisation, should the main concern of the criminal intervention not be to repair the harm, instead of punishing the wrong?

3. WHY NEEDS A WRONG TO BE PUNISHED?

Following Kant, Rawls and others, the wrong must be punished to express the wrongfulness of the act. "(...) what justifies punishment is that it is deserved for [the] wrongdoing".[14] This dogmatic assertion is in fact surprising. Rejection of the moral wrong seems to be balanced by an action (inflicting pain to another human), which is itself also intrinsically wrong.[15] From an instrumentalist point of view, it is the more surprising, because, as Wright wrote: "(...) balancing the harm done by the offender with further harm inflicted on the offender. That only adds to the total amount of harm in the world".[16] Is there an intrinsic, inseparable link between the wrong and punishment? We can look at this in two ways.

Does punishment always express the rejection of a "wrong"? "The penal sanction clearly conveys blame", writes von Hirsch, and most would agree with that.[17] But it is not always like that. Punishment is often seen simply as a cost to be added to the commitment of an offence. It is experienced, not as a blame, but as a risk to be balanced with the possible benefits resulting from committing an offence. That is the main argument for many in pleading for more severe punishments. For some scholars, it is the *de*crease of social blaming in the community which provokes the need for *in*creased penal punishment: because people do not feel blamed anymore,

---

13 J. BRAITHWAITE and P. PETTIT, *Not Just Desert. A Republican Theory of Criminal Justice*, Clarendon Press, Oxford, 1990.

14 R.A. DUFF, "Restorative Punishment and Punitive Restoration", in L. WALGRAVE (ed), *Restorative Justice and the Law*, Cullompton, Willan Publishing, 2002, 82.

15 A. FATIC, 1995 *Punishment and Restorative Crime-Handling*, Aldershot, Avebury, 1995; J. DE KEYSER, *Punishment and Purpose. From Moral Theory to Punishment in Action*, Ph-D. thesis, University of Leyden, 2000; see also DUFF p. 133, in this volume.

16 M. WRIGHT, "Victim-Offender Mediation as a Step Toward a Restorative System of Justice" in H. MESSNER and H.U. OTTO (eds), *Restorative Justice on Trial*, Dordrecht/Boston, Kluwer Academic Publishers, 1992, 525.

17 A. VON HIRSCH, *Censure and Sanctions*, Oxford Clarendon Press, 1993, 9.

you must augment the "objective risks" for their potentially criminal behaviour.[18] Many professional (white collar) criminals see possible criminal punishment as a professional risk. For juveniles involved in subcultures, being arrested and condemned is often a reason for pride towards peers.

The other way round is: do we need punishment to express condemnation of the wrong? Clearly not. Even von Hirsch uncouples blaming from punishment, as appears through his reasoning. Punishment is linked to censure via a detour in four steps. (1) Behaviour is wrong, because it causes harm to "a person's standard of living".[19] (2) The wrongfulness needs to be censured, as a moral message, and to be prevented, as a prudential message.[20] (3) Although the censure can also be expressed in other ways – "A condemnatory response to injurious conduct (...) can be expressed either in a purely (...) symbolic mode; or else (...)"-, the punitive way is chosen, because of its preventive (deterrent) impact ("My... justification would permit the abolition of the institution of punishment were it not needed for preventive purposes").[21] (4) To decide upon the amount of punishment, however, only the degree of blameworthiness (and not the preventive aim) is the reference.[22] Von Hirsch does not consider punishment as the only way to express blame, but he needs punishment for prevention.

Whereas there is overwhelming evidence that the preventative ambitions of criminal punishment are not met, its censuring function is the last possible reason to keep it. However, in daily life, in families and in schools, disapproval is routinely expressed without punishment. Morally authoritative persons without any power to punish are more effective in influencing moral thinking and behaviour than punishment. After a crime has occurred, the settings in view of restoration are more appropriate for communicating moral disapproval and provoking repentance, than are traditional punitive procedures and sanctions. Family group conferences, for example, intensely disapprove of the act through those who care for the offender and for whom the offender cares. Most offenders are open for communication if they themselves experience respect and elementary understanding.[23] They can feel empathy for the suffering of their victims,

---

18 H. BOUTTELIER, "Beyond the Criminal Justice Paradox. Alternatives between Law and Morality", (1995) 4 *European Journal on Criminal Policy and Research* 7-20.

19 A. VON HIRSCH, *Censure and Sanctions*, Oxford Clarendon Press, 1993, 30.

20 A. VON HIRSCH, *Censure and Sanctions*, Oxford Clarendon Press, 1993, 9-14.

21 A. VON HIRSCH, *Censure and Sanctions*, Oxford Clarendon Press, 993, 14.

22 A. VON HIRSCH, *Censure and Sanctions*, Oxford Clarendon Press, 1993, 15-17.

23 G. BAZEMORE and S. O'BRIEN, "The Quest for a Restorative Model of Rehabilitation: Theory-for-Practice and Practice-for-Theory", in L. WALGRAVE (ed) *Restorative Justice and the Law*, Cullompton, Willan Publishing, 2002.

become aware of their contribution to it, feel guilt, and be prepared to do restorative gestures.[24] Moreover, they will better understand the social significance of the norm. Restorative settings position the harm and suffering centrally, presenting victimisation as the focal concern in the norm, and this provides a huge communicative potential.[25]

The statement that wrongful behaviour (because it harms the standard of living) should be punished is difficult to understand. There is some logical inconsistency in defining the crime in terms of harm (being the reason why a behaviour is prohibited), and reacting to it by punishing, making reparation of the harm even more difficult. It seems therefore more logical to accept that the response after an offence must address first of all the reparation of the harm caused. Reprobation of an act does not necessarily include punishment. It includes the recognition of the wrongfulness of the act and the obligation to take responsibility in repairing what has been done wrong.

4. PUNISHMENT A PRIORISM AS AN OBSTACLE FOR COMMUNICATION

Whereas Antony Duff advances punishment as a crucial means in the communication with the offender, my position is the inverse. In my view, the a priori option for punishment, based on retributivist reasoning, is counterproductive for good communication.[26]

Criminal justice's role is to be a beacon of social disapproval, to mark clear limits to social tolerance. The authorities' initiative to respond to the crime, indicates that they do not let things happen. It re-assures the citizens of the norm, and of the authorities' determination to enforce the norm and to protect citizens from victimisation. It may support victims in their victimisation and re-assure them in their citizenship. It makes clear to the offender that his behaviour is not tolerated, and possibly tries to convince him not to re-offend in the future.

---

24 N. Harris, L. Walgrave and J. Braithwaite, "Emotional Dynamics in Restorative Conferences", (2004) 8 *Theoretical Criminology* 91-210.

25 F. Schweigert "Moral Education in Victim Offender Conferencing", (1999) *Criminal Justice Ethics* 29-39.

26 L. Walgrave, "Imposing Restoration instead of Inflicting Pain: Reflections on the Judicial Reaction to Crime", in A. von Hirsch, J. Roberts, A.E. Bottoms, K. Roach, and M. Schiff (eds), *Restorative Justice and Criminal Justice: Competing or Reconcilable Claims*, Oxford, Hart Publishing, 2003; F. Schweigert, "Moral Education in Victim Offender Conferencing" (1999) *Criminal Justice Ethics*, 29-39; M. Wright "Is it Time to Question the Concept of Punishment", in L. Walgrave (ed) *Repositioning Restorative Justice*, Cullompton, Willan Publishing, 2003, 17.

But the a priori option for punishment in criminal justice interferes with effective and constructive communication. While disapproval expressed by the criminal sentence may communicate a clear message to the public at large, it fails to communicate adequately to the other key actors in the crime, the victim and the offender. Good communication needs adequate settings. They are not achieved in court, where confrontation prevails over communication, in front of the judge who will at the end decide upon the kind and degree of hard treatment. The offender then does not listen to the moralising message, but tries to get away with as lenient a punishment as possible. He does not hear the invitation, but merely experiences the threat. It is the a priori option for inflicting hard treatment which is the major obstruction for good communication. Punitive sanctions "are not very effective in deterring offenders, but once the offence has been committed, they deter them from admitting their actions".[27]

Antony Duff takes a more nuanced position. He is of the opinion that punishment is an indispensable response to crime, but advances a type of punishment and a way of punishing which are largely different from the traditional criminal justice practices. Duff is looking for "...a kind of censure that aims to bring offenders to face up to and recognise the wrongs they have done;...of burdensome reparation that expresses such an apologetic and repentant recognition; ...of a reconciliation, mediated by such recognition and reparation, between victim and offender;...".[28] The hard treatment is linked to the offender's "recognition of his wrongdoing, since that should be a repentant recognition, and repentance is necessarily painful".[29] This view projects a sequence: censure leads to recognition of wrongfulness, which leads to painful repentance, which leads to possible reparation. Such sequence is in fact close to what is supposed to happen in ideal restorative justice processes. But it does not fit into the restorative justice philosophy.

First, because wrongfulness is considered separately from harmfulness. As I tried to argue above, wrongfulness cannot be understood separately from harmfulness. One can imagine moral wrongfulness which is not evidently harmful (in religious systems, for example), but we are discussing here a frame for coercive interventions in a democratic state. Purely ethical wrongfulness cannot justify authorities' intrusion upon our liberties, unless it serves preventing harms to fellow citizens and/or to public life. Granted,

---

27 M. WRIGHT, "Is it Time to Question the Concept of Punishment", in L. WALGRAVE (ed) *Repositioning Restorative Justice*, Cullompton, Willan Publishing, 2003, 17.

28 A. DUFF, *Punishment, Communication, and Community*, Oxford, Oxford University Press, 2001, 99.

29 A. DUFF "Restorative Punishment and Punitive Restoration", in L. WALGRAVE (ed), *Restorative Justice and the Law*, Cullompton, Willan Publishing, 2002, 123.

behaviour may be harmful by accident or intentional, and the wrongfulness lies in the *intention* of causing harm. But still, the wrongfulness depends on *the harm* intended, and the degree of wrongfulness on the degree of harmfulness intended.

Secondly, the crucial sequence "censure – recognition of wrongfulness – repentance – restoration" may be more difficult to achieve by the a-priorism that it *must* be burdensome for the offender. Repentance is crucial, indeed, and experience in conferences clearly shows how painful repentance is for the offender. The hardship is however not intended. On the contrary, in fact: repentance in the offender is facilitated because of the respectful and supportive climate in which it may occur. This climate makes it easier for the offender to recognise the unpleasant feelings of repentance, instead of repressing them through machismo and denying victimisation. As argued above, confirmation of the norm and disapproval of the norm transgression can be done otherwise than through intentional hard treatment. Instead of promoting repentance, searching willingly to make the offender suffer, may provoke defiance.[30] In terms of Antony Duff's typology,[31] we fear that the "already repentant offender" does not need punishment to comply with apologies and willingness to make up, that the "defiant offender" might become more defiant under the threat of punishment, and that the amount of "morally persuaded offenders" by punishment will probably be reduced, because the punishment will turn "persuadable offenders" into being defiant ones.

Finally, while Antony Duff presents a truly renovating and constructive approach to the way crime has to be responded to, it focuses on what should be done to the offender, and not, as restorative justice does, primarily on how harm can be restored. The main concern is not about how the experienced harm and suffering may be repaired as much as possible, but on how the "wrong" can be undone. This wrong and the way to respond to it are given, not socially debatable categories. "The reactions of others (including the victim, L.W.), and of the wrongdoer, are... subject to normative appraisal: we must ask not just what they in fact feel, but what they should feel".[32] It clearly remains a top down approach, opposed to the bottom up perspective which is fundamental to restorative justice, and wherein there is large space for mercy.

---

30 L. SHERMAN, "Defiance, Deterrence and Irrelevance: a Theory of the Criminal Sanction" (1993) 30 *Journal of Research in Crime and Delinquency* 1-37.

31 R.A. DUFF, *Punishment, Communication, and Community*, Oxford, Oxford University Press, 2001, 115 et seq.

32 R.A. DUFF, "Restorative Punishment and Punitive Restoration", in L. WALGRAVE (ed), *Restorative Justice and the Law*, Cullompton, Willan Publishing, 2002, 110.

5. DUFF'S COMMUNITARIAN LIBERALISM AND THE TOP-DOWN APPROACH IN RETRIBUTIVISM

It is difficult to understand how Antony Duff combines communitarian liberalism with his retributivist view on responding to crime. Duff describes communitarian liberalism as a tendency promoting an ideal political community in which values such as autonomy, freedom and pluralism are based on mutual recognition of its members, who share a certain way of life. In fact, such political community can function only when it is based on its members' mutual trust that they will respect each others' autonomy, freedom and right to be different. It calls to mind what Putnam called trust, being a crucial element in social capital, which is needed to make "democracies work".[33] Not the "thick trust" in our family members and friends is so important here, but the "thin trust" which we should have in our fellow citizens in general, and in social institutions. The same idea can be found in Braithwaite and Pettit's concept of dominion (or "freedom as non domination").[34] Dominion does not only refer to our set of rights and freedoms, but especially to the fact that these rights and freedoms are assured. Dominion only exists where we can be assured (or we can trust) that our fellow citizens and authorities will take the rights and freedoms seriously

This "assurance", or "trust", or "mutual recognition" is crucial for a communitarian liberal society, as I understand it from Duff's words, to function smoothly. It is driven by common values, but needs "lubrication" by mutual trust or assurance. Such societies must be more than just tolerant for pluralism, as Duff seems to suggest, but must also seek to guarantee opportunities for people to be and to think differently, without negative consequences for their citizenship. That is possible only if social institutions favour continued deliberation among citizens, leading to participatory decision making. In my view, communitarian liberalism cannot be but a bottom up approach to men and society, relying on participatory commitment by responsible citizens.

Such view seems to be opposed to retributivism, because retributivism defends the a-priorism that offending must be punished, and advances a concept of wrong as being an absolutist category, independent from its impact on social life. Retributivism clearly is a top down approach, imposing normative models and action categories to citizens. How can citizens be part of this community if they cannot debate on what they feel

---

33 R. PUTNAM, *Making Democracy Work: Civic Traditions in Modern Italy*, Princeton, Princeton University Press, 1993.

34 J. BRAITHWAITE and P. PETTIT, *Not Just Desert. A Republican Theory of Criminal Justice*, Oxford, Clarendon Press, 1990.

to be wrong and on what kind of response is the most appropriate? This top down approach does not invite citizens to take part in the working of their institutions in view of more constructive social life. It submits them to absolutist rules, and makes them to be selfish opportunists who consume the social institutions for their own benefit, without feeling responsible for social life in general. Retributivism therefore seems to me to be opposed to communitarianist ideals, because it thinks in absolutist terms, and not in terms of active responsibility, and because it does not use quality of social life as the reference.

9. RETRIBUTIVE PUNISHMENT AND SYMBOLIC RESTORATION: A REPLY TO DUFF

Arnold Burms

Responding to Professor Duff's admirable paper is a pleasure. Since I agree with nearly everything he has said, I hope to add a few remarks that are faithful to the spirit of his lecture.

Professor Duff has stressed that his theory has a normative character. My own interest, by contrast, is primarily descriptive and theoretical, not because I assume that this is to be preferred but merely because I lack the experience and the concrete knowledge required for speaking responsibly about the defects of our penal system and about the remedies that might transform it. Of course, I hope that my descriptive remarks might have some indirect relevance for the normative issues.

Two different levels of inquiry can be distinguished in Professor Duff's paper. First, there is the level of immanent or internal understanding. Here the aim is to make explicit what the point of the practice of punishment is, to articulate its immanent goals and values. The first level is to be distinguished from a second level: Antony Duff does not merely want to articulate the immanent meaning of punishment, he also wishes to discover whether punishment as it can be immanently understood, can also be justified within the larger framework of democratic values. The two approaches finally meet in the thesis that punishment is in harmony with our liberal democratic values if it really functions in accordance with what the immanent analysis yields. The crucial idea here is that punishment is a communicative process, that it communicates censure and that the offender who is censured is by that very fact taken seriously and addressed as a responsible agent.[1]

In what follows I shall concentrate mainly on the first level of Professor Duff's account and try to add a few things to what he has said about the immanent meaning of criminal punishment. I shall end with a brief remark about the relation between the two levels of his normative theory.

The need for immanent understanding is implied by the anti-consequentialist view Antony Duff favours. If the point of the practice was reducible to its utility, no immanent understanding would be called for.

1 Duff makes explicit use of this distinction in R.A. Duff, *Punishment, Communication, and Community*, Oxford, Oxford University Press, 2001, XVI-XVII.

The normative issue about justification would then have to be related to the question whether criminal punishment has the efficacy it aims at. The inquiry one would have to engage in would be of the kind needed for the investigation of the efficacy of a new medical treatment. That is not the sort of approach professor Duff favours. He wishes to understand the practice from within and to make explicit what its immanent meaning is.

Talk about the immanent meaning of an existing practice often has a conservative ring. I think that the association is not necessary. Immanent understanding can be critical. Admittedly, the attempt to achieve immanent understanding will have to draw on a familiarity with an existing practice. But one might discover that the actual practice does not live up to the values it purportedly embodies. Take for instance the institution of marriage. An immanent approach will be in contrast with an account that describes marriage in purely contractual terms. But such an immanent inquiry is not necessarily incompatible with the conclusion that marriage as it now exists has lost the point it once had.

Professor Duff's immanent inquiry leads to a defence of retributivism. One of the central theses of his paper is the thesis that his communicative theory can make sense of the retributive element in punishment. Retributivism is often described by its detractors as irrational and even unintelligible. What could possibly be meant by the contention that criminals are to be punished because they deserve it? What is the point of this notion of desert? And what is the point of the belief that the suffering of the offender should in some way compensate for the evil he brought about? Why would one add suffering to suffering?

The correct reply to these familiar charges is, I believe, that the retributive element in punishment is perfectly continuous with certain deeply ingrained attitudes that function within ordinary life. The two attitudes I have in mind are remorse and moral indignation. When we are confronted with immoral behaviour, whether it is criminal or not, we typically feel moral indignation. This attitude tends to express itself in moral blame or censure. Moral blame is meant to be understood in a certain way: the person addressed by it, is invited to see his act in a certain light and to feel remorse about what he did. This pattern is perfectly well-known; it is well-known in the sense that we are intuitively familiar with it, but not in the sense that it is totally transparent how it should be theoretically interpreted.

One thing is clear, however. The understanding we all have of moral indignation and moral blame is an understanding of their *appropriateness*. Saying that we understand the meaning of moral indignation and blame but that we do not understand how they could be appropriate in some cases, does not make sense. But if that is granted, it cannot be meaningfully denied that retributive punishment is intelligible or that it is intelligible how it could be appropriate; retributive punishment expresses blame in the sense in which blame expresses indignation. And similarly: if you think that the point of remorse is intelligible, then you will have to accept at the same time that there is a point in penance as well.[2]

Philosophers who claim that retributive punishment is unintelligible are often mistaken about their target. What they really mean is that some retributivist *theory* is unintelligible to them. At an intuitive level we all understand what feelings of guilt and remorse are; we have an intuitive understanding of moral indignation and of the point of moral blame. But we may be at a loss if we have to make explicit in theoretical terms what it is that we intuitively understand.

What is of crucial importance here is that the retributive element in punishment does not originate in theoretical assumptions. Retribution was not introduced as something about which people thought that there were good reasons to have it. It has to be admitted that our practices –and that is also true for the practice of punishment- are often associated with some theoretical interpretation. But one should keep in mind that the practice itself is primary and may well be misrepresented by most or all current theoretical interpretations. The origin of retributive punishment is to be situated in deeply embedded attitudes. These attitudes – remorse, indignation – were never rationally designed. We never made them for some reason, but they are simply part of our lives.

There is an important difference between the implicit, intuitive understanding of some practice and its interpretations (that are often misinterpretations). Punishment is not the only example that illustrates this point. Respecting and honouring the dead is another example. Nearly everybody understands on an intuitive level that is it morally appropriate to respect the dead and that treating a dead body with disrespect or arrogance can be an act of real cruelty. However, it turns out to be quite difficult to spell out in theoretical terms what the point is of these attitudes and why we think it morally necessary to respect the dead. Similarly retributive punishment has a significance that is intuitively accessible but often inadequately interpreted by retributivist theories. It is a mistake to believe that what is objectionable about these theories is equally objectionable about the interpreted practice.

The slogan "the guilty deserve to suffer" is often used as a summary of the justification of retributive punishment. Introducing the notion of what is morally deserved in this context is in itself not a mistake. But it is tempting to move from this starting point to a fundamental error. For there is a tendency to link this talk about moral desert with the idea that

---

2 This line of thought is inspired by P.F. STRAWSON, *Freedom and Resentment and Other Essays*, London, Methuen & Co., 1974.

retributive punishment is primarily concerned with the mind of the offender. The idea is then that moral blame and punishment are to be situated in the framework of a grading system: the aim would be to determine the moral merits of individuals and to respond appropriately to these merits. Seen from this perspective, blame and punishment are primarily a response to the agent whose conduct is only thought relevant as an expression of his personality or character.

In Antony Duff's paper, by contrast, it is stressed that a concern with the wrongdoer cannot be separated from a wider communicative process. We punish because we owe this: we owe this, first, to the victim of the wrong since to fail to condemn the wrong is to fail to take it and her seriously; we owe it to her as a vindication of her moral standing; we owe the punishment also to the values that were violated; and, finally, we owe this to the wrongdoer himself.

Duff connects the concern with the offender with the responses to the harm done to the victim and to the violated order. The victim and the violated order are mentioned first; then, only in the third place, he mentions the offender. I do not know whether Professor Duff attaches any importance to this, but I am certainly inclined to make much of it. For I believe that the response to the harm done is in an important sense primary and that the response to the offender is in a sense derivative. In what follows I shall try to justify this contention.

Punishment as an expressive or communicative action can be seen as part of a larger pattern. It is an instance of what I will be referring to as "*symbolic restoration*". We cannot really annul the harm that was brought about or the wrong that was committed. But through symbolic restoration we can make sense of the unchangeable past. I shall briefly describe a few examples that illustrate this point.

When a natural catastrophe has happened, a public, ceremonial tribute is normally paid to the victims. Impersonal and indifferent forces killed a number of people as if their lives were of no importance. It is as if through the catastrophe something is expressed: one has the feeling that the dignity of the victims is in some way denied. What was thus denied, will have to be reaffirmed by a solemn tribute to them. And this practice is experienced as something *we owe to them.*

A student, who was on his way to a lecture, was killed by a car. A few hours later, when all the traces of the accident had been cleared away, the place looked shockingly normal again and indifferent: as if nothing important had happened. Flowers are put there by some relative or friend in order to affirm that which seems to be denied by indifferent, anonymous space.

My next example brings us somewhat closer to punishment. A few years ago some inhabitants of the Walloon village Sars-la-Buissière made a remarkable request: they asked that the town council demolish the house in which some of Marc Dutroux's victims had been held captive. It was felt that the house had to disappear because of its link with the horrible crimes that had been committed there. The continuing existence of the house and the possibility that it would be used again was seen as an offensive: leaving the house intact would be a sign of impermissible indifference. An inanimate object cannot be punished but there is, I believe, some plausibility in the contention that the motives for demolishing the house in Sars-la-Buissière are fundamentally akin to the retributive motive for punishment.

In a work of the anthropologist Bronislaw Malinowski on the natives of the Trobiand Islands there is a description of certain mourning rituals that seem deeply similar to a kind of penance or punishment.[3] When a man had died a number harsh mourning obligations were imposed on his widow. She had to stay shut-up for several months in a small, stuffy place; she had to speak in whispers and was not allowed to touch food or with her own hands. The Trobiander widow is obliged by the matrilineal relatives of her husband to undergo all this. Mourning is a kind of punishment here. Its point is to prevent the widow being secretly pleased by the death of her husband and to derive a blasphemous pleasure from the thought that she got rid of him. If she sincerely mourns, so much the better; if she does not feel sincerely sad and bereaved, she should at least suffer under the privations that prevent her from having pleasant thoughts about the death of her husband.

Some years ago, a fourteen year old boy was accidentally killed by a car in a Flemish village. Formally, there was nothing the car driver could be blamed for and he was allowed to go scot-free. But the same evening he was seen in a pub where he made a couple of tasteless jokes about the accident. When this was known in the village, there was an outburst of moral indignation: people were sorry that there was nothing the driver could be punished for. Strictly speaking, the car driver was not guilty of the death of the young man, but the fact that he was materially involved imposed on him a special obligation. He was morally obliged, more than anybody else, to affirm the dignity of the victim by showing respectful restraint. The moral indignation that was brought about by his lack of respect, illustrates, I believe, what the point of retributive punishment is.

The examples I have given lend some plausibility, I hope, to the thesis that retributive punishment is one aspect of the larger phenomenon of symbolic restoration. If that is right, retributive punishment is primarily a response to the harm done. The primary aim is to reaffirm the dignity of the victim or of the violated order and to deny in this way what seemed

---

[3] B. Malinowski, *The Sexual Life of Savages in North-Western Melanesia*, Routlegde and Kegan, 1929, 130-39.

to be denied by the crime. From the offender it is expected that he feels remorse or at least that his suffering caused by his condemnation and punishment is associated in his mind with the wrongfulness of his crime. The logic behind this is simple: it is to be made impossible for him to think about his crime without thinking about his punishment and, hence, from deriving pleasure from thinking about his crime. Through his punishment, remorse or suffering he takes part in the ritual of symbolic restoration.

Recently, there has been some debate about a phenomenon that indirectly supports the interpretation I have been recommending here. "Moral luck" is the term Bernard Williams introduced for referring to this phenomenon.[4] There is moral luck when factors beyond the control of the agent partly determine the moral status of what he did. A classic example is that of the reckless driver: in a case where he has caused the death of somebody his act will make him feel much guiltier and also bring about much more indignation in others, than in a case where the same recklessness did not have such disastrous consequences. Another illustration is the response to criminal attempts: failed attempts are normally less severely punished than they would have been had they succeeded. If it is true that symbolic restoration is the basis of guilt, indignation, remorse and retributive punishment, then the existence of moral luck is exactly what is to be expected. The need for symbolic restoration emerges from a response that what has happened. And that implies that people will be primarily blamed or punished for what they did and not for what they are. The fact that what we do is always to some extent merely contingently related to what we are, is the basis of moral luck.

All what I have said so far is related to the first level of Professor Duff's inquiry. I have dealt exclusively with the immanent understanding of punishment. I hope that my sketchy remarks about symbolic representation fit well in the framework of the communicative process in terms of which Antony Duff describes the point of retributive punishment. Trying to explain the immanent meaning of retributive punishment is trying to make sense of it. This is not the same thing as a full-fledged justification. Something can make sense without being fully desirable. An inquiry that reveals what the immanent meaning of the practice of retributive punishment is can be an adequate response to the charge that that practice is unintelligible. It is quite possible to see what the positive moral significance of a practice is and to believe at the same time that this moral significance

4 B. WILLIAMS, "Moral Luck" in D. STATMAN (ed), *Moral Luck*, New York, State University of New York Press, 1993, 35-55. A. DUFF, *Criminal Attempts*, Oxford, Oxford University Press, 1996, ch.12 contains a substantial and brilliant treatment of the topic. The position he defends in that book and which he calls "objectivism" seems to be very much in harmony with what I am trying to say here.

is outweighed by other considerations. And this leads us to the second level to Professor Duff's inquiry: how can retributive punishment be related to the larger framework of democratic values?

I will limit myself here to a general question. The notions of blame and censure are situated by Antony Duff in the context of a communicative process. One of the central ideas is that the offender is taken seriously by the censure that is communicated to him. But the notion of censure that Professor Duff trades on is older than our liberal, democratic values. It had its role within the traditional context of penance as this was understood by the Catholic Church. The sinner was taken seriously as a human person since his understanding of what he did was addressed. The aim of the penance that was imposed on him was to invite him to repent and to become fully aware of the seriousness of the censure. My question is: in what sense is what Professor Duff has said about the liberal, democratic meaning of punishment different from the traditional, pre-liberal practices of penance?

10. DOES PUNISHMENT NEED HARD TREATMENT? A REPLY TO DUFF

BAS VAN STOKKOM

Many punishment-theories contain monistic views on the question what punishment really is. Retributivists generally believe that intentionally inflicting suffering is the essence of punishment. Some of their theories reveal a so called "principled objectivism", which is in terms of the Dutch criminologist Willem Nagel typical of True Believers.[1] The allocation of a just measure of pain is elevated to a sublime principle of justice. Even if nobody would hold suffering appropriate, still one is obliged to follow that principle. A familiar example is Kant's cramped judgement that even when the world would perish the last criminal should be hanged.[2] In *On the Genealogy of Morals* Nietzsche criticises this "black magic": there is no need to transform a nasty but indispensable punishment practice into a higher principle. Unfortunately his advice fell on deaf ears, because – at least since the seventies of the last century – there is a revival of retributive armchair philosophies in which nice benefit-burden balances are conjured up, of course miles away form the expanding punishment industry.

Like their opponents, many restorative justice theorists try to define sanctions in a monistic way: reparation is given a supreme status. Reparative sanctions would offer just answers for all aspects of the penal system. Sometimes the old abolitionist slogan reverberates: criminal justice has to give way for restoration and reconciliation. In this case we are dealing with True Believers of a more utopian nature.

Both restoration and retribution occupy a legitimate position within the penal system. We have to rely on both punishment motivations.[3] In many situations restoration is not appropriate or applicable, for instance when the offender is not interested in repairing the harm done or when feelings of revenge block a genuine dialogue. Nevertheless, I believe we should deal

---

1 W. NAGEL, "'The true believer' en het probleem van de vergelding" in *Speculum Langemeijer*, Zwolle, Tjeenk Willink, 1973, 365-386.

2 The Dutch criminal justice philosopher L. POLAK, *De zin der vergelding*, Amsterdam, Van Oorschot, 1947, 338 points to the "talionic sophisms of a senile genius", the Kant of *Metaphysische Anfangsgründe der Rechtslehre* (1797).

3 In this article I do not take consequentionalism into account. As is well-known, this paradigm legitimates important punishment functions, but cannot offer the judge adequate motives to explain to the offender why he is punished.

with restoration in a pragmatic way, whereas retribution should be dealt with reticently. So, applying the "good old" proverb of the Modern School: restoration if possible, retribution if necessary.

To accentuate the meaning of retribution and restoration I will examine some basic ideas of one specific retributive author and in many ways a True Believer: Antony Duff. The studies of this outstanding scholar contain some misleading aspects, particularly the old expiatory idea that suffering is a condition to generate personal repentance. I believe his positive interpretation of inflicting suffering is illusory and undesirable. In particular I will criticise the supposition that hard treatment and two-way communication are compatible. Nevertheless, Duff's work contains many starting points for a solid foundation of restorative justice, like the view that proper punishment requires two-way communication, and that punishment is successful when it brings about moral self-reform. It is up to us to put Duff's theory on firmer ground. In the last paragraph's I will argue that hard treatment should be reserved for serious crimes when the public is shocked and the offender does not want to take responsibility. If the offender shows regret or repentance hard treatment seems to be superfluous. Before discussing Duff's theory I will shortly examine two questions: Why do we have to rely on retribution? And: What is hard treatment?

1. WHY DO WE HAVE TO RELY ON RETRIBUTION?

Retributivists are eager to demonstrate that bad practices and negative interventions can produce something good or have some worthwhile ends. Despite these efforts they did not really succeed in developing plausible justifications for intentionally inflicting pain. I do not believe that intentionally inflicting pain can be "explained or developed within a reasonable system of moral thought".[4] The principles that retributivists have invented for that purpose – annulling the crime, taking away benefits, lowering the status of the criminal, etc. – remain vague, imaginary and ambiguous.[5] Nevertheless, retribution cannot be eliminated from morality. Retributive feelings, no matter how disappointing, are a vital part of our emotional life. Grievances reveal desires whose only satisfaction is the belief that offenders are being distressed or made to suffer. The task of retributivism is to bring these vindictive desires within a legal framework of just deserts and proportionality.

---

[4] J.L. MACKIE, "Morality and the Retributive Emotions" in his *Persons and Values*, Oxford, Oxford University Press, 1985 206-219, also T. HONDERICH, *Punishment. The Supposed Justifications*, Oxford, Polity Press, 1989.

[5] N. WALKER, *Why Punish?*, Oxford, Oxford University Press, 1991. Retributivists have developed many other ideas that indeed make good sense: the moral message of the public censure, warranting rights of offenders, the importance of guilt and proportionality, etcetera.

The difficulty that retribution cannot be made decent sense of and the fact that retributive feelings are inescapable: this is what Mackie calls the "paradox of retributivism". When justifying these desires psychological, social and political functions are at stake. The political account of retributivism says that if the state does not take action against crimes it condones behaviour of which the effects run counter to the moral expectations that are connected with the law. Not taking action gives the impression that the state lacks the power to protect its citizens. Thus the authority of the state is compromised.[6] Moreover the impression may last that crime pays and that the moral indignation of victims does not count. Therefore the state is obliged to take action and to declare publicly that punishment will follow. In terms of Spinoza: injustice ought never to thrive, avail or give advantage; it must fail.[7]

However, this political account of retribution cannot give convincing arguments for deliberatively inflicting pain. The desire to cause this suffering fulfils psychological functions: grievance-satisfactions, canalisation of negative emotions like rage, revenge and fear, and regaining some peace of mind. At the same time the public must be informed that the "biased selfishness and norm-violating will" of the offender gets a severe blow.[8] Nevertheless, with Nietzsche we endorse the thesis that retributivism obtains a bad victory: ultimately it works with instruments that are considered illegitimate when used by the other party.

2. WHAT IS HARD TREATMENT?

Retributivists are inclined to see one particular and rigorous aspect of punishment, namely intentionally inflicting pain, as the essence of criminal punishment: "The guilty deserve to suffer." However, nowadays this a priori inflicting pain certainly does not hold absolute sway over the practice of allotting penal sanctions. Sentences can also be related to training, probation or compensation. In these cases the judge often deems it not relevant that suffering really manifests itself, and she can give priority to rehabilitation or pedagogical effects. These kinds of sentences can hardly be associated with "intentionally inflicting pain": the pain or burden is the derivative of imposed obligations. On the other hand, what often is called "hard treatment" can be related to "active" and external ways of inflicting pain: the pain must act upon the psyche of the offender; it functions as an

6 T. BALDWIN, "Punishment, Communication and Resentment", in M. Matravers(eds), *Punishment and Political Theory*, Oxford, Hart Publishing, 1999, 124-132.

7 See L. POLAK, *De zin der vergelding*, Amsterdam, Van Oorschot, 1947.

8 L. POLAK, *De zin der vergelding*, Amsterdam, Van Oorschot, 1947.

attack on his will. The offender must feel the censure in a compelling way and is not allowed to escape form the experience of suffering.

The problem is that retributivists do apply many different definitions of hard treatment. A formal one – popular among lawyers – says that hard treatment simply means deprivation of time and liberty. What actually happens during the execution is deemed not relevant, whether the offender does nothing or is burdened with heavy work. This is a senseless definition, at least from an ethical viewpoint, because the moral implications of the punishment regime are denied, while at the same time the person's status as moral agent is ignored.

We need more substantive descriptions. John Kleinig – who, as a good retributivist, equates punishment with hard treatment – offers some fine distinctions. He points out that merely to criticise, rebuke or censure the wrong-doer would fail to register the seriousness of what was done. Punishment not only involves a stigmatising condemnation, but also some significant deprivation is considered appropriate. This imposition serves to impress on the wrong-doer the nature of what he has done, and also acknowledges the personhood of the victim. But there are limits: cruel and degrading punishments tend to threaten the humanity of convicts, because they undermine their capacity for appraisal (in the Kantian sense of loss of autonomy). In current prison environments, Kleinig adds, we treat inmates in ways that compromise the human regard to which they are entitled. On the other hand, treating people humanely does not mean treating them softly. "Hard treatment may be onerous, tiring, difficult, vigorous, austere, and rigorous without being inhumane".[9]

Like Kleinig, Andrew von Hirsch states that blaming is not enough to explain the institution of punishment. Punishment does convey blame through the visitation of deprivation on the offender. In other words, we express disapproval through hard treatment. At the same time Von Hirsch believes that visiting deprivation on those who offend is only justified when the criminal sanction is useful in preventing crime. Were the censure sufficient to prevent crime, no hard treatment was needed. But too many offenders are not impressed. Therefore a "supplement" of deterrence is needed. "The hard-treatment in punishment serves a prudential reason for obedience to those insufficiently motivated by the penal censure's moral appeal."[10] In other words, hard treatment provides an additional reason

---

[9] J. KLEINIG, "The Hardness of Hard Treatment", in A. ASHWORTH and M. WASIK (eds), *Fundamentals of Sentencing Theory. Essays in Honour of Andrew von Hirsch*, Oxford, Clarendon Press, 1998, 286.

[10] A. VON HIRSCH, "Desert and Previous Convictions", in A. VON HIRSCH and A. ASHWORTH (eds), *Principled Sentencing. Readings on Theory and Policy*, Oxford, Hart Publishing, 1998, 171; A. VON HIRSCH, *Censure and Sanctions*, Oxford, Clarendon Press, 1993.

for compliance to those who are capable of recognising the law's moral demands, but who are also tempted to disobey them. Echoing the liberal worries of Kleinig, he remarks that the harsher the penalty system is, the less plausible it becomes to see it as embodying a moral appeal. Hard treatment then appears as a system of bare threats.

This version of hard treatment as "communication plus deterrence" is criticised by Antony Duff. He claims that this account is not consistent with the ideal of a liberal political community. To address citizens in the coercive language of deterrence is to cease to treat them as members of the normative community. Duff admits that many offenders have no serious regard for the values that the law embodies. But a moral regard is not entirely absent. The problem is that this regard is not wholehearted, or consistent, or always sufficient to overcome the temptations of self-interest. Offenders are not wholly deaf to the law's moral appeal and we do not attend to it enough. A second critical point is directed against Von Hirsch's idea of hard treatment as a supplement. "We must ask whether 'prison sentences of up to three (or five) years can really be seen as *supplements* to the law's moral appeal".[11] Duff rightly fears that in the context of severe punishments prudential "incentives" will replace the moral voice of censure. On the other hand, if punishments were modest enough to be mere supplements it might be questioned whether the preventive aims are as effective as Von Hirsch presupposes. A modest supplement fails to dissuade.

To overcome these shortcomings Duff develops a more ambitiously communicative account of hard treatment. Punishment must give offenders an opportunity to examine their souls. The deprivation in punishment must provide a kind of secular penance.

3. DUFF'S ACCOUNT: SOME IMPLAUSIBLE PSYCHOLOGICAL ARGUMENTS

In his study *Punishment, Communication, and Community* Duff points out that penal hard treatment is an essential part in the communication of disapproval. His aim is to persuade the offender to accept the censure as justified, to recognise and repent his crime as a wrong, and to engage in moral self-reform. We have to invite the offender to attend to these core questions, but we should not penetrate his conscience. He has to develop his moral competences himself. However, mere words are not enough to persuade: they are too easily ignored or forgotten. A suitable kind of hard treatment can help keep the offender's attention focused on his crime, and

---

11 R.A. DUFF, *Punishment, Communication, and Community*, Oxford, Oxford University Press, 2001, 88.

so help to induce repentance. Secondly, the offender must give a forceful apology to the victim and also to the wider community. He must "make up" for his crime, but a merely verbal apology is too easy: undergoing or undertaking suitable penal hard treatment gives more force to the apology. At the same time, he must offer reparation to those whom he wronged. In short, punishment is two-way communication, and penal hard treatment is essential to both communications because it induces the pain of remorse and enforces the pain of reparation.

Duff stresses that his rationale for hard treatment is not of a consequentionalist nature: what makes the punishment appropriate is not its effectiveness, but addressing offenders as responsible moral agents. Punishment requires the communication of censure and the encouragement of moral learning, not providing training programmes to change the offender's behaviour. Offenders should not be instrumentalised to reach a "greater good". We have to address them as autonomous agents in terms of their own values so that their moral respect is guaranteed.

Persuading is a central concept in Duff's theory. We should persuade the offender, even if we are sure we will fail. We should not give up on him as a moral agent. In that case we would treat him as beyond moral redemption. "We owe it to him to continue to treat him as someone who is not irrevocably cut off from the values he has flouted, who could still redeem himself – even if he will not do so".[12] In short, we have to treat him as a potential penitent.

Duff's theory has significant implications for sentencing practices. It should lead to reducing the use of imprisonment, given its exclusionary meaning, and of fines, as implying a monetary value to crime. Sentences as community service and probation should be favoured, since they support self-correction and repentance. Their communicative content is direct and explicit. Duff aims to impose meaningful tasks that are related to the wrongdoing.[13] At the same time, negotiated sentencing and penal versions of victim-offender mediation could be promoted, so offenders and victims might have a more active role in the determination of reparation-work.

Doing so, Duff constructs a "third way" between pure retributivism and consequentialism, a way that offers many points of departure for restorative justice advocates. Nevertheless, his theory holds some severe flaws. I will concentrate on some implausible psychological arguments. First – and this is the main objection – it must be questioned whether two-way communication and hard treatment go together. During communication between

---

12 R.A. Duff, *Punishment, Communication, and Community*, Oxford, Oxford University Press, 2001, 123.

13 See also R.A. Duff, "Alternatives to Punishment – or Alternative Punishment", in W. Cragg (ed), *Retributivism and its Critics*, Stuttgart, Frans Steiner, 1992, 43-69.

autonomous persons everyone's integrity is respected. Does penal hard treatment fit in with respecting integrity? The answer is probably negative because the communication goes by in implicit terms of dominance and submission. Dominating persons often fail to convey moral authority. For this reason hard treatment tends to incite mistrust: the offender is anticipating hostile intentions, feigns conformity, resists or withdraws. At the same time it is improbable that submission or "being the subject of deliberative inflicting pain" encourages moral reflection, since the attention of the offender is concentrated on his own suffering. The attention shifts from the harmfulness of the criminal act to present hardships. This makes the offender obstinate, incites anger or raises depressive feelings. Nietzsche – in his study *On the Genealogy of Morals* – summed up these effects in a succinct way: "Punishment is supposed to possess the value of awakening the *feeling of guilt* in the guilty person; one seeks in it the actual *instrumentum* of that psychical reaction called "bad conscience", "sting of conscience". Thus one misunderstands psychology and the reality of things even as they apply today (...). It is precisely among criminals and convicts that the sting of conscience is extremely rare; prisons and penitentiaries are not the kind of hotbed in which these species of gnawing worm is likely to flourish (...). Generally speaking, punishment makes men hard and cold; it concentrates; it sharpens the feeling of alienation; it strengthens the power of resistance."[14]

Duff mistakenly presupposes that persons who must endure punishment, are receptive to reasonable arguments and moral learning. Suffering would encourage the offender to concentrate on the crime, the censure and misery that the victim had to endure. The offender recognises what he did wrong. This is only plausible when the offender accepts the justice of his suffering. In Duff's terms: burdensome tasks only serve the aims of the communicative enterprise when the offender is convinced that he was wrong and that he deserves punishment. If this is not the case then hard treatment does not at all contribute to more moral insight: suffering precludes concentration and the opening of the self that are necessary for learning. Generally offenders do not experience suffering as a contribution to a "lesson they need to learn", but as an indication that they have no control over their fates[15] For that reason serious deprived offenders will not take initiatives to repair harm or offer genuine apologies to victims. Moreover, there are too many offenders who are not susceptible to moral

---

14 F. NIETZSCHE, *On the Genealogy of Morals*, Vintage (translation Walter Kaufmann, first publication in 1887), New York, 1967, 81.

15 T.R. CLEAR, "The Punitive Paradox: Desert and the Compulsion to Punish", (1996) 33 *Journal of Research in Crime and Delinquency* 94-108.

messages, from amoral risk-takers to status-seeking machos. Others are not susceptible because they have too much awe for legal authorities.

In short, Duff works with dubious psychological premises. It is highly questionable if the moral communication and moral education he aims at, will occur. Hard treatment is no reliable route to moral self-reform. Attention and support from others are more important.[16]

A subsequent question is why we should communicate with offenders when they reject our moral message. According to Duff – and here he shows himself a real True Believer – we must try to persuade them to repent their crimes otherwise we would treat them as being beyond moral redemption. We have to treat the offender as someone who could come to repentance, even if we know that our attempt will fail. That is not convincing: Duff leaves the door wide open for the troubles of making converts. Even less convincing is Duff's argument that we have to treat offenders who are punished as if they have apologised themselves. "to treat him as a fellow citizen (..) is to treat him as someone who has through his punishment made apologetic reparation for his crime – which means that we must treat him at least as if he is to be trusted again".[17] Duff believes this "insincere apology" makes clear to the victim that the community takes seriously the wrong she suffered. The possibility that many victims would experience this insincerity as cruel does not occur to him.

In short, combining hard treatment and two-way communication, repentance and serious deprivation, is a misleading idea. Anyone who deems deliberative inflicting pain necessary should not expect remorse. In most cases that is unreal. One cannot conciliate and feel excluded at the same time. Now it is possible that Duff cannot find himself entirely in these critical remarks because he interprets "hard treatment" in different ways. He works with several accounts, what makes his theory difficult to assess. A first account is specific: hard treatment is connected with the pain of remorse and the pain of reparation (see his contribution in this volume). Although in these cases the offender is voluntarily enduring pain – one might call it a kind of "hard self-treatment" – Duff also wants to induce this pain. In his words: one function of hard treatment is to make it harder for the offender to ignore the message that punishment aims to communicate. But persisting attempts to persuade and convert offenders who reject moral messages, can easily degenerate into bullying. Keeping on talking to a wall

---

16 See also U. NARAYAN, "Moral Education and Criminal Punishment", in T. MAGNELL (ed), *Values and Education*, Rodopi, Amsterdam, 1998, 69-80; J. BICKENBACH, "Duff on Non-Custodial Punishment", in W. CRAGG (ed), *Retributivism and its Critics*, Stuttgart, Franz Steiner, 1992, 69-74; B.M. BAKER, "Consequentionalism, Punishment and Autonomy", in W. CRAGG (ed), *Retributivism and its Critics*, Stuttgart, Franz Steiner, 1992, 69-74.

17 R.A. DUFF, *Punishment, Communication, and Community*, Oxford, Oxford University Press, 2001, 169-170; also 123-4.

of silence is in fact also degrading for the reformer. The second account is more encompassing: in some passages in his recent book Duff calls every kind of punishment that is burdensome – independently of its censorious meaning – a kind of hard treatment. But that is senseless, because for instance a probation programme aimed at controlling aggression generally is not accompanied with hard treatment. Surely, such a programme is burdensome and implies deprivation, and is in that respect a fully fledged punishment. But this does not mean that the programme's aim is to inflict a priori pain. In the case of constructive sanctions the pain is rather – as Walgrave stresses – a side effect.[18] When the aim is learning offenders are treated in a careful way, not harshly.

If Duff's views do not convince it is tempting to embrace Von Hirsch's account of hard treatment. In this volume (p.137) Duff admits that Von Hirsch's interpretation is in some sense attractive. Those who are deaf to the moral voice of the law must be addressed in a language of self-interest and deterrence. There is certainly some logic in this proposition: criminals are supposed to understand the language of threats. But also this account seems to fail: not only for the reasons Duff mentioned but also because many criminals are not inclined to calculate benefits and costs, or weigh up the risks of criminal behaviour. In fact prudential reasoning leads to loss of status in criminal sub-communities.[19]

It seems more realistic to give hard treatment another meaning: impose deliberately painful tasks in a disciplined environment, as a reaction to serious crimes that have alarmed public indignation and rage feelings. Hard treatment must temper these feelings. In some ways this comes close to Kleinig's description of hard treatment: keeping offenders on a tight rein, refuse them to take initiatives, pursuing intensive control, etc. Probably Duff would criticise this realistic account because it makes to many concessions to "the primitive and vindictive desires to inflict pain". He would not tolerate the idea that hard treatment only has this "nihilistic" function. It comes too close to the disconcerted practices of the "real existing punishment industry". But I think it is a serious omission to give no attention at all to these negative feelings. Like many restorative justice advocates Duff has carefully banished these emotions from his moral universe.

In sum, Duff is reasoning in an idealistic way and disregards the troublesome psychological "basis" of inflicting pain. Therefore we must

---

18 L. WALGRAVE, "Imposing Restoration Instead of Inflicting Pain", in A. VON HIRSCH et al. (eds), *Restorative Justice and Criminal Justice: Competing or Reconcilable Paradigms?*, Oxford University Press, Oxford, 2003 and p. 153 in this volume.

19 T.R. CLEAR, "The Punitive Paradox: Desert and the Compulsion to Punish", (1996) 33 *Journal of Research in Crime and Delinquency* 94-108.

bring the Scottish "Hegel" down to earth: uncouple two-way communication and hard treatment and relate each of them with separate sentences: restorative sanctions that draw the offender into a dialogue on the one hand and retributive sanctions that bring along discipline on the other hand.

4. REPENTANCE AND TRUST: FACILITATING TWO-WAY COMMUNICATION

Some core-ideas in Duff's philosophy are highly instructive to substantiate restorative justice theories. Punishment should not only refer to backward looking retribution, but if possible it also has to obtain the future good of self-reform. Particularly relevant is the difference between experiencing punishment in a passive or active way. In the classic "punishment as expression"-theory the offender is a passive recipient of a public censure.[20] Expression is a *one-way* activity of a "ruler" over the "subservient convict". Duff stresses that real communication is a *two-way* activity, which does not require a passive recipient but a participant whose reasonableness and responsibility is addressed. The parties argue and judge together. Duff is inclined to give the offender a greater say in the determination of his own punishment: he is a participant in the discussion which kind of reparation is needed. Duff points out that offenders get a better understanding of the consequences of the wrong-doing when they are involved in this discussion. Offenders are forced to put themselves in the position of the victim and to consider what is required.

A restorative sanction – work for the victim or the local community – normally presupposes an offender who admits his guilt and who wants to take (some) responsibility. The offender regrets or repents, which means that he is somehow connected with the values which the law is appealing to. For that reason – contrary to Duff – there is no need for intentionally inflicting pain (although restorative justice conferences have their own tough habits: being painfully reminded to the wrong-doing; forcing the offender to recognise the harm he brought about).[21] Suppose the remorseful offender is beforehand informed that he is not allowed to escape from external suffering. Then it would be senseless to discuss with him in constructive ways which reparation must be offered. Besides, we must prevent the offender from performing meaningless or degrading tasks with

---

20 J. FEINBERG, "The Expressive Function of Punishment", in *Doing and Deserving*, Princeton, Princeton University Press, 1970, 95-118.

21 See L. WALGRAVE, "Imposing Restoration instead of Inflicting Pain", in A. VON HIRSCH et al. (eds), *Restorative Justice and Criminal Justice: Competing or Reconcilable Paradigms?*, Oxford, Hart Publishing, 2003, 161-78.

no relation to the wrong-doing. If the tasks are related to his competences and interests he is better able to provide for victim-needs.

So when an offender repents there seems to be no need for concomitant, external infliction of pain. But there are exceptions. In the case of serious and abhorrent crimes apologising words will fail, no matter how honestly and eagerly expressed. Repentance is outweighed by a shocked sense of justice. For that reason hard treatment should have (temporary) priority over two-way communication. The offender is not yet conferred the status of sincere participant and co-director of his punishment. First the retributive emotions must erode before we can grant him a dialogue on the subsequent modelling of his punishment. In other words, some crimes are so serious that the inner pain of repentance does not convince and retribution is ordered. That is why both punishments – restoration and retribution – have a certain relentlessness when it comes to their demarcation. Often retributive feelings are silenced during the execution of a reparation-sanction. Some of the parties involved will find it difficult to accept. Conversely, in the case of hard treatment empathic feelings are silenced. Some parties – for instance victims of violence at home – will not appreciate that.

Restorative justice – like any other system that rewards remorse, as plea bargaining – attracts offenders who fake repentance. Their crocodile tears cause mistrust: we are forced to investigate the authenticity of repentance signs. How to deal with this problem? I believe the offender's plans to offer repair-work must prove his genuine intentions. We have to trace signs of active repentance – what the Germans call "tätige Reue" – that give moral force to the apology.[22] Offenders who apologise but are half-heartedly involved in the discussion on reparation-plans or offer no serious proposals, are problematic. They can hardly function as the "author" or "manager" of their own punishment.

Genuine repentance points at a positive moral disposition, a commitment to avoid wrongdoing in the future. It is an indication – an aspect that Duff does not work out – that trust can be renewed. Now many offenders can be trusted: their behaviour only reveals a deficit, which can be remedied through attention, support and learning. The willingness to repair the harm done not only indicates that the offender acknowledges that he committed a wrong, but also that he will respect other persons' rights in the future. Others cannot be trusted, for instance when the offender says: "when I am free I will steal again". Threatening to continue criminal behaviour is promising to harm or suffer other persons and implies a breach of trust.

---

22 See B. VAN STOKKOM, "Moral Emotions in Restorative Justice Conferences: Managing Shame, Designing Empathy", (2002) 6 *Theoretical Criminology* 339-360.

It is my opinion that trust should be decisive in choosing which kind of sentence is suitable: for instance impose a community service coupled to hard treatment (disciplining) or impose a community sentence directed at restoration. If the offender shows goodwill and trustfulness, he is qualified for the last sentence. Is the offender defying or uncooperative, the first can be meted out.[23] However, if the seriousness of the crime is at stake the judge should operate with comparable tariffs, so the principle of just deserts is obeyed.[24] In other words, an uncooperative offender does not deserve a supplementary term, but a different kind of sentence.[25]

Thus, the decisive standard is trust, i.e. the assessment of expected moral conduct.[26] Trust is a personal quality and part of someone's attitude or "character". Now "character" is a tricky question. Punishing character, Nigel Walker says, is "to engage in moral book-keeping, using previous records as an index of total moral worth".[27] There is a clear danger of double punishment: allocate additional punishment on the basis of former conduct. Another danger is to define character statically. Of course initially remorseless offenders can change themselves. For that reason the execution of sentences should be adapted to actual "good" behaviour. Conversely, an initially cooperative convict who fulfils no obligation at all forfeits our compliance.

Nevertheless, attention to "character" is inevitable because it gives information on the faithfulness of the motives for the crime and because it points out which kind of sentence is indicated.[28] The judge has to take into account offender characteristics such as repentance and the possibility of recidivism, just as she takes the social circumstances of offenders and their families into account. If you adhere to the principle that the offender "has to learn a lesson" it is good to know if he is stubborn, has learning

---

23 In this last case one can – of course – also take behaviour change programmes into consideration.

24 Some retributivists argue that genuine repentance should lead up to reduction of sentencing terms, see J.G. MURPHY, "Repentance, Punishment and Mercy", in A. ETZIONI and D.E. CARNEY, 1997, 143-170; L. POLAK, *De zin der vergelding*, Amsterdam, Van Oorschot, 1947). I agree with Duff that (later occuring) repentence does not make the crime less serious. The same is true for the defying criminal: defiance does not make the crime worse.

25 B. VAN STOKKOM, "Herstel, zelfcorrectie en communicatief straffen", in B.VAN STOKKOM, *Straf en herstel, Ethische reflecties over sanctiedoeleinden*, Den Haag, Boom Juridische Uitgevers, 2004, 287-313.

26 For restorative approaches in which the factor trust is important, see W. CRAGG, *The Practice of Punishment: Toward a Theory of Restorative Justice*, London, Routledge, 1991 A. FATIC, *Punishment and Restorative Crime-Handling. A Social Theory of Trust*, Aldershot, Avebury, 1995 en I. WEIJERS, *Restoration and the family: a pedagogical point of view*, in L. WALGRAVE (ed), *Restorative Justice and the Law*, Willan Publishing, Cullompton, 2002, 68-81. For a retributive approach see S. DIMOCK, "Retributivism and Trust", (1997) 16 *Law and Philosophy* 37-62.

27 Cited in M. BAGARIC, Double Punishment and Punishing Character: The Unfairness of Prior Convictions (2000) 19 *Criminal Justice Ethics* 10-28.

28 R.A. DUFF, "Choice, Character and Criminal Liability", (1993) 12 *Law and Philosophy* 345-383.

disadvantages, or lacks self-control. Moreover: suppose the judge does not take in account the moral disposition of the offender and his social situation. This would stimulate offenders to cope with the imposed sanction in cynical and indifferent ways.

CONCLUSION

Hard treatment, although in many cases inevitable, often brings more psychological and social desperation than the judge aims. It destroys trust and goodwill, and reduces opportunities for restoration, reconciliation, and augmenting self-respect. Next to that hard treatment is not suited for offenders who repent and are prepared to do reparation-work. If this is ignored only an ideology is served, be it the ideology of blind retribution or inducing repentance in circumstances of sorrow and misery.

If punishment is only inflicting pain there is no guarantee that the offender "will learn his lesson". Suffering cannot repair harm or reconstruct what is destroyed. It only can communicate a sense of injustice. Nevertheless: in cases of serious crimes and serious harm our trust is affected so much or the community feels so terrified that a priori inflicting pain is unavoidable. We have to do justice to the outraged feelings of victims and the larger community. But it is a mistake to believe that in this way offenders are stimulated to reform themselves as True Believers like Duff think.

Thus, both punishment legitimizations – retribution and restoration – have their own proper place in the penal system. Monistic views on what criminal punishment should entail, are superfluous.

11. A RESPONSE TO WALGRAVE, VAN STOKKOM, AND BURMS

ANTONY DUFF

I would like finally to comment very briefly on the helpful responses to this paper from Lode Walgrave, Bas van Stokkom, and Arnold Burms.

Walgrave offers two main objections to my account. The first concerns my emphasis on the idea of wrongdoing as the focus of criminal punishment. However, since he himself wants a process that will communicate moral disapproval and induce guilt and repentance (p. 150 in this volume), he cannot be objecting simply to a focus on wrongdoing: for moral disapproval, guilt and repentance take wrongdoing as their object. There is, of course, the further question whether wrongdoing in general, or wrongdoing of a kind that properly concerns the criminal law, must involve harm – assuming that we can clearly separate harms from wrongs[1]: but Walgrave himself agrees that wrongs are more than just harms (p. 151), and that is all I need for my argument. Once we appeal to a notion of wrongdoing, we must of course also ask who is to determine what should count as a criminal wrong, and face the possibility that governments or powerful groups will impose oppressive or unacceptable conceptions of wrongdoing: but that is a problem for anyone who believes that the state should concern itself with right and wrong, and that the criminal law should condemn certain kinds of wrong – that is, it is as much a problem for Walgrave as it is for me, and for (almost) any serious political or legal theorist; I make no apologies for not resolving it here.

Walgrave's second objection is that punishment, the imposition of hard treatment, is not an effective or appropriate way of pursuing the communicative and reparative goals that, we seem to agree, our responses to crime should pursue. I certainly agree that such goals are not likely to be achieved by the kinds of punishment typically imposed in our existing system of criminal justice, given the context, character and spirit of their imposition; it is clear that the actualisation of either Walgrave's or my vision of a just and constructive social response to crime would involve the radical reconstruction of our existing practices. However, first, I do not think that Walgrave can get away with portraying pain or hardship merely as a side-effect of the restorative process that he favours: if the process should aim to induce repentance (as he argues it should), then it aims to induce pain,

1 R.A. DUFF, "Harms and Wrongs", (2001) 5 *Buffalo Criminal Law Review* 13.

since repentance is necessarily painful; that is to say, if the offender is not pained by what he has done, the process has failed in its aim, since it has not induced a genuine repentance. Second, I agree that to seek to inflict burdens or pains as such, merely to make the defendant suffer, is neither conducive to repentance nor something that a state should do to its citizens: but on my account the aim is to find a kind of burden that could serve as an appropriate kind of communication; I do not share Walgrave's complete pessimism about the possibility of succeeding in this.[2]

Van Stokkom shares Walgrave's pessimism about the possibility that punishment which imposes deliberately "hard treatment" could constitute an appropriate mode of communication with offenders, and I agree that such a process can easily go wrong in various ways: not only might it fail to persuade (for the possibility of *that* kind of failure is intrinsic to any attempt at rational persuasion); depending on the context and spirit in which it is administered as well as on the material content of the punishment itself, what is supposed to be an exercise in rational moral communication can very easily become an oppressive kind of bullying or manipulation in which brute power is exerted over the powerless. Such dangers would be even more real if our aim was simply to inflict ("a priori") pain or suffering: but that is not what I think our aim should be. We should indeed aim to induce a particular kind of pain, the pain of remorse: but that is something that the offender must induce in himself, by repenting; the most that we can or should do is to aim to induce that repentance by a punishment that – as I still want to argue – must involve deliberately hard treatment. But as van Stokkom notes (p. 173 in this volume), by "hard treatment" I simply mean any measure that is meant to be burdensome independently of its censorious meaning. Van Stokkom finds that "senseless" (p. 173), but it is not: to use his example, a probation programme is burdensome, in that it makes demands on the offender's time, attention, energies and conscience; all I am claiming, as against both him and Walgrave, is that its burdensome character should be intended, as a way of making clear to the offender that he has, in the eyes of the law and the polity, done wrong.

Let me just note two further, perhaps smaller, points about van Stokkom's comments. He finds my suggestion that even an insincerely apologetic act of required reparation might serve the proper ends of punishment

---

[2] Indeed, we already have examples of kinds of punishment that can have this character: probation is one obvious example (A.E. Bottoms and W. McWilliams, "A Non-Treatment Paradigm for Probation Practice", (1979) 9 *British Journal of Social Work* 159) as is community service (see A.E. Bottoms, L. Gelsthorpe and S. Rex (eds), *Community Penalties: Change and Challenges*, Cullompton, Willan Publishing, 2001.

unpersuasive, given "[t]he possibility that many victims would experience this insincerity as cruel" (p. 172): but the requirement that the offender undertake such reparative action constitutes a *sincere* demonstration of our collective recognition of the wrong that the victim suffered, even if the offender makes it clear that she is not apologetic; and my further suggestion was that, out of a proper respect for privacy, neither the victim nor others should inquire too closely into the offender's sincerity – the public ritual's significance does not depend on its private sincerity. This leads into my second point. Van Stokkom wants us to explore the offender's sincerity in offering to undertake reparative work: to "investigate the authenticity of repentance signs", to "trace signs of active repentance" (p. 175). I am still enough of an old-fashioned liberal to find this disturbing, which is why I have made so much of the ritual character of punitive reparation:[3] friends or lovers take a proper interest in the sincerity of each other's expressions of feeling and apologies, but the criminal law is concerned with us simply as citizens, and with our relationships with each other simply as fellow citizens; we should not allow its inquisitive (and coercive) tentacles to push so far into our consciences as to investigate the sincerity of our apologetic rituals.

I can simply welcome the first point that Burms discusses, about the connection between punishment and such important human emotions as remorse and indignation. Although such emotions as these can clearly mislead us into various kinds of self-destructive and oppressive excess, and although they can display rich and complex pathologies, they play a central role in our moral self-understanding and in our human responses to our own wrongdoings and to those of others.[4] I am less sure about his second point, about the way in which our responses to wrongdoing are (or should be) focused on the victim and on "what happened", rather than on the offender; I would argue that we owe it to the offender as our fellow to attend to him as much as to his victims or to the impact of what he did, and that essential to our responses to crime should be the effort to bring offenders to face up to what they have done.

---

3 See R.A. DUFF, *Punishment, Communication, and Community*, Oxford, Oxford University Press, 2001, 94-5, 109-10.

4 For a sensitive and sensible discussion of their role, and their dangers, see J.G. MURPHY, "Moral Epistemology, the Retributive Emotions and the 'Clumsy Moral Philosophy' of Jesus Christ", in S.A. BANDES (ed), *The Passions of the Law*, New York, NYU Press, 1999, 149-67. A recognition of the importance of such emotions clearly depends on a recognition of their rationality – a recognition that whilst emotions can of course be irrational, excessive or distorted, they can instead express our rationally appropriate normative understanding of the world: on the significance of this for criminal law theory, see D. KAHAN and M. NUSSBAUM, 1996, "Two Conceptions of Emotion in the Criminal Law", (1996) 96 *Columbia Law Review* 269.

Finally, Burms rightly reminds us that ideas of censure and repentance played a significant role in "traditional, pre-liberal pratices of penance" – notably in the traditions of Catholic religion (p. 163 in this volume); this raises the question of how my purportedly liberal, democratic conception of criminal punishment is related to these older, neither liberal nor democratic, conceptions. This long historical tradition of penance is certainly important – though it leads critics to object that whilst ideas of penance might have a proper role within a religious community, they have no place in a secular liberal state.[5] In drawing on it, I am certainly doing something more than merely trying to transport such ideas from the pre-liberal, pre-democratic context in which they once made a particular kind of sense, into a liberal democratic context – an exercise that would hardly be sensible: for what a liberal state can demand or expect of its citizens is very different from what a church can demand or expect of its members, and what penance and repentance can properly mean or involve must thus also differ significantly between the religious and the secular liberal context. This is not to say, however, that the ideas of penance in the two contexts have no connection or continuity of meaning: we might do better to see both the religious and the secular versions of penance as variations on a common human theme.

[5] See e.g. A. VON HIRSCH, "Punishment, Penance and the State", in M. MATRAVERS (ed), *Punishment and Political Theory*, Oxford, Hart Publishing, 1999.

PUNISHMENT, RESTORATIVE JUSTICE, AND THE MORALITY OF LAW

CONCLUDING OBSERVATIONS

RENÉ FOQUÉ

The question with a juridical form "Who is the subject of rights?" is not to be distinguished in the final analysis from the question with a moral form "Who is the subject worthy of esteem and respect?" ... Furthermore, the question with a moral form refers in turn to a question of an anthropological nature: "What are the fundamental features that make the self capable of esteem and respect?"

(Paul Ricoeur)[1]

1. INTRODUCTORY REMARKS

To fashion conclusions at the end of such a stimulating exchange of ideas, as is represented in and by this book, is at the same time an exciting and easily impossible task. In the first place, the oeuvre here presented is a "work in progress". The authors of the keynote lectures, just as much as the commentators and the other contributors to the discussions knew well to resist the temptation to rehash supposed generally accepted truths or retrace already well-travelled paths. They all laid themselves open to the force of the better argument or a more nuanced reflection. This is no scant praise, for it confers on the present collection a special store of originality and eloquence in the advance of so relevant a debate as that over the meaning of punishment and restorative justice, as well as the connection between the two. Moreover, that debate is expressly not only an academic, scholarly question, but one which directly concerns how citizens actively come into their rights within the institutional framework of a democracy under the rule of law, a constitutional democracy. Against this background, it is simply not possible in the limited confines of these concluding observations to do equal justice to all the nuances, considerations, hypotheses, and arguments which were brought forward. For this reason, these closing remarks will attempt, by way of some concluding observations, to crystallise some reflections that link up with the ideas brought forth by the various authors in the present volume.

---

1 P. RICOEUR, "Who Is the Subject of Rights?" in P. RICOEUR, *The Just*, Chicago-London, University of Chicago Press, 2000, 1.

2. THE NEED FOR A NORMATIVE THEORY OF LAW

The three main themes treated in this book find their principal theoretical and practical significance in their complementary mutuality. Can the morality of law offer us a normative framework for the theory and practice of criminal justice in general, and for the legitimation of the classic version of (criminal) punishment as much as the practice of restorative justice in particular? And lastly, can it also offer one for a better understanding of the complementary nature between both responses to the shock and distress caused by criminal behaviour? The contribution of Claes offers us in the first part a convincing conceptual model by which an affirmative answer can be given to those questions posed above. His general approach finds a persuasive particularisation in the more tapered contributions of Hildebrandt, Duff, and Burms, as well as in the critical approaches of Marshall, Daems, Brochu, Walgrave, and van Stokkom.

The tension often felt in practice between the repressive character of criminal law on the one hand and the more horizontal, humanising claims of restorative justice on the other, confronts us with a serious conceptual and theoretical deficit.[2] What is needed is a more refined conception of law than that offered by a purely repressive interpretation of law. The latter risks becoming the victim of an ill-considered spiral of fault and penalty, one which is not so seldom tossed on the stormy pragmatic and populist seas of an uncompromising politics of crime-fighting. A more refined interpretation of law, one which can mobilise sufficient critical potential against a similar, somewhat naïve (but in its naïveté often successful) repressive image of the law, will have to transcend the practices of criminal justice in order to be able to assess and guide it in critical fashion. In other words, it will have to form part of a normative theory of law, one which is transcendent over individual case precedents.

3. A PLEA FOR A RECONSTRUCTIVE THEORY OF LAW AND THE ROLE OF GENERAL PRINCIPLES

A normative theory of law will not be some general moral or ethical theory which establishes general moral values and norms external to the system of positive law, but against which positive law in consequence (in vertical, top-down fashion) could be tested. A normative theory such as the

[2] See, from a critical view, Walgrave, pp.145-163 in this volume. For a good introduction to the formulation of a theoretical underpinning to the practice of restorative justice as an alternative to a repressively functioning criminal law, see also Aertsen and Beyens, pp.101-117, in this volume.

one argued for in this book has to be (in contrast to all forms of natural law) a reconstructive theory. This means that such a theory would have to be drawn out of a reconstruction of its own development of law in terms of the implicit normative principles it gives effect to in its technique of rule making and judicial decisions. These principles are the foundation for what Ronald Dworkin has called "a society of principle", a society based on shared value orientations. "Members of a society of principle accept that their political rights and duties are not exhausted by the particular decisions their political institutions have reached, but depend, more generally, on the scheme of principles those decisions presuppose and endorse."[3]

The Dutch civilian Paul Scholten has convincingly made this point (already long before Dworkin and other present-day authors) in his essay on general legal principles published in the 1930's. "In and behind each system of law embodied in rules and precedents," postulated Scholten, "there lie fundamental ideas whereof the particular precepts and decisions can be understood as the results." He concluded, "These ideas are as much part of the law as the rules and precedents themselves."[4] Indeed, if a legal system would make claims to validity and legitimacy, then it must be more than a coincidental confection of random or mutually inconsistent norms. Each rule or ruling must be recognizable as an expression of a general set of value orientations and expectations based thereupon, which expression can be expected as a common one for the society in which the rule or decision claims legal validity.

That does not mean that general principles of law so construed could be seen as *a posteriori* constructs projected after the fact into rules and judgments "only for the systematisation of interests", "to demonstrate the common factor in concrete instances", as Scholten puts it.[5] Even less is it the case that the force of validity of the general principles of law should rely on the individual authority of some person or institution. "It can of course be said that the principle is *recognised* ... but that recognition can hardly serve as support for what already otherwise exists: that the

3 R. DWORKIN, *Law's Empire*, Cambridge (Mass.) – London, Harvard University Press, 1986, 211.

4 P. SCHOLTEN, "Rechtsbeginselen", (1935) in P. SCHOLTEN, *Verzamelde Geschriften*, Deel I, Zwolle, Uitgeverij Tjeenk Willink, 1949, 402: "In en achter ieder in wetsvoorschriften en rechterlijke uitspraken belichaamd rechtssysteem liggen grondgedachten waarvan de bijzondere bepalingen en beslissingen als uitwerkingen kunnen worden gedacht. Die gedachten zijn evenzeer deel van het recht als die voorschriften en uitspraken zelf."

5 P. SCHOLTEN, "Rechtsbeginselen", (1935) in P. SCHOLTEN, *Verzamelde Geschriften*, Deel I, Zwolle, Uitgeverij Tjeenk Willink, 1949, 402: "alleen voor de systematiek van belang", "door in concrete bepalingen het gemeenschappelijke aan te wijzen".

principle itself is speaking, is compelling matters in a certain direction."[6] As a result, attached to general principles of law (just like with human rights) is a relatively autonomous meaning, and as such they form a necessary point of entry for a reconstructive theory of law, one which at the same time can be called a normative theory.[7]

4. HOW THE LANGUAGE OF THE LAW INSTITUTIONALISES A SENSE OF OTHERS

The language and the procedure involved in criminal law – precisely because of the scarcity of (traumatic) concrete circumstances infusing their abstractions – can not provide a structure in which the turmoil experienced by the victim and that by the offender can be undone. But it can provide one (even if it be fragile and vulnerable) which nevertheless can make a start at looking for some meaning to the events, at reaching catharsis, and at finding some place for what happened in the future of each person's life. For this reason, the presence of the other is necessary.[8]

The abstract language of the law (as just mentioned, with little grasp and sense of the trying and often traumatic circumstances present in the events, experiences, and actions of the parties) can show a mere formal, perfunctory sense of community, where actual communication seems impossible. The conceptual language of the law provides the minimal circumstances which make communication just possible. That stands as more than a lifeless bundle of pure logic formulas from which the presence of the other as a partner to a meaningful dialogue, as one who make claims on me and requires a response, is abstracted away. In such a case there is also no place for me and my identity. In short, there is no responsible human agency, deserving that name, without a sense of others, of co-actors on the stage. "Life, living in and through legal structures is not only the application of a cognitive-logical system, but a joining in a *social practice*."[9]

---

6 P. SCHOLTEN, "Rechtsbeginselen", (1935) in P. SCHOLTEN, *Verzamelde Geschriften*, Deel I, Zwolle, Uitgeverij Tjeenk Willink, 1949, 402: "Wél kan gezegd worden, dat het beginsel is erkend ... doch die erkenning kan slechts steun zijn voor wat al van elkders vaststaat: dat het beginsel zelf spreekt, tot handelen in zekere richting dwingt."

7 R. FOQUÉ, "Penitentiaire beginselen. Over de rechtsvormende betekenis van rechtsbeginselen", in H. Borghouts (ed.), *Grenzen tussen goed en kwaad. 13 essays over misdaad en straf in de 21ste eeuw*, Den Haag, Ministerie van Justitie, 1998, 9-20.

8 E. CLAES and R. FOQUÉ, "Herstel van autonomie", in L. DUPONT and F. HUTSEBAUT (eds.), Herstelrecht *tussen toekomst en verleden. Liber Amicorum Tony Peters*, Leuven, Universitaire Pers Leuven, 2001, 143-162.

9 CH. TAYLOR, "To Follow a Rule", in CH. TAYLOR, *Philosophical Arguments*, Cambridge (Mass.)-London, Harvard University Press, 1995, 165-180.

The conceptual language of the law, with its discourse in terms of what someone's legal status is, of his, rights, remedies, and so on (and not to mention also the law of (criminal) procedure, with its rules for charging people, for the admission of evidence, for the determination and application of sanctions, and with its principles of due process), offers the institutionalised forms which stock our democratic *decent society*[10] in situations where people themselves seem no longer able from the very strength of their own existence to communicate.[11] In these circumstances of upset and existential isolation, the language of the law creates a framework where not only a *sense of others* but also *co-actors on the stage* can once again take form.

To be sure, there can never be enough attention directed at the interests, the authority, and the not yet fully explored possibilities of language, conventions, symbols, and rituals which the judge and public prosecutor have in hand allowing the latter to help the victim along in coping and recovery. But is there not still something more deeply placed at work than just the semiotic and purely formalistic force of the law?

5. THE LAW AS *SYMBOLIC ORDER*

It strikes me that the characterisation of a legal system as a symbolic order (the phrase coming from psychoanalytic theory) can offer an interesting contribution to the development of a normative (criminal law) legal theory[12], because the expression can afford a more profound analysis of the need in a community of a *sense of others as co-actors on the stage of the public realm.* As mentioned above, in a democratic state under the rule of law, it is just the abstract nature – conceptually and procedurally – of the language of the law itself (including its implied normativity and compulsoriness) that will try to re-establish an involvement for itself and for the dislocated individual in the language of the community and in a space shared with the other.

To sumbolaion in Greek means to deal with others based on set terms of recognition. And *to sumbolon* means what belongs to each.[13] A symbolic order in society funds community; it constructs a language of common signs of recognition, procedures, and manners. And not only this, but it

10 A. MARGALIT, *The Decent Society*, Cambridge (Mass.) – London, Harvard University Press, 1996.

11 R. FOQUÉ, "De autonomie van de rechtstaal", (1995) 44 *Ars Aequi* 675-677.

12 See my inaugual lecture at the Erasmus University of Rotterdam: R. FOQUÉ, *De ruimte van het recht*, Arnhem, Gouda Quint, 1992.

13 PH. VAN HAUTE, *Psychoanalyse en filosofie. Het imaginaire en het symbolische in het werk van Jacques Lacan*, Leuven, Uitgeverij Peeters, 1989, 52-53.

also constructs communal values and meanings which are constitutive of the society. By living in the shared symbolic order of a community, recognition and respect – of oneself and the other – becomes possible. To put this another way, the symbolic order concerns not only the relationship between individual members of a community, but also the relationship of each to the values and meanings shared in the society by which inter-subjective relations become meaningful.[14] That implies that the symbolic order of a society is at the same time its vulnerable Achilles heel: an attack upon its communal values means disregarding and denying the community at the very core of its viability.[15] Then it is not only the case of conduct which injures a victim, but also conduct which damages the communal norm – the symbolic order of the society as thus constituted.[16] Under this view, criminal law takes up a particular and necessary role. Criminal acts have not only the character of *harm-doing* (injury which can and should be compensated for). They also have the essential character of *wrong-doing*, of violating a communal norm (the negation of a community which requires retaliation).[17]

The character of a legal system as a symbolic order can offer yet another contribution to the development of a normative legal theory. Psychoanalysis also distinguishes between a *symbolic order* and an *imaginary one*. The latter is directed at forcing the other into a mirror-image of myself, or on the mirror-image of what I or the ordinary public considers as the standard for *homo normalis*. Then to trace out law as a symbolic order means that the legal order allows for the non-normal, non-standard behaviour of the other. But to trace out the law as a symbolic order means also to recognise the other as different from me in some fundamental way, but with the obligation to live in a world of shared meanings. Using psychoanalytic theory, then, it can be concluded that, "The symbolic makes that recognition possible which not only links me to the other, but also in a sense 'releases' the other."[18]

14 C.P.M. CLEIREN, "Genoegdoening aan slachtoffers in het strafrecht", in *Het opstandige slachtoffer. Genoegdoening in strafrecht en burgerlijk recht. Handelingen van de Nederlandse Juristen-Vereniging*, 133 (2003-1) 33-104, as well as my critical notice of Cleiren in *Het opstandige slachtoffer. Genoegdoening in strafrecht en burgerlijk recht. Handelingen van de Nederlandse Juristen-Vereniging*, 133 (2003-2) 36-39.

15 See Burms, p. 161 in this volume.

16 J.F. GLASTRA VAN LOON, *Norm en handeling. Bijdrage tot een kentheoretische fundering van de sociale wetenschappen*, (1957), Groningen, Wolters-Noordhoff, 1987. For an interesting refinement and application of Glastra van Loon's concept of a norm in the context of criminal law, see M. HILDEBRANDT, *Straf(begrip) en procesbeginsel*, Kluwer, Deventer, 2002, 46.

17 See Duff, p. 132 in this volume, and the concurring opinion of Burms, see p. 161 in this volume.

18 PH. VAN HAUTE, *Psychoanalyse en filosofie. Het imaginaire en het symbolische in het werk van Jacques Lacan*, Leuven, Uitgeverij Peeters, 1989, 53.

6. PARTICIPATORY CITIZENSHIP, MORAL AGENCY AND THE PRINCIPLE OF HUMAN DIGNITY: TOWARDS A PERSONALISTIC CONCEPTION OF LAW

To trace out law as a symbolic order can have far-reaching implications for the question how to justify the right to punish. In the framework of the criminal law as part of the symbolic order, the main question is not primarily the state's right to punish, as an authority external to the community of citizens, but the community's right to punish, implying a shared responsibility among its citizens. "How can citizens punish each other?" Anthony Duff asks himself in the introductory remarks to his contribution herein. The right to punish – such is the implication of his question – should remain compatible with the image of mankind which is tied up in our idea of citizenship. A democratic state under the rule of law would otherwise lose its credibility when it retains practices in its criminal law which conflict with the basic principles it defends and with the *symbolic order* which makes the sociation of its citizens first possible. But this means that citizens are bound by the law in which the symbolic order – in conjunction with their participatory citizenship – is institutionalised in an enforceable way. Here we can speak of a *common* law, but in a deeper sense of that word, or as Duff puts it, "a common law that speaks to them in the voice, not of an alien sovereign, but of their own supposedly shared values".

The *shared values* which the symbolic order of our society in general, and the legal order as part of that symbolic order in particular also conditions, should not be conceived of with a static, and all-too-quick natural law, meaning. Such a suggestion issues for example from Durkheim's notable category of the *conscience collective* which gives cohesion and direction to each society.[19] As is well known, Durkheim was subjected to rather sharp criticism by the German philosopher Adorno who saw in this conception the threat of a moralising and ultimately authoritarian position. Despite all empirical differentiation, according to Adorno, the risk is nonetheless that the *conscience collective* will develop into a sort of *Urphänomen*, in which dealing as one sees fit, and in particular choosing one's own position, will be seen as subordinate. And likewise associating based on *shared values* would more stand in the way of than promote an autonomous and active citizenship. Moreover, and expressed in psychoanalytic terms, it would suspend the symbolic order of a society and substitute the ultimately mere mimesis of an imaginary order.

---

19 See the stimulating critical remarks Daems makes in his comment on Claes' contribution in Daems, pp.65-66 in this volume.

When what is at issue is a conception of law understood as the "common law that speaks in the voice of our own shared values", it is in fact the recognition of each person's autonomy and status as a responsible moral agent that is at stake. Indeed, it is in the actual experience of having legal status, in the actual practising of rights and freedoms, that each and every citizen concurrently and repeatedly encounters the situation that "he or she is universally recognized as a morally responsible person", according to the German philosopher Honneth. And he concludes, "In the experience of legal recognition, one is able to view oneself as a person who shares with all other members of one's community the qualities that make participation in discursive will-formation possible."[20]

The central notion of citizenship in Anthony Duff's contribution, in which the autonomous citizen in a democracy under the rule of law is recognised and preserved as a responsible moral agent, finds an important and principled explication in the notion, as analysed in the Claes contribution, of human dignity in relation to the principle of legality. On the one hand, the fundamental principle of human dignity compels the acknowledgment of the uniqueness of each individual's personhood in the actual life story of each person.[21] On the other hand, that same principle of human dignity compels at the same time an acknowledgment of the legal order as a more general context in which legal recognition should make it possible for each person to encounter themselves as one who can put shared values into practice with others.[22]

With this optic of a bipartite meaning to human dignity, Claes focuses on the relationship between punishment and restorative justice. The first branch appears to be taken seriously in the practice of restorative justice, whereas the second branch seems to be cherished by criminal law. How might we reconcile both perspectives of human dignity with one another?

In his work cited above, *The Struggle for Recognition*, Axel Honneth raises precisely this question in a very penetrating way. His central contention holds that the recognition of human dignity, as much by one's self as by another, in the unique lifeworld of every individual or in the unique confrontations between individuals, is not possible without a strongly

[20] A. HONNETH, *The Struggle for Recognition. The Moral Grammar of Social Conflicts*, Oxford – Cambridge, Polity Press, 1995, 120.

[21] See, for a philosophical analysis of human dignity, TH. DE KONINCK, *De la dignité humaine*, Paris, Presses Universitaires de France, 1995. Preference has been here given to "human dignity" in place of a more nuanced differentiation comprehended in the terms "human worth", "human value", and "human dignity" because of the general use of "human dignity" in the literature.

[22] On human dignity as a fundamental principle of law, see J. FIERENS, "De la dignité humaine comme concept juridique", (2002) 121 *Journal des Tribunaux* 577–582; and J. FIERENS, "Encombrante dignité humaine", *Cahiers de la Faculté de Droit de Namur*, Namur, 2002.

institutionalised legal recognition of each other's position in society which each shares with others. This latter point assumes equally that such legal acknowledgement does not become imprisoned in a ghetto of its own positivistic self-reference. A legal form of recognition can only function fully in moral, political, and societal terms when it can maintain an expressly recognised connection with the symbolic order of the society in which it operates. Fully in line with Hegel's philosophy of recognition, borne by a shared *Sittlichkeit* (ethical life), and by Mead's symbolic interactionism, Honneth proposes that, "[i]n order to be able to acquire an undistorted relation–to-self, human subjects always need – over and above the experience of affectionate care and legal recognition – a form of social esteem that allows them to relate positively to their concrete traits and abilities. ... For self and other can mutually esteem each other as individualised persons only on the condition that they share an orientation to those values and goals that indicate to each other the significance or contribution of their qualities for the life of the other. ... The fundamental, universalistic principle underlying these relations could only be reconstructed by conceiving them as the outcome of an uncoupling of legal recognition from the forms of social regard in which subjects are recognised according to the socially defined worth of their concrete characteristics."[23]

This brings us to a threefold conclusion regarding the principle of human dignity, considered also as a legal principle. In the first place, each form of legal positivism bound up in an unfeeling logic of self-referentiality and ethical-moral neutrality should be avoided. That would also mean rather pointed criticism of pragmatic instrumentalism in the criminal law, whereby it is understood and used as an ethically neutral instrument in the hands of government which can put it to its own opportunistic use, and interpret it broadly or narrowly depending on the political objectives to be achieved. As against this positivism and instrumentalism, is required a conception of law which can in its practice give account of itself in a more complete reconstructive way, in terms of its own underlying fundamental principles, and that in the context of a decent, respectful society.

In the second place, a normative theory of law, one which wisely avoids the pitfalls of positivism and instrumentalism, would set in plain view the connection between self-respect and respect for others. It is just in this complementarity between here a rights-based legality and there a dialogue grounded in reciprocity of recognition (such as that which restorative justice strives for) that it becomes visible how they are able to make human dignity possible, becomes visible. The American philosopher Joel Feinberg commented tellingly that all the rights discourse, what it is to be holders

[23] A. HONNETH, *The Struggle for Recognition*, Cambridge – Oxford, Polity Press, 1995, 121.

of rights, allows us "to stand up like men, to look others in the eye, and to feel in some fundamental way the equal of anyone". Human dignity presumes an equality made institutionally enforceable. In this way, Duff's concept of moral and responsible citizenship and Claes' argument for the recognition of human dignity as a basic legal principle complement one another. Precisely because each citizen in a democracy under the rule of law is guaranteed the enforcement of his rights and the acknowledgment of his claims, does each citizen also actually experience his universal acknowledgement as a moral and responsible person. "Indeed", says Feinberg, "respect for persons may simply be respect for their rights, so that there cannot be the one without the other. And what is called 'human dignity' may simply be the recognizable capacity to assert claims".[24]

In the third place, it should be noted that the anthropological perspective for the complementarity of the criminal law and restorative justice can be found in the connection between moral and responsible agency (even beyond the limits of citizenship) on the one hand, and human dignity on the other. This anthropological perspective can be characterised as person-oriented, as it has been developed in the so-called school of personalism. Personalism refers to an intellectual tradition developed in Europe during the twentieth century and to which are associated the names of Jean Nabert, Emmanuel Mounier and Paul Ricoeur in France[25], of Max Scheler and Helmuth Plessner in Germany, and of Philip Kohnstamm and Hendrik Brugmans in the Netherlands.[26] In its conception of man as a person-in-community, personalism attempts to escape, on the one side, liberalism's monological conception of the individual, and on the other, communitarianism's rejection of all forms of human autonomy rooted in a dialogical participatory citizenship. It holds that a person can give account of himself and restore his own autonomy (as would be necessary in cases of upset and breakdown) in dialogue with others. Mounier speaks of personalism's double movement: on the one hand, a reflexive disengagement (*dégagement réflexif*), and on the other, a community engagement (*engagement communautaire*).[27] In order to achieve this double movement, a person must be

---

24 J. FEINBERG, "The Nature and Values of Rights"' in J. FEINBERG, *Rights, Justice and the Bounds of Liberty. Essays in Social Philosophy*, Princeton – London, Princeton University Press, 1980, 151.

25 The still influential journal, Esprit, published by Éditions du Seuil in Paris, grew out of the personalism movement and still is its principal voice.

26 As Paul Ricoeur has remarked, the term "personalism" is probably not all that satisfactory because it carries the strong connotation of a new –ism with all that tendency to set absolutes and certainties which usually follow. See P. RICOEUR, "Meurt le personnalisme, revient la personne ..." (1983), in P. RICOEUR, *Lectures 2: La contrée des philosophes*, Paris, Éditions du Seuil, 1992, 195-202.

27 E. MOUNIER, *Le personnalisme*, Paris, Presses Universitaires de France, 1949, 34-35.

capable, at one and the same time, to distance himself from his own self and from his actual situation (Plessner calls this the capacity to internalize an "exocentric position"[28]), and yet to turn this capacity back onto himself, literally, to return to himself. A human being can hardly live in dignity when he is bound over without compromise to a community and its commands. But equally, a person can hardly accomplish that either when he shuts himself off to everyone but himself.

The conceptual and procedural language of the law allows us to distance ourselves from the confected meanings centred in the actual applicable law, and so, to shift our concentration to the process of creating meaning itself. Viewed thus, the contra-factual character of juridical concepts and principles can provide the necessary theory of knowledge complement to the anthropological insights of personalism regarding the exocentric positioning of persons in a world where law has effect. Life worlds, created and realized in and through a diversity of individual positions each in itself unique, become legally significant because they can constitute themselves as just as diverse subjects of law, as bearers of rights and duties, and as such, become publicly recognized and recognizable among each other.

To reiterate, a legal system, with its classifications and procedures, should be conceived of as the necessary mediation between the inner self and the community in which one lives, between the *dégagement réflexif* and the *engagement communautaire*.

7. THE RISKS OF AN ABSOLUTE VICTIMOLOGICAL TURN IN CRIMINAL JUSTICE

One of the significant contributions of the restorative justice movement to criminal justice is the attention it calls for on the situation of the victim and on the reparation of the relationship between victim and offender. It does so by giving respect for victims a strong institutional grounding in the criminal justice process.[29] But just for this very reason, it is of utmost importance to define restrictively the meaning of "victim" so as to avoid the situation that its more generalised application lead to an all-encompassing "claim culture".[30]

---

28 H. PLESSNER, "Zur Anthropologie des Schauspielers" (1948) in H. PLESSNER, *Zwischen Philosophie und Gesellschaft. Ausgewählte Abhandlungen und Vorträge*, Bern, Schwabe Verlag, 1953, 180-192.

29 I. AERTSEN, *Slachtoffer-daderbemiddeling: een onderzoek naar de ontwikkeling van een herstelgerichte strafrechtsbedeling*, Leuven, Universitaire Pers Leuven, 2004.

30 A.C. ZIJDERVELD, "De wisselende aandacht voor slachtoffers. Enkele cultuursociologische overwegingen", in *Het opstandige slachtoffer. Genoegdoening in strafrecht en burgerlijk recht. Handelingen van de Nederlandse Juristen-Vereniging* 133 (2003-1) 1-32; and my critical notice of Zijderveld in *Het opstandige slachtoffer. Genoegdoening in strafrecht en burgerlijk recht. Handelingen van de Nederlandse Juristen-Vereniging* 133 (2003-2) 13-17.

Some authors have pronounced with relative certainty on a radical paradigm shift typified as the victim-oriented, the victimological, approach in criminal law. In this victim-orientation of the criminal law, the argument is made that the legitimacy of criminal justice is not to be found in those classic principles of the rule of law which are tied to punishment and criminal law, but rather in sympathy with, or a compassion for, the victim's suffering. When heard against this background, the expression "the revolt of the victims", as used by, for example, the Dutch Legal Association, inevitably recalls the famous slogan which then the newly minted discipline of sociology in the second half of the nineteenth century coined in its struggle against the then dominant legalistic theory of law: "the revolt of the social facts against the law, *la révolte des faits contre le droit*".[31]

The self-image of rebellion and revolution to the new discipline – today's victimology, as much as nineteenth century sociology – can often lead precipitously and irresistibly to a rather unnuanced abolitionist standpoint. The struggle against a legalistic conception of law would then lead all too quickly to a dismissal of law such as it is. And the critique of victimology against the self-referential formalism and authoritarian reductionism of current criminal law would likewise quickly mushroom into a rejection of the particular, domain-specific significance of the criminal law and the law of sentencing as such. A similar rejection would seem likewise to be dictated more by the compelling, but superficial, epos of the victim defying the alienating and oppressing character of the criminal law, rather than by a sophisticated and innovative reflection on the significance of criminal law for a community where victim and offender alike can find some future, as well as their relationship to one another.

The victim's defiance of the traditional view of criminal justice, formulated in strongly epic terms, has a strong chance of leading to at least two reductionist stereotypes. First, we have the rather one-sided – and theoretically naïve – image of law. Law in general, and criminal law in particular, are presented as a set of commands, prohibitions, and sanctions in the hands of a centralised and authoritarian government.

Under these terms, so it would appear, juridical rationality does not seem to comport with the relational nature of humanity. Law appears to be cut off from every opportunity to ensure cohesion in the fabric of society, for empathic concern one's fellow man, and for a restoration of collapsed relationships. This gives a quite statal and instrumentalist picture of law. Admittedly, recent practice whose common mainstay is a mutually reinforcing coalition between a calculating government and a calculating

---

[31] See, in more detail, R. FOQUÉ and A.C. 'T HART, *Instrumentaliteit en rechtsbescherming. Grondslagen van een strafrechtelijke waardendiscussie*, Arnhem – Antwerpen, Gouda Quint/Kluwer Rechtswetenschappen, 1990.

citizen or interest–group, undeniably seems all too often to confirm this one-sided view of the law.

A critique of such a practice may not just simply proceed to a dismissal of (criminal) law as such, but serves instead to reconstruct the achievements of modern legal analysis in its questioning of authority. And in so doing, it can explore further in them the liberating and equalising possibilities which are insufficiently made use of in practice. Indeed, we may not ignore one of the most important aspects of modern law, namely its critique of authority. By virtue of this feature, law is not thus in the first instance a set of commands and prohibitions, but instead is above all the affirmation and guarantee of the compulsory character of a set of relationships, between citizens and government, and among citizens themselves, all of which are necessary for the viability of a decent society, and for mutual recognition and respect in and among its members.[32]

Not only the import of the conceptual and procedural language of the law, but just as much the import of those general legal principles and fundamental rights not otherwise proclaimed in existence by the authorities, take up a principal place in that conception of law. In fact, they are the commonly accepted building-blocks of what was earlier referred to as the symbolic order of both democracy and the rule of law.

The shrill polemical attacks by a large part of the victimological literature risks passing all too quickly the authority-questioning character of modern criminal law. It also thereby risks missing the domain-specific function of the criminal law within the checks and balances characteristic of democracy and the rule of law.

8. THE MEANING OF *RESTORATIVE* IN RESTORATIVE JUSTICE: WHAT MUST BE REPAIRED?

Next to the naïve stereotype of criminal law as statal and authoritarian, a second, and equally unnuanced stereotype threatens to enter the discussion. It concerns the potentially misleading connotations to the expression "restorative justice". What is meant here precisely by "restorative"? Whereas the section above called for a reconstructive approach to the (authority-questioning) fundamental characteristics of modern legal thinking, here what is necessary is earnest consideration of, and by consequence, a refined appraisal of, the practice of restorative justice and mediation in criminal law.

---

32 A similar relational approach to law is distinctly present in the tradition following Montesquieu. On this, see: R. FOQUÉ, "Evenwicht van machten en rechtstatelijke vernieuwing, Bijdrage aan de Staatsrechtconferentie van de Vlaamse Juristenvereniging," in A. ALEN and L. WINTGENS (eds.), *De Trias Politica ruimer bekeken ...*, Brussel, Larcier, 2000, 1-24.

Let me here refer to the practice, intensively followed in Flanders[33], of mediation, and the practice-grounded reflections, the *Reflexion auf eigenes Tun* so to speak, which the mediators themselves conduct.[34] I should also refer to the Flemish association *Sygnomè* (literally from the Greek: a communal space which at the same time makes possible standards for social behaviour), an association of mediators who expressly tie their practices to experience-driven reflections and intuitions. A number of thoughts come to mind in light of this.

First, mediation in criminal law confronts us with the significance of a communicative approach *within* criminal justice. A normative theory of criminal law and punishment would have to take the procedural character of criminal justice with greater earnestness. In these procedural arrangements, are actually incorporated the fundamental values of, and basic preconditions for, a reasonable and proper criminal justice system. Second, care will have to be taken to preserve the criminal law as *public law.* Maintaining public space as a place of openness and of *public* nature, of reciprocal recognition and mutual respect among citizens, needs to be protected. The Jewish-American political philosopher Hannah Arendt comments tellingly here on the "formality of the public" as a basic precondition for the public space of a viable democracy: "by definition, the presence of others is always required, and the presence needs the formality of the public, constituted by one's peers, it cannot be the casual, familiar presence of one's equals or inferiors".[35]

But it also remains necessary to protect the public recognition and protection of the borderline between public and private space. In a criminal act, there often occurs actually a dramatic attack on the victim's values of privacy, freedom, and autonomy. Precisely these values are the ones which need restoration. But what is meant here by restoration? That brings me to a third point. Mediation does not concern the restoration of the status quo prior to the criminal act. The distress encountered by both the victim and the offender concerns precisely the experiencing of that which can not be undone in deed, and that which can not be consoled in the suffering caused.

What is at issue in the first place is not the undoing of all that was caused, but rather a public acknowledgment of the irreparability that was caused by the criminal act. Dismissing what can not be restored is seen as

---

33 See, on this point, the helpful contribution, of Aertsen and Beyens, pp.109-110 in this volume.

34 See, eg, the impressive contribution of LEO VAN GARSSE, "Praktijk en wetenschap. Drie bedrijven uit de ontwikkelingsgeschiedenis van een bemiddelingspraktijk", in F. HUTSEBAUT and L. DUPONT (eds.), *Herstelrecht tussen toekomst en verleden. Liber Amicorum Tony Peters*, Leuven, Universitaire Pers Leuven, 2001, 515-530.

35 H. ARENDT, *The Human Condition*, Chicago – London, Chicago University Press, 1958, 49.

hurtful and alienating in the practice of mediation. Terms such as "damages" or "compensation" risk enlarging that alienation and hurt. They suggest in fact that suffering could be compensated, or paid off. In light of this, the ultimate objective of restorative justice and mediation, as a fourth thought, comes more clearly into focus.

The starting point of mediation – more particularly of the *re-instatement* of both the victim and the offender – lies above all in the search for the possibility – literally and figuratively – *to put things in place once again.* It is about a *re-positioning* (I take the formulation from Leo Van Garsse) in relation to one's self and to others, by re-positioning one's self in relation to the circumstances which have occurred and to the consequences following therefrom for all concerned.[36] It is also a re-positioning in the story of one's own life, in the society to which one belongs, and ultimately also in the damaged self-images of the offender as well as the victim. How can it become possible for all these – irreparable – injuries to find a place in their own futures and in their shared future? An answer to this is only possible through finding a common language, a common – be it procedural – setting where at least the minimal conditions for communication (howsoever fragile and vulnerable) can be established just where they appear to be missing. This latter point, fifthly, is not only a private occasion for the interpersonal confrontation or communication between offender and victim, but above all also a *public responsibility under a rule of law regime of the criminal law as public law.*

Reinstatement of both the victim and offender, and the authority-questioning character of legal thinking thus affect each other's possibilities and responsibilities.

9. THE DOMAIN-SPECIFICITY OF CRIMINAL LAW AS PUBLIC LAW: A NECESSARY CONDITION FOR THE COMPLEMENTARITY OF PUNISHMENT AND RESTORATIVE JUSTICE

Relating the victim-orientation to criminal law as an abolitionist fare-thee-well to the criminal law as such needs to be rejected. It misses the complementarity of restorative justice and criminal law. Both offer their own respective contributions to dealing with criminal offences and their consequences, without allowing the other to take over their own function.

This question is not only of an academic, theoretical nature. It does reach, in my view, the very practical and theoretical core of the domain-

---

36 L. Van Garsse, "Op zoek naar herstelrecht. Overwegingen na jaren bemiddelingswerk", (2001) *Panopticon* 423-446.

specificity of the criminal law as one of the cornerstones of both the rule of law and democracy. A criminal offence denies the constitutive values and principles of our society at their very core. Any reaction to such a breach of those norms held in common by society can not be reduced to a restoration of or compensation for the relationship of reciprocity between offender and victim. In criminal offences, there is more at stake than simply an injury in the horizontal relationship between the parties. As an act of *wrong-doing*, a criminal offence requires at the same time a vertical reaction, to restore that common (in the sense of constitutive for that society) norm. This is why the state's right to punish is indispensable in order to restore a community's shared values. Indispensable, because without a restoration of the breached norm, without bringing about the return of the offender to the community's symbolic order via punitive sanctions, every horizontal, reinstatement directed, communication between offender and victim is doomed to remain insignificant and illusory

My conclusion thus is also that the verticality of criminal law, including the right to punish as part thereof, and the horizontality of restorative justice, of a right to reinstatement, do not exclude one another either at a practical or on a theoretical level. To the contrary, they should be thought of as complementary to one another and put into practice that way.

(*translation by David Haljan*)

LIST OF THE CONTRIBUTORS

Ivo Aertsen is Professor of Criminology at the Catholic University of Leuven, Belgium, where he teaches Victimology and Penology. His main research domains are victimology, mediation and restorative justice. Dr. Aertsen is chair of the European Forum for Victim-Offender Mediation and Restorative Justice, and leads COST Action A21 on Restorative Justice Research in Europe.

Kristel Beyens holds a degree in Sociology and Criminology. In her Ph.D. dissertation she developed a sociological-criminological approach on sentencing. She is Professor in Criminological Sociology and Research Methods at the Criminology Department of the Free University Brussels (Vrije Universteit Brussel). Her research focuses on penal matters, such as sentencing, prison overcrowding, community sanctions, electronic monitoring and developments in punishment in general.

Serge Brochu got a doctoral degree in clinical psychology in 1981. He is a full professor at the School of Criminology of the University of Montreal. He is the past director of the International Center for Comparative Criminology (1996 –2004) and actually the co-director of Recherche et intervention sur les substances psychoactives – Québec (RISQ). His research themes are on Drugs/crime relationships; Treatment of addict offenders; Programme evaluation.

Arnold Burms is a professor of Epistemology and Philosophy of Art at the Higher Institute of Philosophy at the Catholic University of Leuven. His main publications are in the field of philosophy of science and philosophy of mind.

Erik Claes is a professor of Criminal Law Theory at the Catholic University of Leuven. His main research areas are theory of adjudication, philosophy of the criminal law, penal theory, and restorative justice. He obtained his doctoral degree in Law on "Legality and Adjudication in the Criminal Law" (*Legaliteit en rechtsvinding in het strafrecht*, Leuven, University Press, 2003), which was rewarded with the Fernand Collin Prize for Law in 2002.

Tom Daems studied criminology at K.U. Leuven, Belgium and the London School of Economics and Political Science, UK. At this moment he is based at the Department of Criminal Law and Criminology, K.U. Leuven where he works as a Research Assistant of the Fund for Scientific Research –

Flanders (Belgium). In his Ph.D. project he explores the relationships between punishment, victimisation, and society.

Antony Duff has taught Philosophy at the University of Stirling since 1970. He is the author of *Trials and Punishments* (1986); *Intention, Agency and Criminal Liability* (1990); *Criminal Attempts* (1996); *Punishment, Communication, and Community* (2001); contributing editor of *Philosophy and the Criminal Law: Principle and Critique* (1998) and co-editor with D. Garland, of *A Reader on Punishment* (1994).

René Foqué is a professor of Legal Theory and Legal Philosophy at the Law Faculties of the Catholic University of Leuven and of the Erasmus University of Rotterdam. He is correspondent member of the Royal Dutch Academy of Sciences. His main publications cover the domains of legal philosophy and of criminal law theory. His recent research interests are in the areas of the foundations of human rights and of international law.

Mireille Hildebrandt has worked since 1994 as a teacher and researcher at Erasmus University Rotterdam, where she took a doctor's degree in philosophy of law and criminal procedure in 2002. Since 2002 she has been seconded to the Free University of Brussels as a postdoctoral researcher on an international interdisciplinary project concerned with the relationship between science, technology and law within the framework of the democratic constitutional state.

Sandra Marshall is a professor in the Philosophy Department at the University of Stirling and a Deputy Principal of the university. She has worked for many years in the overlapping areas of moral and legal philosophy. She is currently working on aspects of the role of victims in the legal process and is a partner, with Antony Duff, Lindsay Farmer and Victor Tadros, in the *"Trial on Trial"* research project funded by the UK Arts and Humanities Research Board. She is also co-editor of the *Journal for Applied Philosophy*.

Tony Peters is an emeritus professor at the Catholic University of Leuven, Faculty of Law. Criminology, victimology, penology and crime policy are his main subject matters of teaching. His research work focuses on punishment, victimisation, mediation and restorative justice. He has been the President of the Scientific Committee of the International Society of Criminology and is actually co-director of the M.A.-programme in European Criminology at the Catholic University of Leuven.

Bas van Stokkom is currently research fellow at The Centre for Ethics, Radboud University Nijmegen, The Netherlands. He held a research post at the Wiardi Beckman Stichting and was chief editor of "Justitiële verkenningen". His research concentrates on the fields of restorative justice, punishment ethics, policing and deliberative democracy. Among his recent books are: *Straf en herstel. Ethische reflecties over sanctiedoeleinden* (2004) and *Streetwise: verbaal geweld tussen politie en burgers* (2004).

Lode Walgrave is Professor emeritus of Criminology at the Katholieke Universiteit Leuven, and director of the Research Group on Youth Criminology. He has been chair of the International Network for Research on Restorative Justice for Juveniles. Among numerous other publications on restorative justice, he edited *Restorative Justice and the Law* (2002).

www.ingramcontent.com/pod-product-compliance
Ingram Content Group UK Ltd.
Pitfield, Milton Keynes, MK11 3LW, UK
UKHW051927100926
8556IPUK00022B/1418

9 789050 954235